RENEWALS 458-4574
DATE DUE

GAYLORD			PRINTED IN U.S.A.

A Florida Fiddler

A Florida Fiddler

~

The Life and Times of Richard Seaman

Gregory Hansen

THE UNIVERSITY OF ALABAMA PRESS
Tuscaloosa

Copyright © 2007
The University of Alabama Press
Tuscaloosa, Alabama 35487-0380
All rights reserved
Manufactured in the United States of America

Typeface: Minion

∞

The paper on which this book is printed meets the minimum requirements of
American National Standard for Information Sciences-Permanence of Paper for
Printed Library Materials, ANSI Z39.48–1984.

Library of Congress Cataloging-in-Publication Data

Hansen, Gregory, 1962–
A Florida fiddler : the life and times of Richard Seaman / Gregory Hansen.
p.   cm.
Includes bibliographical references (p.) and index.
ISBN-13: 978-0-8173-1553-5 (cloth : alk. paper)
ISBN-10: 0-8173-1553-5 (alk. paper)
1. Seaman, Richard, 1904–2002. 2. Fiddlers—Florida—Biography.
3. Storytellers—Florida—Biography. 4. Old-time music—Social aspects—Florida.
I. Seaman, Richard, 1904–2002. II. Title.
ML418.S43H36 2007
787.2′162130092—dc22
[B]

2006022575

Contents

∼

Acknowledgments
vii

Preface
Shuffle
ix

Introduction
Fiddler's Stories
1

Chapter 1. Arts Mania
9

Chapter 2. And the Merry Love the Fiddle
18

Chapter 3. Workshop
33

Chapter 4. "Your Word Was Your Bond"
An Anthology of Tall Tales
55

Chapter 5. Uncle Josie's Farm
86

Chapter 6. Richard's Fiddle
105

Chapter 7. Core Repertory
132

Chapter 8. Folklife in Education
150

Chapter 9. A Florida Fiddler
163

Chapter 10. The Voice of a Fiddler
182

Chapter 11. The Icing on the Cake
196

Postscript
199

Tunes
201

Notes
209

Works Consulted
237

Index
249

Photographs follow page 122.

Acknowledgments

~

I am grateful to Bill Foshag for introducing me to folklife studies and old-time music. Bill is an old-time and bluegrass guitarist, and he also played his old-time tunes on his stereo for me while we were working to restore his old gristmill near Carlisle, Pennsylvania. I was listening.

Two teachers initiated me into playing the fiddle. Lasaunne Allen introduced me to the instrument during one of her winter stays in St. Augustine, and Wayne Martin taught me new techniques and provided me with a good feel for the tunes through lessons at his restaurant's dance hall in Blountstown, Florida.

Folklorists associated with the Florida Folklife Program gave me opportunities to present fiddlers and other traditional musicians and folk artists in schools and communities. Peggy Bulger, Tina Bucuvalas, Kristin Congdon, Ormond Loomis, Nancy Michael, Nancy Nusz, David Reddy, Jan Rosenberg, Bob Stone, David Taylor, and Brent Tozzer were especially generous in sharing their knowledge of Florida folklife. I have benefited from the expertise, passion, and good humor of my folklore colleagues. They are too numerous to mention, but Betty Belanus, Paddy Bowman, Brent Cantrell, Bob Gates, Alfred Kina, and Gail Matthews-DeNatale deserve special recognition.

Dick Bauman, Sandra Dolby, Henry Glassie, and Greg Schrempp at Indiana University provided valuable insights, guidance, and direction. I have also benefited greatly from readings and discussions with my friends and colleagues at

Arkansas State University. Rick Burns, Chuck Carr, Bill Clements, Cyndy Hendershot, Joe Key, Frances Malpezzi, Clyde Milner, and Bryan Moore all offered either careful readings or good discussions of various ideas relevant to fiddling, folklore, history, and theories about creative expression. Drew Beisswenger made an important contribution with his excellent transcipts and his conscientious reading, and Alan Jabbour provided an especially helpful reading of my discussion of Richard's repertory.

Jack Piccalo not only introduced me to Richard, but he also recognized why Richard truly is a treasure within Florida's rich legacy of cultural heritage. It was my own great fortune to become friends with him when I was living in Jacksonville.

My wife, Betsy Hansen, has always encouraged my various folklore and academic endeavors. She left her native Florida to live in Indiana before we returned to Florida. She then graciously accepted our latest move to Arkansas, and she is happy with her new home in the Arkansas Delta. This book is dedicated to her for her constant support and good spirit.

Preface

~

Shuffle

Slowly, carefully, the old man lifts his fiddle from the mantelpiece, gently cradling the instrument as he lays it on his couch. Opening up an old violin case, he takes out a well-worn bow and turns its screw, tightening the frog to make the horsehair taut. Pulling a block of rosin that was processed from a nearby turpentine camp five decades ago, he slides the amber chunk up and down the bow, giving it the ability to bite into the instrument's strings. Picking up the fiddle once again, he tucks it under his chin and lets the violin's neck lie on his palm. Double-stopping the second and third strings, he pauses a moment, calling into his mind a bowing pattern before engaging the bow to the strings. His hard, long downbow is followed by a sharp upbow and another heavy downbow, and he plays the first tune that he learned.

The fiddler is waiting for a visit from a friend who is coming to see him that evening. He is going to introduce him to someone who works for the people who run the folk festival in White Springs. The fiddler has attended the festival for years, and he enjoys sitting in his lawn chair under the live oaks each Memorial Day weekend while listening to the old-time and bluegrass music that is featured on the stages of the Stephen Foster Folk Culture Center State Park. The festival allows him to hear music that he grew up with years ago, and he enjoys spending time at the park on the banks of the historic Suwannee River. The fiddler has made friends with some of the musicians and music fans who attend the festival, but he has never met the people who put together the show.

The fiddler plays through a couple more tunes. An old Volkswagen Jetta pulls into the driveway, and the fiddler puts down his instrument to meet his friend at the door. Gathered at the back porch, he meets his friend's son who is accompanying the folklorist who, handing him a business card, explains that he is also working with Jacksonville's schools and Florida's folklife program. After more introductions, small talk, and an explanation that the folklorist appreciates the chance to record some tunes, the fiddler hands his six-string Ovation to his friend, who strums out some chords to back up the fiddle on guitar. The folklorist opens up a floor stand to make a stereo recording by placing two Sennheiser microphones in a tip-to-tip setup.

Over the course of the evening, they record over two dozen old-time fiddle tunes. When everyone becomes tired, the musicians set their instruments down, and the tape recorder is put on pause. As conversation flows, they decide that they have plenty of tunes on tape for the night, and it is time to pack up. Breaking down the microphone stand, coiling up the chords, packing away the tape recorder into a carry-bag, the folklorist listens as the fiddler tells a tall tale about a cow that fell down a well.

The folklorist listens, laughs, and says that he would like to return the next day. The folklorist then asks if he can take some photographs, assuring everyone that the camera won't break. Posing for a few candids, the guitar player and the fiddler are quizzical about the need to take more than one picture, but they patiently pose with their instruments for some more shots. After five more minutes of picture-taking, the folklorist puts away the camera, tucking it into his carry-bag with the tape recorder, microphones, and cables. They talk some more, and the boy tells his dad that he is ready to go home.

Everyone strolls outside, and the fiddler tells another story. The visitors chat some more on the lawn. The folklorist promises to come back to learn more about fiddling and to record the stories.

Introduction

~

Fiddler's Stories

The fiddler's name is Richard Seaman. He was born in Kissimmee Park in 1904, and he began playing the fiddle by 1912. Richard is one of the relatively few Floridians who can lay claim to the title "native Floridian," and he has spent most of his life living in what is geographically the largest city in the state, Jacksonville. We met that August night in 1988 when I was working as the folk arts coordinator for the Duval County Folk Arts in Education Project, a public sector folklore program sponsored by the Florida Department of State's Bureau of Florida Folklife Programs and Duval County's school system. The project was initiated by a grant from the National Endowment for the Arts in 1984, and it was first coordinated by David Taylor. He and the bureau's staff designed the program to enhance and complement the Florida studies component of the fourth-grade social studies curriculum through a series of two-week residencies in which a folklorist works with four to six classes a day to teach a course in folklore. The project involved classroom instruction, media presentations, and visits with local tradition-bearers. Designed to familiarize students with the region's folklife, the project consisted of field research in Jacksonville's various communities with folk artists, traditional musicians, folk dancers, storytellers, and other keepers of tradition who offered their time and talents to the program. Taylor's original fieldwork provided the basis for a teacher's guide, instructional resources, and publicity materials used in the program. Under his two-year tenure as the project's coordinator, the program was rated "Model for the Nation" by an independent evaluator for the National Endowment for the Arts.

David Taylor coordinated the project for two years, prior to accepting an administrative position with the Bureau of Florida Folklife Programs in White Springs. While working as an administrator, he secured funding from the Educational Opportunities Consolidation Act's "Chapter Two" funding program, a grant allocation designed to enrich educational experiences for ethnically diverse communities. As the funding was made available in the fall of 1987, the bureau hired me to work as the new folk arts coordinator. By this time, David had accepted a new position at the American Folklife Center in the Library of Congress, and I have benefited greatly from his fine research and the wealth of instructional activities and educational materials that he and other folklorists had developed in folk arts in education projects across the nation. During my first six months, time constraints prevented me from doing fieldwork to find new folk artists to demonstrate their arts or to perform their music in the schools. By the beginning of the summer of 1988, I began completing fieldwork to add to the cadre of people able and willing to give presentations in the schools.

Jack Piccalo is Richard Seaman's friend. I met Jack during a bluegrass jam session and found that he is a first-rate bluegrass banjo player, with a rich knowledge of the history of bluegrass music and a deep understanding of the aesthetic system that constitutes the genre. I was pleased to find that Jack was not only able to come into the schools to perform bluegrass music for schoolchildren but that he was also an excellent resource person for working with the region's bluegrass community.

I also found that Jack was a wealth of information about the form of music that predates bluegrass, namely old-time fiddle tunes. While the origins of bluegrass are surprisingly recent, dating only to the late 1930s and early 1940s, the term "old-time" names a much older form of music. One of America's most prolific and insightful folklorists, Simon Bronner, writes that the phrase "old-time music" came into popular currency during the modernism of the 1920s but that it describes a corpus of tunes and styles that date back centuries.[1] When used in relation to fiddle playing, the term "old-time" typically names the square dance tunes played at square dances and fiddle contests throughout America's history. Old-time tunes are often called "hoedowns," but the phrase "old-time fiddling" also names a style of playing associated with country waltzes as well as the early blues tunes that became popular at the turn of the twentieth century. Among fiddlers, the term "old-time" generally describes a set of tunes that were either imported from Ireland, Scotland, England, and other European repertoires or else created by American fiddlers. Styles of old-time fiddling vary across regional and ethnic boundaries, but the most common shibboleth that allows a musician to declare a tune old-time is whether it can be played to accompany a square dance. Despite ambiguities in attempting to determine exactly what constitutes traditional fiddling, old-time fiddlers make it clear that their music is distinct from bluegrass. Bluegrass fiddlers, in turn, also play in a style different from old-time.

Hearing an old-time fiddler evokes the presence of the past. This music's emotional core inspired Bill Monroe to create the high, lonesome sound of his bluegrass music, and there is something about listening to old-time music that appeals to a sense of history and a strong, direct, ostensibly simple aesthetic system. The desire to find in old-time music a visceral link to history inspired Jack to bring his son Troy along when he introduced me to Richard Seaman. Watching Troy listen to Richard provided me with an excellent opportunity to discover what an elementary-age student might think of an old-time fiddler's tunes. During the evening, I found that Troy listened politely to the tunes and that he liked Mr. Seaman, but I also found that the musical style was unfamiliar to him. Troy reminded me that if I were to invite Mr. Seaman to perform for fourth-graders I was going to need to learn about his music and develop a sympathetic way to present him and his tunes. In doing fieldwork with Richard Seaman, I knew that I would need to discover what makes the music so appealing to the fiddler and to find a way to contextualize what I had learned so that my students could better appreciate what Richard would offer.

I was able to bring Richard to well over a dozen schools during the four years that I coordinated the Duval County Folk Arts in Education Program in more than one hundred elementary schools. While I was initially unsure whether students would appreciate his music, I found that every class responded enthusiastically to his school presentations and that he became one of the most popular of all the artists who performed as part of the folklife in education programming in Duval County. Before coordinating these performances, I knew that the best way for me to learn how to present him in classrooms would be first to learn what he knows about his music. Through fieldwork, I needed to gain an understanding of his life history and his perspectives on his music, and I also needed knowledge of Florida's old-time fiddling and storytelling traditions.

This complex task did not seem daunting or arduous. I loved hearing him play his tunes and tell his stories, and Richard generously taught me both how to back up fiddle tunes on a guitar as well as how to learn to play hoedowns and waltzes on the fiddle. We have a mutual passion for sharing the music with others. My folklore training taught me how to do fieldwork, and folklorists' theories of performance taught me how to begin the research that I would apply in public presentations. Roger Abrahams, Richard Bauman, Henry Glassie, Dell Hymes, Edward D. Ives, and other thinkers in my discipline derived performance-centered approaches to folklore by adapting ideas from thinkers as ostensibly diverse as Kenneth Burke and Noam Chomsky.[2] Based on the necessity of completing a solid and accurate empirical description of the phenomenon under study, performance theory provides resources to describe and systematize Richard's fiddling and storytelling. To describe fiddling, I knew that I would need to understand the system of music used to create tunes as well as the contexts that make the tunes interesting, appealing, and effective in various performances. Observing numerous performances and identifying common patterns and themes provided resources for developing a methodology for my research. In conducting a series of tape-recorded interviews, I found answers to questions about the cultural, social, personal, and historical contexts for the tunes. The answers to the questions about these contexts led to texts that address the major goal of performance theory: a statement of the artist's competence, the theory of what is appropriate and effective in artistic expression.

Through note-taking, interviews, and various forms of documentation, I became interested in narrowing the idea of competence into ideas that resonate with Richard Seaman's own perspectives about his tunes and stories. Analyzing performances using constructs to systematize performances into a speaker's use of communicative norms, roles, genres, texts, purposes, and other facets of discourse provide heuristic guidelines for research. The arcane vocabulary and esoteric theories of the performance theorist, however, can obscure ways in which performers, themselves, conceptualize their artistry. I appreciate the great value of using performance-centered approaches in fieldwork and analysis, but the academic dialect of the theorist does not square with the ways in which Richard Seaman presents his own ideas. To resolve how a folklorist's etic categories and systems are at odds with the folk musician's ways of speaking, I am burying most of the theoretical apparatus in footnotes (and epigraphs). I have also organized this book in terms of performances and statements of competence that make sense to both Richard and me. The purpose of my analysis is not simply to contextualize Richard's music within his life history. Rather, I use an eclectic array of methods and theories to ascertain his own conceptual, interpretive, and theoretical perspectives on his music. These artist's statements emerge through his public performances, formal interviews, informal conversation, and reflections and stories. This orientation to performance can be termed a "logocentric perspective" in that I use focus on specific contexts of situation in which the spoken word is central to communication.[3] In combining a focus on the spoken word with the visual qualities of verbal images and actual photographs, I am seeking to present in print a view of ways in which the auditory qualities of speaking are interanimated with photography.

My presentation of Richard's music is a life history, but it is not a biography. Nor is it an ethnomusicological analysis of Florida fiddling. Rather, it is an inquiry into ways in which Richard Seaman thinks about his life in relation to his musical experiences. Neither Richard nor I have any illusions that he represents "Florida fiddling," but his experiences as a fiddler and his skill as a storyteller provide one important view of fiddling in the state. To present his fiddling tradition from his own perspectives, I rely mainly on stories that sketch out biographical details of his life history, especially as the narratives relate to his life as a musician. To connect and contextualize the stories, I have included research and commentary derived from academic research and interviewing strategies that involve asking the subject of the interviews for his own commentary— whenever this approach is practical and effective. My bigger interest, however, is an interest that Richard shares: namely, we both wish to provide an understanding of the core values and perspectives that Richard so generously offers to friends and willing audiences.

I have arranged the chapters to present performances that we have developed in public sector folklore programming. Descriptions of these performances demonstrate how Richard presents his tunes and stories to the public, and they also provide a basic understanding of genres and programs offered by public folklorists. The chapters that describe his performances break away from a chronological order of a life history. I arranged the chapters in this way to provide an understanding of how Richard uses history to contextualize contemporary performances, thereby showing how he envisions the past within the present. This approach is much more attuned to the way that we both see his predominant ways of telling his stories. To integrate these contemporary performances with Richard's biography, I have arranged stories and reflections that I have edited from a series of folklife studies and oral history interviews. My approach is less to provide a life history or a psychological study of a musician and more to demonstrate how understanding stories and tunes yields insight into ways that a musician creates and contextualizes his own performances. Other chapters focus more on relevant aspects of the competence that emerges in performance. These chapters provide additional context useful for understanding the systems of aesthetics that emerge within Richard's artistry as well as background information for understanding the contexts of the fiddler's performances.

Chapter 1, a contemporary performance at an arts festival, provides an initial introduction to ways in which Richard presents himself in public programs. Chapter 2 contextualizes the first chapter through Richard's personal experience narratives about his early life history. I focused my interview questions around the idea of discovering how a fiddler played an important role in rural life in Kissimmee Park, Florida. Chapter 3, "Workshop," presents a contemporary performance of fiddle tunes. This presentation at a folklife festival is the only event when Richard Seaman, Chubby Wise, and George Custer performed together on the same program. Chubby grew up in north-central Florida, and after he moved to Jacksonville in the 1930s, he went on to become one of the pioneering bluegrass fiddlers with Bill Monroe's Blue Grass Boys. George Custer is a well-known Florida fiddler who played with Bob Wills's western swing bands and numerous bluegrass groups and also in classical venues. Richard, Chubby, and George play tunes and answer interview questions from the folklorist Bob Stone. This chapter's content further places Richard's old-time fiddling tradition within Florida's musical heritage, and it also provides an understanding of the stage techniques that a fine presenter uses to craft a public folklore program. Chapter 4 is an anthology of Richard's tall tale repertoire. I use the motif and tale-type indexes of folklore scholarship to place his tales in geographic and historical contexts in order to examine how the texts fit into regional culture patterns of distribution. Along with the historic-geographic interests, I also provide commentary to place the texts within the cultural context of Florida folklife. Richard's ideas about the importance of the spoken word provide an important theme in this chapter, and his perspectives on truth and lying establish a unified way to understand his self-presentation as a performer of old-time music.

Chapter 5 discusses Richard's move from rural central Florida into the urban area of Jacksonville in the 1920s. I became intrigued with James Deetz's argument that old-time fiddle tunes and communal square dancing thrive in the social structure of the little community.[4] He argues that old-time fiddling and square dancing fell out of popularity because of shifts in a community's social order, and his perspective is resonant with Richard's own assessment of major changes in his music-making. This change involves displacing rural folklife with urban living, and Richard's physical move from Kissimmee Park to the city of Jacksonville provides a fine resource for discovering how he experienced dramatic changes in music with the coming of mass media, the Great Depression, and new venues for musical performance in an urban environment. I provide a close look at Richard's fiddling in Chapter 6, in which I examine the systematic qualities of old-time fiddling in order to elucidate aesthetic values that Richard shares in performance. I provide a basic introduction to his fiddling to train the ear of the novice listener, but I have also included information on Richard's particular approach to fiddling. Chapter 7 expands on the preceding chapter as I track down major shifts in his fiddling repertory over time. This approach documents the time frame in which Richard learned new tunes and mastered new genres. Because understanding the social context for performing tunes in his repertory is essential to discovering how he learned his repertory, this approach provides resources for examining and developing Deetz's assertion that shifts in genre index shifts in social structure. A longitudinal study of one individual's repertory provides a strong base for understanding why a repertory changes in relation to shifts from playing in communal house parties into performances at folklife festivals and shopping malls.

In Chapter 8, I provide another description of a performance. This chapter looks at a typical "Folklife in Education" presentation that I coordinated with Richard in Jacksonville. It provides an understanding of public programming as a co-presentation between the folklorist and the folk musician. Moreover, it demonstrates how Richard contextualizes his music and life history to schoolchildren. Chapter 9 looks at the array of images associated with fiddling in Florida. Richard's stories about Florida Cracker culture provide historical context for contemporary images of rural life. He candidly discusses serious issues, including race relations and the harshness of life in rural Florida. The chapter also explores how fiddling has been associated with negative stereotypes about Florida. In Chapter 10, I provide Richard's most complete statements about his own theories about fiddling, public presentations, history, and art. Vernacular theories do not emerge through the spoken word with the same panache and elaborateness of the high theorist's written prose. It is a mistake, however, to dismiss the honest and plainly spoken ideas of a mechanic with an eighth-grade education. Rather than privileging the theory of the academic by having the high theorist set the agenda for understanding Richard's music and stories, it makes more sense to learn to listen to Richard's own ideas. I am honored that he trusts me to write about them. The book's final chapter, "The Icing on the Cake," completes an important part of his life history, and Richard and Annie Seaman offer a love story that explains the origins of the "Annie Seaman Waltz."

Richard's stories and his fiddle tunes feature repetition and variation as important artistic resources. His tall tales build on incremental repetition, and he uses parallel constructions and intricate formal patterns in many of his stories. A fiddle tune involves the repetition and variation of musical phrases, and the two-part form of most of his tunes provides a central resource for understanding his music. Valuing repetition and variation as importance resources for learning tunes and stories, I have included slightly different versions of selected tales in various chapters. Readers will notice how Richard varies the tellings with different performances, and I am repeating a number of the tales to give readers the flash of recognition that models ways in which Richard learned and refined his tales. This dynamic quality of storytelling also models how he has learned fiddle tunes, and these epiphanies are easier to understand by reading similar stories rather than by solely analyzing this aspect of verbal and musical artistry.[5]

In working with Richard, I became interested in what David Whisnant terms "systematic cultural intervention."[6] In a number of works, Whisnant demonstrates how those who coordinate public programs rely on agendas that entail cultural change in various communities. The goals of the Duval County Folklife in Education Program involved fostering an understanding of the culturally diverse traditions of Florida. Nancy Michael writes that this goal included familiarizing students with folk culture that Floridians may perceive as the culture of "others," as well as the folklife that is a long-established part of the state's indigenous culture.[7] Richard's folk traditions are part of Florida's regional culture, and my specific interventionist goals included using his artistry to teach students about an aspect of folk culture that was unfamiliar to them. Whisnant's writing reminded me that positive intentions can yield unforeseen negative consequences, and I was initially concerned about conflicting agendas and potential confusion between myself as a folklorist and Richard as a folk musician. What was remarkable, however, was that most of our goals for creating public programs are in accord. In working with Richard, I also discovered that the perspectives, interpretations, and vernacular theories of the folk musician challenged me to examine my own ideas about cultural intervention and public folklore. His gentle reminders that there is great value in preserving old traditions challenged my implicit belief in the grand master narrative of progress in academic inquiry. Richard also taught me to understand how focusing on contemporary popular culture at the expense of older forms of folklore can foster ideologies complicit with ageism and regional prejudice.

In more than a decade of working with Richard Seaman, I found that our roles began to switch. I began to play Richard's tunes on the fiddle, and Richard developed theories about Florida's folk culture. The folk musician developed theoretical perspectives on folklore that continue to challenge my own thinking about my discipline and practice as a folklorist. His tunes, stories, beliefs, and perceptions reveal what it means to live a good life in his communities. In seeing the twentieth century through his eyes, Richard offers important perspectives useful in thinking about the life in the twenty-first. In this respect, he offers ways to truly "listen to the vernacular."[8]

1

Arts Mania

~

There are no hidden meanings.
—I. Sheldon Kopp

The Jacksonville Landing sits as an urban shopping park on the north bank of the St. Johns River. Developed by the Rouse Corporation as part of an urban renewal and economic development project in Jacksonville's core city business district, The Landing is a semicircular shopping mall that features dozens of specialty shops, a few restaurants, a video arcade, and a food court on its second floor that provides workers in the city with a place to have a sandwich, salad, or a slice of pizza during their lunch hour. The first floor consists primarily of retail spaces that are leased on a revolving basis, and the arch of stores opens into an interior courtyard featuring a fountain where children play between intermittent sprays of water. The area is accessible from a large parking lot on its east side as well as from a dock and riverwalk on the edge of the St. Johns River. The courtyard is a gathering spot that attracts different crowds throughout the week, and it is also the site where the Rouse Corporation's staff coordinates special events, including festivals, concerts, and dances. At its best, The Landing provides a public space that is designed to encourage local residents and tourists to patronize downtown businesses and provide a space for artistic and cultural expression within the urban environment.[1] Constructed largely on old parking lots, the shopping park also replaced old buildings. The facility was opened in the fall of 1987, and businesses continue to move in and out of the building.

The morning of the first Saturday of October 1992 opens a windy and cool northeastern Florida weekend day. The sky is dense, and rain is in the forecast. Richard Seaman and Jack Piccalo are about to play for an afternoon performance at a community-wide arts festival at The Landing. Known as "Arts Mania," this regional festival has been produced by the Arts Assembly of Jacksonville, Inc. for the past four years, and I have coordinated an afternoon folklife presentation at the event for the past three years. Folk musicians and dance groups who accepted my invitation to participate are performing at the event's main stage, located in the courtyard, and I am also staging performances on a smaller "Folklife Stage." I had asked the event's staff to set up this area in front of The Landing's north entrance as I wanted a smaller and more intimate venue for many of the performers taking part in the folklife component of the event.[2] Old-time country musicians, a cappella gospel groups, and bluegrass bands play under the cover of the building's entrance. They face downtown Jacksonville's Water Street while the audience sits under a tent canopy that also shelters the sound crew from the sun and impending rain. David Reddy, an anthropologist, colleague, and friend from the Florida Department of State's Bureau of Florida Folklife Programs, grins as he mischievously describes the stage as "a very post-modern context for a folk festival."

I had arrived an hour before the day's events were to begin. The extra time allowed me the chance to meet the sound engineers setting up the stage, arrange chairs under a canopy for the audience, and be present to greet the performers. The festival is now underway, and soon Richard and Annie Seaman arrive. He helps his wife out of his car, and I take her to a seat nearby and then help Richard unload his fiddle, guitar, video camera, and tripod from his trunk. Mr. Seaman asks me to watch the equipment while he parks the car, and as I wait for him to return, I chat with Annie about the plans for the day. Her blue eyes sparkle over her warm smile, and she explains how pleased she is to be able to hear Richard play this afternoon. I acknowledge that I am glad that he could participate and that I am looking forward to hearing his tunes and stories once again. Annie asks if Jack has shown up yet, and soon we both see him coming up the sidewalk with Richard.

We exchange our hellos, and I answer Richard's question by explaining that things are indeed going well that day but that I also am a bit concerned about the threat of rain and the heavy winds. We all decide to get busy anyway, and Jack goes to talk to the soundman about the microphone setup and the sound mix for the show. While Jack is explaining that Richard needs a vocal mike and that the volume level for the guitar should be a bit lower than the level for the fiddle, Richard is positioning his video camera under the canopy that shields the twenty members of the audience from the threatening weather. He asks me to monitor his video camera, and I explain that I can watch it after I introduce them on stage. Everything is set up, and the four of us wait for the first band to finish its set. After introducing Richard from the stage, I take a seat next to the sound engineer where I can keep an eye on Richard's video camera.

Richard and Jack begin with "Yellow Gals." Richard is on stage left, and he is wearing blue jeans, a western shirt and bolo tie, cowboy boots, and a broad black cowboy hat. Jack is dressed casually and is playing backup guitar on Richard's Ovation. When they finish the first tune, the performance continues.

Richard acknowledges the applause, saying, "Thank you very much." He continues his stage patter, "When you applaud for us, you know, you can't overdo it. It's like making love to an old maid—you can't overdo it. So just bear down."

While the audience laughs, Jack looks to Richard and asks, "Want to try 'Liberty?'"

Richard steps up to the microphone and says, "Now this tune will be a little number called 'Liberty.'"

Jack looks to Richard and says, off mike, "Key of D."

They play the hoedown tune "Liberty." Richard repeats it six times, varying each repetition only slightly as they play over the parts.

Richard again acknowledges the warm reception from the small crowd, "Thank you very much." He continues by integrating a tall tale into his stage patter:

> I started my playing down below Kissimmee, many years ago. And, of course, that's nothing spectacular to be raised on a farm. We had something to eat, and we had a lot of freedom. And on the farm, my sister had a place down there that was the richest place in the state of Florida. We had to plant corn on the run. The soil was so rich that that kernel of corn would sprout and run up your britches leg before you'd get out of there. So you had to plant it on the run.
>
> And watermelons. Well, we couldn't do much with them. The ground was so rich that the watermelon vine would grow so fast until the vines would wear the watermelons out dragging them across the ground before they got ripe. We saved one or two. And we wanted to take it up to the house, but we didn't have enough neighbors around there to pick it up. It was a big watermelon. So we hooked a mule to a wagon, and we went down there to get it. And we finally got enough of the neighbors around there, and we got that watermelon mounted up there on that wagon. And it fell off and busted and drowned my mule. So that was it.[3]

Richard looks at Jack and they both laugh. Jack says to Richard, " 'Mississippi Sawyer.' "

They play the hoedown tune "Mississippi Sawyer." On the second repetition of the A part, Richard shifts into "Liberty." Jack tries to keep time, and Richard slides back into "Mississippi Sawyer." Jack grins and looks relieved. They repeat the A and B parts six times. At the end of the tune, Jack nods to the audience and says, "Thank you."

Richard's "thank you" initiates another story: "On my sister's farm, not very far from where we was, she raised bees and sold honey. That orange blossom honey down there is very special and everybody liked it. And she had more orders than she could fill. She had all the bees that she could put down there—had them everywhere—didn't have room for any more. But still she couldn't fill the orders. There was just more demand for the honey than she could get. Finally she thought up an idea that worked. You know what she done? She crossed them honeybees with lightning bugs, and they could work all night long."

The audience members laugh while Jack says to Richard, "Let's do 'I Don't Love Nobody,' key of D." They play this dance tune, repeating the piece nine times. Richard plays variations by adding slides and double-stops on different repetitions.

As they finish the tune, Richard thanks that crowd and then gives them another story: "You know, my wife's been wanting a waterbed. She kept going— You know, when a woman puts in for something, you just as well go get it because she's going to get it yet—if it takes six months! So anyhow, she wanted a waterbed. So the day that it was supposed to be delivered, I come home a little early to see what it's all about. And as I walked in there, I seen a man in the room there. And I said, 'Who's he?' She said, 'He's a lifeguard.' "

Jack looks at Richard, smiles, and nods. "Let's do that 'Soldier's Joy.' " Richard plays the first two bars softly and looks at Jack. Jack says to Richard, "Key of D."

They start "Soldier's Joy." Richard adds some fast shuffles and interesting variations on the tune as they repeat the melody several times to complete the tune.

When Richard lowers his fiddle from under his chin, he begins another story: "You know, my wife and I had an awful argument the other day. I was so mad I could have bit a railroad spike in two. And the more I thought about it, the madder I got. I got off work that afternoon. And I got out of the car, and I slammed the car door, jerked open the front door and looked. And, lo and behold, there was my wife standing there with a pretty dress on—every hair in place." Richard slicks his hair back with his left hand, and he continues his story. "The table was set with my favorite supper. The candles were lit, and I looked. The more I looked—the more I forgot. And, you know, she had one of these little skirts all pulled up. Man, I forgot all about being mad, you know. Well, I ain't going to tell you the rest of it anyhow!"

As the audience laughs, Jack makes an apt suggestion to Richard, "Why don't you do 'Annie's Waltz'? Introduce her." Richard picks up on the idea and says, "I'm going to play a little waltz that I wrote for my wife called "'Annie Seaman Waltz.'"

They play the waltz. The tune is Richard's variation of older waltz tunes played in the area. The musicians repeat the waltz's melody seven times, Richard adding double-stops and slightly syncopated shuffles throughout the piece to vary the tune. On the fourth repetition, he plays almost every note double-stopped, and his harmonies ring out true and clear through the sound system at the Jacksonville Landing.

After he finishes the tune, Richard acknowledges the audience's applause and tells another story:

> Many years ago before I came up to Jacksonville, I had a friend that lived down in Kissimmee, and he was a young man. And I really liked him: I thought a lot of him. He was recently married then and had a little boy. So I went down to visit with him, and it got to doing that I had to spend the night with him. He lived way out in the country. Well, they just had a little five-room house and two bedrooms. So they said I could share the room with the little boy. Well, that night when we got ready to go to bed, the little boy and I went up in to the room.
>
> And I looked over there, and that little boy was kneeling down by the bed with his head laid down on the mattress. And I said, "Well, if that little boy is man enough to say his prayers, I'll say mine too." So I got on the opposite side of the bed and got onto my knees. The little boy looked up and said, "Mr. Seaman, what are you doing?" I said, "I'm doing the same thing you are." The little boy looked up and said, "Well, mama's going to be mad—the potty's on this side of the bed."

The joke goes over well, and Jack says to Richard, "Flop-Eared Mule."

Richard plays the first few notes softly before looking to the audience: "Yeah, there's an old tune we used to play for square dances a long time ago called the 'Flop-Eared Mule.' I don't know why exactly they give it that name. But we had to work with some of them down there, and they were ornery as the Devil—especially the white ones. But the name of this tune is 'The Flop-Eared Mule,' and we used to play it for dance parties."

Richard and Jack play this hoedown, repeating it nine times. On some repetitions, Richard again alters the rhythm by playing the first measure as four quarter notes instead of the shuffles usually played to begin the tune. Although he says he does not know how the tune was named, he makes his fiddle bray like a mule on the first four notes of the B part.

As the applause settles, Jack looks over the set list that he has placed down at his feet and says to Richard, "'Westphalia Waltz.'"

Richard introduces the tune, "We're going to play a waltz now. I'll slow down a little bit."

Jack makes another suggestion to Richard, "Tell them the story about how you got the waltz" as Richard pulls loose horsehairs from his bow.

Richard says to Jack, "I think I'm coming apart a bit." He adjusts his bow and plays some fiddle lines seeking to find the key of "Westphalia Waltz."

Richard picks up on the cue that Jack offered and tells another story: "I heard Chubby Wise play this. I thought it was a pretty piece, and I wanted to learn it. So I walked down where he was at a bluegrass festival, asked him did he have a tape with that tune on it, 'Westphalia Waltz.' He said, 'Yes, I got one.' I said, 'Well, I'd like to buy it. How much is it?' He said, 'Fifteen dollars.' So I paid fifteen dollars to learn this tune."

Richard and Jack play the "Westphalia Waltz." It is a pretty piece. Throughout the tune, Richard uses double-stops, slight syncopation, and detaché bowing in the beginning of the B part. His embellishments bring out the beauty of the waltz, and it is a fine performance. Once again acknowledging the applause, Richard then offers another story: "A couple of weeks ago, I slipped out on my wife and went out on the town. I thought I was getting away with it. And while I was gone, a burglar broke into my house. Sure did. But I don't think he got anything more than a cracked eye and a broke jaw. You see, my wife thought it was me slipping back in."[4]

As the laughter settles, Jack says to Richard, "Let's do 'In the Garden.'" They play the familiar gospel tune. The old hymn resounds through downtown Jacksonville as some of the audience members sing along.

As they finish the tune, Richard thanks the audience and begins another story:

> That there reminds me of a preacher that I knew. He lived about ten or fifteen miles outside of Kissimmee, but his church was in town. And every Sunday he had to drive through some wooded section, a pretty wooded section, to get to town.
>
> One Sunday morning, he was driving to town, and he looked in the rearview mirror. And he saw an old drunk driving behind him. Well, it made the preacher feel sort of bad to know that this fellow would be intoxicated on the Sabbath. He said a little prayer for him

and speeded up. And he looked in the mirror: the drunk was right be-hind him. He'd go a little faster. The drunk was right behind him. He kept looking up in that mirror and trying to outrun that drunk. He happened to come up on a sharp curve in the road, and he was looking in the mirror and didn't see it. And he couldn't make that curve, so he went out through the woods. He hit a stump and turned the car upside down. All four wheels straight up. And the old drunk stopped, went back, got down on his hands and knees. He said, "Mister are you hurt?"

The preacher said, "No, I'm not hurt. I've got the good Lord riding with me."

The drunk said, "You better let him drive with me. The way you're driving you're liable to hurt him!"

The joke goes over well, and the soundman looks at me and we laugh. Jack offers the next tune on the set list, " 'Fourteen Days in Georgia,' key of G," to Richard. They play the hoedown tune, repeating it nine times.

I signal that there is time for another tune, and Jack quietly responds with a nod. "One more?" he asks.

I quickly nod my head.

Richard continues with another story:

A lot of memories come from way down the state when I was a boy. Down on the Kissimmee Prairie about forty-five or fifty miles west of Miami at that time in the early 1900s.[5] It was pretty isolated. It was no road out there. Miami was just a little fishing town.

Well, this man and his wife decided they'd go out there on that prairie and homestead some land and raise some cattle. Maybe they might start a little ranch, so they went out there. They got a few cows and worked them hard. And in due time, as luck would have it, she became pregnant.

Well now, out there in those days, there was no help within miles around. So she knew that she had to have help. So when the time came for the baby to be born, she started out for Miami, which was about forty miles away by horseback. And the old horse was pregnant too, by the way.

So they hadn't been gone very long before the Indians got after them. Now that was a race to behold. That horse was running for all it was worth with that woman hanging on to him, hoping they could outrun them. And them Indians was a bunch of varmints.

And, well, in the excitement, that horse had to give birth to that colt. There, now, they stopped, right there. And the woman, in the excitement, her time was there too—and the Indians were closing in on them. Well, that old mare give birth to a colt; she give birth to a baby. And the horse jumped up, and she jumped on to its back and there they went. And that colt jumped up, and the baby jumped on his back, and they outrun them. You know, we beat them!

Richard laughs to Jack, "You don't believe that."

Jack smiles and says to Richard, "This is the last one, 'Up Jumped Trouble.'"

Richard cues the song: "We got one more favorite we're going to play and cut out this here foolishness up here and let you people find something worthwhile to listen to. We thank you for being with us. You've been a great audience, and we've enjoyed it. And maybe someday we'll have the good luck to play for you again. We've got one more piece we want to play, and we call it 'Up Jumped the Devil.'"

Richard and Jack play the tune, repeating it several times as the melody catches the audience's ear. After Richard plays his usual tag, they finish their set. Jack thanks the audience for applauding, and Richard lifts his hat in a final salute before turning away to pack up his fiddle and bow. I make sure that the next act is ready to go onstage, and I thank Richard and Jack, telling them how much I enjoyed their show.

A violent thunderstorm rages through downtown Jacksonville an hour after their set, and the weather forces me to close down the folklife stage for the day.

Throughout the thirty-minute performance, I had kept my eye on Richard's video camera while I listened to the mix coming through the soundboard. The presence of Richard and Jack's performance emerges through their words, but what is absent is the laughter that followed each of his jokes and stories. Also absent is the toe-tapping and head-nodding of the audience members, including the out-of-time clapping of a three-year-old girl who toddled by the stage. The transcript misses the sense of cooperation and connection between the performers, producers, and audience members. I had worked with the soundman during the past two Arts Mania events, and he noticed how Richard had presented an especially smooth and entertaining performance this year. The videotape and transcript also exclude the comments from an Arts Mania volunteer who gushed how she had a such a great time volunteering to work at this stage and how much fun it was to hear Richard's tunes and tales. She beamed as she noted how she loved hearing the waltz that he wrote for his wife.[6]

Sitting next to the camera and listening through the sound system, I began to reflect on Richard Seaman's performance. I was amazed at how he was able to create such a sense of presence through his music and stories. He established the feel of playing at a Florida frolic, and he also evoked a strong sense of Florida history. I was impressed that he made this popular structure of feeling so palpable in his performance and that he and Jack could evoke a strong sense of time and place in such an effortless and artistic manner. As I was sitting in the audience, I also wished that there was a way to let the members of the audience understand the value and appreciate the beauty of the scores of tunes in his repertoire. The tunes he played represented only a fraction of the hoedowns, waltzes, and other songs that he plays.

As I was listening to his stories, I also came to recognize that I knew little about tall tale telling in Florida. I became curious about the meanings that Richard was expressing in his stories, and I wanted to learn more about his storytelling tradition. Finally, I felt a bit unfulfilled because I wanted the audience to understand more about the importance of Richard's status as an old-time fiddler from Florida, especially because he is a musician who learned many of his tunes at house parties shortly after the turn of the century. Although fiddlers still accompany dancers at square dance clubs and festivals, the old context of holding house parties with live fiddlers has virtually disappeared in Florida and America. Richard's participation in these events as a fiddler is an important, even irreplaceable, facet of the state's social history.[7]

In watching the performance, I began thinking about what Richard has seen in a lifetime of playing fiddle tunes and telling stories. He was ninety-seven years old when I last interviewed him in the first year of the twenty-first century. The century of life that he has experienced in Florida has been the scene of major changes in the peninsula's landscape. He has seen changes that few living people have experienced, and I knew that he reflects on the changes in history, tells fine stories, and eloquently reflects on his life experiences. In formal interviews and informal conversations, I found that he not only articulates rich descriptions of Florida's history but that he also develops intriguing perspectives about the contemporary performances of his music and stories. I also discovered that he draws from his experiences and his perspectives about presenting folklife within the public sphere but that there is also a private sphere that remained separate from the Folklife Stage at Arts Mania. His stories and reflections reveal how he draws from both public presentations and private personal experiences to craft his performances. Through these performances, Richard creatively expresses himself using his vast repertoire, storehouse of experiences, and acute perceptions and insights. A wry crackle in his gentle, husky voice reveals how much he has to say.

2

And the Merry Love the Fiddle

~

For the good are always the merry,
Save by an evil chance,
And the merry love the fiddle,
And the merry love to dance.
                    —W. B. Yeats, "The Fiddler of Dooney"*

Outside of Richard and Annie Seaman's home in Jacksonville, the ther-
mometer is climbing to the other side of one hundred degrees. I have
spent the last couple of afternoons inside of their house in the Avondale section
of the city where I have been completing hours of interviews with Richard.
Near the close of the millennium, we are recording his memories of life in
Florida in the second decade of the twentieth century. I have focused many
of my questions on the place of the old-time square dance at house parties in
Richard's home community in Osceola County. We have recorded a number of
his tunes, and I had played fiddle and guitar with him earlier that day in their
living room. Annie offers me a Coke, and, hoping to round out the interviews
with Richard, I ask her if she had ever attended square dances.

She responds with a succinct answer that curtails my attempt to document her description of an old-time square dance in Florida. "Whew, my Dad
wouldn't allow that. He was real strict on us—the girls especially."[1]

Annie grew up in Baldwin, Florida, about thirty miles west of Jacksonville. She explains that the dances held eighty years ago in her northern Florida
community were regarded as too rough for her to attend. Although she enjoys
hearing Richard talk about the dances and loves hearing him play, I am not con-
vinced that she would have enjoyed everything about the house parties in central Florida that Richard has been eloquently describing during our interviews.

His stories about the dances that were held a hundred and fifty miles south of Jacksonville in central Florida is a vivid description of an important facet of his life. By talking about ways that fiddling and dancing were interwoven into Florida's social fabric, the stories contribute to the history of an area that has undergone more change in one century than in the state's entire six millennia of existence.[2] Richard's story begins as he places himself, his two sisters, and his parents in his home community near Lake Tohopekaliga.

We lived back out in the woods, and we had no electricity. We had no running water or anything like that. So there wasn't much to do but work.

My Dad took care of a seventy-five-acre orange grove for a man by the name of McCool. William McCool, from Beaver Falls, Pennsylvania, he owned that land. And they would come down there in the wintertime and hunt. It was good hunting and fishing around on that lake and them swamps down there.

And that was the only outlet we had—other than taking care of the orange grove and working for Old Man McCool. That's what we had to do, and when I got big enough, I had to get out there and help with them. Plowing and fruiting trees, hoeing trees, taking care of fencing and mending fence—and anything that happens on the farm. And we had no outlet. When the sun went down, that was it.

We'd generally eat about dark. In the time the supper dishes were washed, why, it was dark. And there was nothing else to do but just sit around. Read a book if you had one. Maybe us kids would play games. Mother would sew a quilt. She was always making something, like making a quilt or mending clothes. Dad would read an old book if he had one.

The only outlet we had was if the neighbors would get together, and your next door neighbor might be three quarters of a mile or a mile away. They'd get together on a Sunday and go and have a picnic down at the lake. And they'd seine some fish and have a fish fry. We thought that was wonderful.

A lot of Saturdays—evenings—why for something to do, they'd have a square dance somewhere. And there'd be one or two old fiddlers—or someone who tried to fiddle. There was never experts at it. And they would sit down and saw on this fiddle, and they'd dance all night long.

Some of the women still had their old bonnets on and their aprons. But they didn't care. They was having a lot of fun.

And then Sunday, it was just recuperate to go back to work Monday. It was the same routine, over and over. Fishing and hunting was my outlet.

I had a lot of territory there that I could hunt, trap, fish, and in the wintertime we would catch a few furs, coons and stuff like that, and try to sell the hides to a hardware store by the name of McKinson. That would give me a little spending money. In the summertime, we'd hunt alligators and sit up all night and fight mosquitoes and try to kill us a few alligators. And we thought that was fun. All that is gone now. Everything is gone.

They've got electric lights, and they even got a fire department out there now where we used to live. People have come out there in trailers. And the old place, you wouldn't know it. The old orange groves, the last bad freeze we had, which was several years ago, wiped it out. And that's all dead.

There's nothing out there now like it was.[3]

Richard's story explains how he envisions life in his home community of Kissimmee Park around 1914. It is a vivid and fascinating account of life in an area that is now subsumed largely by urban sprawl and barely planned growth. The only physical features from his childhood home that he still can locate are some live oak trees that remain on the property where his parents' home once stood. But a fascinating story remains, and Richard's clear memory, sharp analytical skills, and personal experience narratives provide a vivid context for his life story.[4] In contextualizing his story, he provides a fascinating means for understanding old-time fiddling and square dancing in his region of Florida. Richard is providing the most complete description I have heard of a major form of entertainment that existed prior to the advent of the electronic hearth, the Golden Age of Radio, and even the introduction of recorded music in rural Florida.[5]

I listen as Richard explains why a square dance was an important event in Florida. He describes how in the past, communities would gather together a few times a month to dance in homes and establish through recreation the neighborly associations essential for daily work. In the present, Richard offers his view of the dance's importance in his home community. He explains that the dance party or "frolic" went by different names.

The old "free-for-all," we used to call it, they don't have that in their homes like they used to. Whenever some of the people in the neighborhood decided they wanted to have a little fun on a Saturday night, they would get it out, "we'll have a square dance." And all the neighbors from miles around could come.

Of course, some of them would get drunk too, but that all went along with it. But they would have a big time and dance till two or three o'clock in the morning. That was just about the only fun we had. Picnics and square dancing were about the only two real outings we had in those days. Because there wasn't nothing else to do, we had to do something to create a little excitement.

Richard's memory is sparked by my comment that I had heard that the house parties could not begin until a room had been cleared of furniture, and he tells his version of the classic "roll back the rug" story.[6]

Carpets and stuff like that, very few people had them. If they did, we'd roll them up. And we'd sprinkle corn meal on the hardwood floor. We'd sprinkle corn meal out there, and in about the first fifteen or twenty minutes of dancing, that corn meal would be sifted around. And the floor would be real slick. They thought that made dancing easier. It didn't matter to me—just so I could get up there. They had to have a good floor to dance on. Most people would have a front room big enough. They had to have at least four couples for one set. If they'd get two or three sets that way, you'd have to have a pretty good size. If the floor wasn't too big, some people would rest while others would dance.

Finding out that the dances were quadrilles and that as many as two dozen dancers would be swinging their partners, performing circles, stars, do-si-dos, and allemandes, I ask Richard when the dancing would start.[7]

Most people there had chores to do. Everybody that lived around there had a cow, some horses, and some hogs. That was their livelihood, and every afternoon all that stock had to be fed and taken care of. After you got all that done and had your supper, it was generally after dark a little bit. They'd gather over to somebody's house. As a general rule, everybody had to get the chores done before they went out. You couldn't go and stay nowhere. I know my folks, if they went anywhere, they had to get home and milk that cow and feed the stock. Hogs, horses, cattle, all that had to be fed, and hay had to be pitched down for the night, especially in the wintertime. So it would always be about dark, or a little later. Some of them wouldn't get there until way late. Just as soon as they got enough there for four couples, they could start.

Richard explains that the most important player in the dance was the caller. The caller would begin the dance when enough couples were on the floor. He notes that the dancers graciously learned to figure out unique systems for calling a dance.

In the old-time dancing, sometimes there wouldn't be enough for two sets. Sometimes there would be more. They would get out there and call their own dances. The callers in those days, one wouldn't be like the other at all. He'd just have his own way of calling. Back yonder it was just that each caller would have his own way, and you had to sort of figure out what he meant. So we'd get four to a set, all the way around. And when they'd start to dance, each couple out would try to remember what he meant: like the bird in the cage.

"The bird fly out and the hog fly in, hog fly out and swing his bird and go again.

"Right foot up and your left foot down, you cut a figure-eight when you come around.

"And runaway eight when you get straight." That was promenade: "runaway eight when you get straight."

That would be four couples, eight people. They would have all different calls and a little different names for their sets. I never did know all of them.

Later on in the interview, Richard provides a longer sample of a square dance call:

Back your ears and go hog wild,
Swing your partner cowboy style,
With your left foot down,
You cut a figure-eight when you come round.
First couple out and swing.
Go down the center and split the ring,
The lady go gee—the gent go haw.
Swing on the corner then swing your partner.
Run away eight when you get straight.[8]

I comment that the dances sounded like fun, hoping that Richard will develop a more complete description of the dance.

> It was a lot of fun. Some of the dances were real nice if you could get somebody who knew how to call the dance. Most everybody would try, but there wasn't professional square dance callers like we have today. They really don't dance like they used to. They more or less walk now around in formation. They used to get up there and get some action into it. Most of it was just simple callers who would get up there and would call out the set to the best of his ability. And we'd try to do it—whatever he'd call. It wasn't anything that had to be. It was just whatever come up. That's where the fun was. You could just sort of make your own fun, and if you didn't follow that caller, why, it was no harm done. It just kept right on going anyhow. They didn't pay no attention to the musicians, once they got started. They was too interested in what they were doing. They had done established the tempo, and they would keep going. Just as long as they could hear some music in the background, they weren't caring much what you played. Just so you played.

Richard explains that most of the dances in his area were variations of the square dance. A few people would show off some fancy clogging steps, and Richard adds that he tried some of the new steps with limited success. He explains that when he tried clogging, his feet looked like "two little pigs fighting."

Shifting from a consideration of the dance to a description of the music, he notes that he was always more interested in the fiddling than the dancing. He begins by explaining where the fiddlers were positioned in the room. "They'd be sitting in a corner, generally in a room or in the corner. Or where he could sit where he'd be out of the road. Sometimes them old boys would get a little bit tight, and it wasn't safe for the fiddlers."

Laughing, Richard continues with a story that shows how understanding fiddling in central Florida entails an understanding of the dance. He wants to ensure that I have a good mental image of the entire event. Later on, he will return to a closer consideration of what was expected of a fiddler at an old-time square dance. In speaking of the dance, he reiterates that his style of dancing a hoedown was a bit different than the more sedate style of contemporary square dancers.

> I've seen him swing the girl's feet clean out. One set would darn near knock over another one down. They were having fun. Them old

country boys, they were rough. They'd have their old boots on and their rough clothes on. They didn't dress up to go to a dance. They'd just go like they were. Some of them would have hats on and some wouldn't. And everything went. And if you wanted a drink of whiskey, you'd go outside and feel around the palmetto bushes. After a while, you'd feel a bottle. Somebody'd hid a bottle there. Take a drink, and stick it back in and go on.

Realizing that interesting activities went on outside of the house at a house party, I ask Richard how many people would show up for a dance. He answers in his careful and exact manner and then illustrates how the coming of roads and the automobile changed the dance. In highlighting the changes, Richard tacitly explains how the community was isolated in its early years. "Oh sometimes there'd be thirty or forty, I guess, in the little neighborhood where we lived. And that would be about a houseful. Of course, later on when automobiles came in and the roads were good and handy, why they would double that because people could come from farther away. They would come in from town and come from a long distance. But when I was a kid, we didn't have automobiles. We had to walk or go in horse and wagon. Or maybe ride the old mule if you had no other way to go and was just yourself."

Trying to envision how a house party might look, I comment, "I could just picture all the horse and wagons and mules outside of the person's house."

Richard responds with a slightly anthropomorphized illustration. "It'd be all carted-out under the trees. Horses standing there, wishing to God they could go home." We laugh, and I comment that maybe they were wishing that they could go inside and dance. My quip sparks a wonderful story of a prank that could be played on buggy drivers.

With buggy wheels, the back wheels are bigger than the front wheels. Most all people who drove horse and buggies around had a buggy wrench—what they would call a "buggy wrench." It fit the nuts to take the wheel off, and they'd have a little old box with a little top to it in the dashboard there to put your buggy wrench in that. In case something would happen, if a wheel come off or would get loose, you could tighten it up.

Well the threads on the right side had right-hand threads. The wheels on the left side had left-hand threads. So the rotation of the wheel wouldn't roll the nut off. If it happened to hit the nut, it would tighten it.

You'd get someone to help you. Them little buggies wasn't heavy.

He could pick up the rear wheel, and you'd loosen the nuts. And you'd take that nut off the little wheel and run it back there and stick it there on that axle and tighten it up. And then you'd put the big wheel up front and tighten it up. You'd put the wrench back in there and go on.

They'd come out there, and there'd be a little wheel and a big wheel and a big wheel and a little wheel.

Richard smiles and pauses a moment. He collects his thoughts and continues by explaining how this part of the practical joke provided the basis for a double set-up. "Or you'd take the horse out, turn him around, face him in, and then run the shafts through the holders on the backboard. You'd go out there in a hurry, and you'd danced all night and was tired. And you'd go out there and get in your buggy. And there was that damn horse looking at you."

Richard leans back, closes his eyes, and chuckles. Annie's eyes twinkle as she winks at me and we laugh, sharing in Richard's laugh.

He concludes his description. "And if you didn't have somebody to help you, you couldn't change them wheels. Of course, you could turn the horse around and face him in by yourself. I've done that a lot of times. We were pretty hip to things like that."

Richard admits that he had been the prankster as well as the prankee. His description of the dance moves forward in time as he explains how improvements in transportation contributed to the house party's demise.[9] "After later years, when they had roads in there, people began to have cars. More youngsters began to be able to buy old junk cars. They'd come from further away because they came in cars. And that sort of messed up some of the dances because some of the toughs would come from town and come out looking for trouble. And they generally found it too."[10]

Richard's eyes light up as he laughs, thinking about the tension between city kids and country boys and the myriad mismatches that created the inevitable clashes. I am interested in the fiddlers and ask if any string bands ever played at the square dances. He responds with another full description that, once again, reveals and elaborates on how the system of dancing and playing worked together. "We never had a band there. No, not then. It was always just one fiddle. Maybe there'd be two there, but one would relieve the other one. They never had a band. I never even seen a guitar until I was sixteen years old."[11]

Richard explains why he might only hear one or two fiddlers at a dance by noting that there was a dearth of musicians in Kissimmee Park. His answers to my legal pad full of questions provide his understanding of the fiddler's talents and the musician's place within the community.

The old-time square dance was way back yonder when music was scarce. Sometimes we'd have a little trouble in the olden days in getting someone to play because everybody didn't have instruments like they've got them today. Where one fellow in the community might own an old fiddle, the most of us couldn't even hardly afford a harmonica, and we'd do the best we could with what we had. But it was fun.

It didn't matter how well you played a violin—they would only call you a fiddle player. Maybe you couldn't play but one or two tunes, but you was classed as a fiddle player right along with some fellow over here that could play. It didn't matter. So you was a *musician* if you could play but one tune!

That was where the fun came in. Everybody was out for a good time, and they just enjoyed the dancing. It didn't make much difference what kind of music you had—just so you had a good tempo, you was all right. Down home, anybody that could play a mouth organ or a harmonica, or a fiddle, he was considered a *musician,* whether he could play it good or not. So it was not how well you could play it. It was just the tempo. If you had something to dance by, that was about all them fellows cared for. Once in a while somebody would come through that could take a fiddle and play a different tune than we knew and sound pretty good. But that was very seldom. It was just the same old thing. "Shear 'Em" was generally the old stand-by.

The tune Richard mentions, "Shear 'Em," is a lively hoedown tune. In south Georgia, the same tune is known as "Cotton Bagging." It is the first tune that he learned to play. After first learning it at home, he would play the tune at dances, repeating it scores of times to allow dancers to perform sets that could take thirty minutes to complete. The repetition allowed him to perfect the tune and develop some slight variations on the melody. "Shear 'Em" shows up in early collections of fiddle tunes throughout Florida, and he learned it through an aural tradition that was in effect prior to the existence of recordings made on compact disk, audio tape, vinyl records, and wax cylinders.[12] The fiddlers whom Richard first heard had picked up their tunes from other musicians who had never learned fiddle tunes through formal music lessons or from written sheet music. Nor did they learn these tunes from airplay on the radio. Rather, the tradition of fiddling in Florida stretches back to an oral tradition at least three centuries old.[13] Richard notes that although there were good players in the area, he evaluates much of the musicianship as substandard. "Some of them couldn't hardly carry a tune. One old man used to sit down and play, and he'd get in that key of A. And he never changed. He'd get in A, and he'd just keep that beat. But they were dancing by it. They knew no differences."

Although skilled old-time musicians were welcome to play at the dance, the focus of the dancers' attention was directed away from the tunes. Richard's assessment of the place of the fiddler within the square dance tradition emerges in his stories and vibrant descriptions. He offers a bare-bones description of the music at dance to reveal what element of fiddling was essential in a hoedown. Paring away the extraneous components of virtuoso fiddling, such as innovative variations of tunes, intricate ornamentation, complex harmonies, and fancy melody lines, Richard explains that even playing musical notes could be a superfluous element of old-time fiddling. "Sometimes the dancers went along with no tune at all. It was a beat or a swing. If you could get them dancing, they didn't give a dang as long as you've got a rhythm. I have seen it where they didn't even use an instrument and still have a square dance. They'd take two sticks—similar to sawed-off broom handles—and sit down there and tap them on the floor. And they'd just get a rhythm started and then go ahead and dance. They didn't have any music, but they'd dance anyhow. It was just fun."

The dance was entertainment. Fiddlers accompanied the dancers as they cut the figures at the command of the caller. In Richard's view, playing the fiddle was akin to tending a machine that set people to dancing, for in Kissimmee Park, fiddlers were *musicians* because they could make music. His own ideas about fiddling are close to how he regards members of his home community's assessment of this perspective on musicianship. Fiddlers are not necessarily endowed with special gifts that set them apart from other people, and musicianship is a skilled craft that can be learned with practice and perseverance. An old-time fiddler is a *musician* if he or she can keep time, play a tune, and keep dancers moving to a caller's patter. Musicianship in fiddling does not depend upon a unique talent that emanates from a visionary, isolated, or even tortured soul, but rather it is a quality that a fiddler can choose to develop and then offer a community.

Although he remembers that almost everybody in his neighborhood appreciated the fiddler's gift of music, he also recalls that there were a few who had their reservations about the moral character of fiddlers and the whole enterprise of fiddling.

There was an old lady that lived down home there that wouldn't let her husband bring the fiddle in the house. She said the fiddle was kin to the Devil, and she wouldn't let him. He had to leave it in the barn. He couldn't bring it in the house.

That was superstitious. The old people had their superstitious ways, and that was hers. The best that I can remember, he was just like the rest of them. He'd just saw off a tune. She was the only one I knew of who was that way. The rest of them all seemed to accept it. The better you could play, the better they'd like you. She thought it was sinful, but that's the only one that I know of.

I've heard of different ones claiming that they would hide the fiddle if the preacher came around and stuff like that. Some of them thought that fiddle music was harmful. But all I knew of was that one old lady that didn't want her husband to bring the fiddle in the house. She said the fiddle was the Devil's music.[14]

It is curious that the fiddle was regarded as "the Devil's box" in countless communities throughout the Americas and across Europe. In Kissimmee Park, the diabolic associations seem even stranger because there seem to have been limited opportunities to hear the frenzied and passionate playing of those whose virtuosity might rival Niccolò Paganini's prowess.[15] Richard also explains that there were no church buildings in his immediate area, so it is unlikely that a Saturday night of square dancing competed with church attendance. In fact, although Richard admits that the dances could become wild, square dancing and fiddle playing were seen as positive contributions to establishing and keeping a community spirit alive.

He explains the importance of this neighborly spirit by comparing life in rural Kissimmee Park to contemporary life in the city of Jacksonville. "We had very little amusement, only jokes and things like that. If you went somewhere in your horse and wagon and met some of your neighbors down there on the road, sit right there and talk. The old horse would be almost sleeping. They'd be talking. Now it's 'Get the Hell out of my way.' And they go."

Richard raises his eyebrows and laughs. I agree with him about the impatience of Jacksonville's drivers and respond, "Things have really changed in that way, didn't they?"

He is quick to reply, "It is."

He pauses long enough to invite my next question. Knowing that he wants to develop a topic that he cares about, I ask him if he thinks that the communities were tighter eighty years ago. He nods, his eyes comfortably affirming my question, and responds with a quick "Yeah."

Well, I've seen people help one another. If a person had—say for instance he was getting his hay in—you'd cut and mow your own hay, and you had to carry your own hay in. You'd get somebody to help. If you had kids, why, you're all right. They could tamp it down in and then you'd push it in the wagon. You'd have a wagon plumb full. Carry it to the barn. Push it in the barn. And everything would be all right. But now if you saw a rain coming up and your hay was down—if the weather began to look bad, there'd be another one or two rigs of horse and wagons drive up and get in there and go with you. See? They didn't ask for any money. They'd help you get your hay in and save it. See? If you didn't save it, you might lose it. And if anybody got sick, the neighbors would come around—flock around—and feed your stock. Take care of stuff that had to be done outside. They didn't want any money.

The relationship was established not through economic contracts but rather through a covenant of reciprocity.[16] Reminded of ways these types of relationships formed an *economy of neighborliness* in the Irish community of Ballymenone, I ask Richard for his perspectives on the dynamic of social reciprocity.[17] "Was that because they knew that if they would help you, you would also help them?"

Richard answers my question before I had finished asking it. Clarifying and expanding upon the relationship between neighborliness and cooperation, he explains:

> You'd help one another. And if anybody got sick or anything like that, somebody's wife or daughter would come over there and take over and help her. Pretty hard for a man there to take care of his wife and take care of his farm and keep things going. If there'd be a young one in the family, why, there'd be always some of the neighbors over there to help. And they didn't expect any money. There was no money passed at anything—as I know of—like that.
>
> If you was going to town and if you met your neighbor, you'd always say, "Can I bring you anything?"
>
> "Yeah, bring me a sack of feed or some bread."
>
> Or whatever you'd want. So he'd buy it and bring it over. You'd give him the money for it and that's all. He'd bring feed for your stock. He'd do things like that. And nobody even thought about hiring anybody. There were just neighbors. It was just "neighborly surviving," I guess you could call it. Everybody helped everybody. If you needed anything that you couldn't afford and if you really needed it, more than likely somebody would help you with it or do what they could for you. They would always get together, and it was just friendship all the

way around. Well, in fact, it had to be to live out like that. If you didn't have someone to help you, you'd be in a heck of a fix.[18]

Being neighbors in Kissimmee Park meant that people contributed what they could and that they asked for help when it was needed. Richard Seaman sees the square dance as an occasion for practicing and celebrating the system of neighborly survival. Folklorists have demonstrated how neighborly life is affirmed and communities are formed within festivals and celebrations where people gather.[19] Richard speaks of the connection so directly that he sounds as if he had written the textbook interpretation of the square dance as a microcosm for community life. He explains that the dance was one outlet for creating the connections that were essential for keeping people together in his home community of Kissimmee Park.

An authority on American fiddle music expands on what Seaman describes by positing the dance as a model of community interaction. Burt Feintuch writes that, historically, old-time square dancers acted out wider cultural patterns and social relations in festive display.[20] The dance affirms the institution of the couple as a basic social unit, and Feintuch explains that the patterns of the dance modeled the values and patterns acted out in visiting one's neighbors. Following Feintuch's analysis, the dance floor provided a site for practicing the values that would create the reality of Seaman's idea of neighborly survival. This reality was practiced not only in the four-couple sets in which dancers formed stars, allemandes, promenades, and other figures in their community, but neighborly survival was also enacted en masse when dancers formed the "big circle" by rounding up all of the dancers in one room.[21] For the neighborly spirit to survive and for the dance to work, the participants had to cooperate. Various relations that were created, practiced, and tested in the dance were then extended to life outside of the Saturday night free-for-all.

The dance was communal, but the authority invested in the caller was supreme. Even though the fiddler was subservient to the needs of the group, the dancers and musicians had to obey the caller's voice. The dance could still work with wild actions on the dance floor, but individual expression was possible only within the parameters of the socially proscribed constraints chanted by the caller. Dancers found and selected partners as they milled through the figures. They changed partners. They looked to their original partner to anticipate the end of a dance. Husbands trusted wives as they danced with other men, but then they returned home. The set's completion consummated a desire for excitement followed by harmony and an affirmation of order.

Richard regards this tight social network as essential for the community of rural people to survive their daily life. Community members had to cooperate.

Dancers who greeted and mingled with neighbors at the Saturday night dance would stop their horses and their horse-drawn carts to greet and mingle with neighbors while completing their daily work throughout the week. Although the system of neighborly survival and communal cooperation was in place within each working community, there were business owners, experienced workers, bossmen, and constables whose word was law. The balance and precision celebrated in the square dance were job requirements for farmers, ranch hands, citrus grove caretakers, and sawmill operators when they returned to work after the weekend.

Richard recognizes that there was room for individual expression within the community, but he also notes that there were tight constraints against stepping outside of the community's bounds. The dance was a place to socialize as well as to court, and most of the fights that broke out were the results of would-be suitors overstepping a boundary. The need to trust your partner and your neighbor established and supported relationships of trust within the community.

Richard completes his rich and vivid portrait of the square dance in Kissimmee Park by explaining the importance of the fiddler's contribution to the community. The fiddler's importance emerges as Richard rounds out his story by comparing the dance to a picnic. The relationship between dancing and picnicking is more subtle than it may first appear as he explains why picnics were important events. Understanding a picnic provides a commonplace means for understanding the important responsibility played by the fiddler.

> It brought people together for more of a friendship. They were laughing and talking and cutting the fool. It'd give them a chance really to associate with the neighbor. That was the main thing, I guess. But anyhow, everybody seemed to enjoy it. It was just a simple procedure. Everybody in there was just enjoying themselves. It would give the community a chance to meet, talk, and associate with one another.
>
> Same way with a picnic. They'd generally have a picnic down at the lake. And somebody would take a seine and go out and seine some fish. And they'd have a fish fry, and everybody would bring something. The ladies would bring pies and cakes and whatever they had. It could be tasties, some cookies that they made. They'd sit all out there, and they'd fry them fish and go to eating. And everybody would just be having a big time. They did it just to get together and be together.

Richard's stories and descriptions explain what it meant to be a good neighbor. A good neighbor helped seine and fry fish for a picnic. A good neighbor contributed to the fish fry by baking pies or cakes. A good neighbor contributed to the social event by offering what he or she could. Good neighbors were there for others when needed.

The fiddler was responsible for bringing the music in the same way that his wife might bring a pie, cake, or shredded coconut for the fruit punch. The fiddler thus was not a glitzy star whose ego was spotlighted on a silver stage. He was a workhand who made a musical offering within the economy of neighborly survival that contributed to the creation and sustenance of the community. If a neighbor could make the fiddle ring, then he was expected to play.

Richard reiterates that fiddlers were rarely paid and concludes his discussion of the musician's place in his home community.[22]

Everybody was just having a good time, and the fiddler was willing to sacrifice his time to keep the thing going. It was just that everybody knew everybody and everybody trusted everybody. When I was a kid, we never locked the door. Sometimes we didn't shut it.[23] When we'd go to town, if anybody was to come by and get caught in the rain, he go in there until the rain was over and then go on. He didn't touch nothing. Everybody knew what you had. Everybody knew everybody. And everybody trusted everybody. I didn't know what it was when I first come up here to have to lock things and it began to get like it is now. We didn't lock up nothing when I was a kid. Everybody trusted everybody.

3

Workshop

~

Late in the evening about sundown
High on the hill above the town,
Uncle Pen played the fiddle, Lord how it would ring,
You could hear it talk, you could hear it sing.
—Bill Monroe

When planning for the second annual First Coast Folklife Exploration, I had decided to spotlight fiddle traditions in northern Florida. Even though bluegrass and country music is popular throughout Jacksonville, many Jacksonville residents know little about old-time, bluegrass, and western swing fiddle traditions. I wanted the audience to appreciate the chance to listen to fiddlers who had rich and interesting experiences to share. I was fortunate to have written contracts with three fiddlers who had agreed to perform throughout the two-day event. Although they all had played festivals previously, workshop presentations were new to them. Over a series of phone conversations, I presented the idea of holding a workshop, and I explained to each of them that the upcoming workshop would consist of on-stage interviews, informal storytelling about their musical experiences, discussion of musical history and various styles of music, as well as the performance of a few tunes.[1] All were cooperative and interested in this event, and they were looking forward to the opportunity to share their knowledge of Florida's fiddle traditions.

Unlike the stage performance genre of the Arts Mania festival where Richard and Jack performed, a workshop stage involves greater mediation by a presenter. Fortunately, I was able to contract the services of a past president of the Florida Fiddlers Association, Bob Stone, a folklorist who was working with the Florida Department of State's Bureau of Florida Folklife Programs in White Springs.

Bob plays old-time and Cajun fiddle, and I have also heard him play some fine boogie-woogie piano as well as sacred steel guitar licks.

Bob knows about the state's fiddling traditions. He is a skilled presenter, having assisted with the state's Florida Folk Festival for years. These types of presentations appeal to me because the presenter can help provide a more in-depth understanding of the folk musicians' artistry. His introductions, inter-viewing, and commentary set the stage for the three fiddlers to present their own artistry, and Bob's approach to leading the workshop brings out the strengths of the workshop genre. He understood my goal of showing historical continui-ties between Richard's old-time fiddling tradition and other styles of music such as bluegrass and western swing. He recognized that his role is best played by allowing the musicians to tell their own stories and offer their own reflections about music. Bob recognized that these fiddlers are all fine storytellers and that their narratives would emerge naturally and spontaneously in their perfor-mances. Their stories provide opportunities to compare the experiences of in-dividual musicians and suggest wider patterns of history and culture, thereby providing a wider context for understanding Richard's life experiences as a Florida fiddler. This particular workshop session especially appeals to me be-cause of the wonderful interactions among the musicians. They explore com-mon experiences and reflect on deeply held values associated with their musical life histories, and their collective commentary all supports Richard's own reflec-tions. All of the fiddlers comment on and affirm each other's stories. Storytelling is vibrant with the fiddling tradition, and the stories that are recorded during interviews take on a rich vitality when they are presented within the living con-text of a festival workshop.

It is Saturday, April 3, 1993, and Bob is leading the workshop in Jackson-ville's Museum of Science and History's Carpenter Gothic Church. The wood frame building dates from the late nineteenth century, and it was donated as a gift to the museum. It is an icon of an important style of vernacular architecture in Florida, and the church is also used for small programs offered by the mu-seum's educational department. It is located on the south bank of the St. Johns River, directly across from the Jacksonville Landing.

Stage left, Bob is seated on a metal folding chair that I have positioned at the far side of the church's chancel. He introduces the guest performers and ori-ents the audience to the workshop format used in a folklife festival. Moving from his immediate right to complete the introductions of the musicians who are seated in a semicircle, Bob cleverly opens the show: "I'd have to use my calculator to add up the total years of fiddling we have here, probably about two hundred years of fiddling. Richard Seaman, here, is from Jacksonville. He started playing about 1914. We'll be hearing from him. George Custer, from down in Salt Springs, comes from a family of fiddlers. His uncle was Georgia Slim Rutland, who did a lot of radio work and recording with the great Howdy Forrester, and Georgia Slim was a great fiddler in his own right. Chubby Wise, 'Mr. Bluegrass Fiddler.' "

There is a stirring in the crowd and some scattered applause. Chubby Wise looks out, nods his head, and smiles.

Bob continues his introduction, "All right. So I think we'll get started and work our way across and have everybody play a piece and talk a little and see what happens. We'll leave it real loose and casual."

He pauses a moment and looks down the line, making eye contact with the musician seated opposite him on stage right and admits, "And I forgot your name."

Jim gives a quick nod and replies, "Jim Quine."[2] Bob introduces the guitar player who plays with the Salt Run bluegrass band of St. Augustine and has agreed to back up the fiddlers for this session.

Following Bob's introduction, Chubby Wise picks up on the theme of Bob's introduction. He interjects, "You know, I think it's funny here, speaking of the old-timers, I believe the three of us are the only ones that Noah invited in the ark to play a fiddle for him when he built it. We've been around about that long, I reckon."

Chubby's wit is just about lost to the audience because a din of foot shuffling, stirring, and whispering nearly obscures his voice.

Bob notices the inquisitive faces and clarifies Chubby's comment with a question, "Noah invited you to play for him at the christening of the ark?"

Chubby answers, "George and I, he's been in the business, I guess, thirty-five/forty years, at least."

Outside a rooster that is stalking around the Carpenter Gothic Church lets out a crow, and George Custer makes his first comment, "Yeah, in fact, the later part of the '40s it was. '48, '49, '50, so what is that? Does that make forty years?"

Chubby tallies up the arithmetic and notes, "Close. Right close. By the way, the Nashville Association of Musicians just sent me a pin for fifty years with them at the Grand Old Opry, so I've been down that road a few miles."

George recollects, "I remember hearing my Uncle Bob—Georgia Slim. Every time Chubby and his wonderful wife, Rossi, would come through, they'd have to stop off and see Slim there at Valdosta. It was kind of semi-retirement after leaving Texas. But there were some great tales to be told."

Chubby acknowledges George's comment, "Well, I'll tell you George, and I mean this with all sincerity. There is fine fiddlers. There's great fiddlers. And then there was Georgia Slim and Howdy Forrester. To me, they were just the top of about any field that you'd want to put them in."

George acknowledges the compliment and remembers there is an audience in front of him, "For the folks that may not know, Howdy got his nickname—really—Slim gave it to him. Back then you had to have a stage name, so it was Big Howdy Forrester mainly because Howdy was always right out front with the biggest, widest grin you've ever seen."

Chubby accepts the responsibility of playing to an audience and suggests, "I think it might be a good idea for us to play one. How about 'Down Yonder'? I'll bet you remember 'Down Yonder,' don't you?" Richard nods his head and says, "Yes." George pipes up with "Yes sir. Yeah."

Chubby is about to start the show by suggesting in his high-pitched but deeply southern accent, "In the key of G. Is that all right with everybody?"

George answers, "That sounds fine. Should we take turns?"

Chubby offers a good way to showcase the tune, "We'll all play together and then each man will just kind of take a turn at it."

George lights up with a good idea, "Would you mind if, on my turn, if I just have you play again and let me give you some harmony? I *love to play* harmony." Chubby beams his affirmation, "Why I'd *love* it!" George is pleased that Chubby is open to his idea, "I love to play harmony more than if I had to play lead."

Further developing the stage patter, Chubby bestows a new sobriquet on George, "Well, I believe that's your middle name: George 'Harmony' Custer."

The audience laughs, and Chubby kicks off the fiddle tune with "All right, here we go."

The three fiddlers fly into "Down Yonder." Chubby sets a fast pace for the tune, and all the musicians keep up with the breakneck speed. George's harmonies beautifully complement Chubby's melody lines, and Chubby encourages the musicians by shouting out his approval with "Oh yeah, get with it" during the performance. As George plays harmony, Chubby coaxes the crowd along in Bob Wills' style by commenting, "Yes sir, that's all right," as George finds a particularly exciting harmony line. When Jim Quine hits the walk-down guitar line to provide a perfect answer to the melody that Chubby plays, George's smile shows that he recognizes that Jim is a hot guitar picker. It is the first time that all these four musicians are playing together.

It is a virtuosic performance. The musicians nod to each other as Chubby lifts his chin and raises his eyebrows to wind it down. The three different fiddlers each play three different tags, and the different melody of each tag creates a rich musical mélange of old-time counterpoint.

The lively acoustics in the church enrich the bright, enthusiastic applause of an excited crowd. Their anticipation of hearing the fiddlers is consummated, and they are expecting a great show.

As the applause fades, George refers to Bob Stone's introduction. The fiddler notes, "They really gave us a puzzle a minute ago with these years, but as long as they put the word 'young' after it."

All of the workshop performers laugh, and Bob intervenes with his first question as a presenter. "Richard, you've got a pretty good story on that fiddle of yours. Could you tell us that story?"

Richard pauses a moment and answers, "Well, I come to Jacksonville from below Kissimmee, in 1926, and went to work for the railroads. While I was up here, my old fiddle was down home at my dad's place. When the '26 hurricane came, it destroyed Miami that time." Richard lifts his voice to see if everyone is on common ground.

George remembers the storm, "Oh my, yes," he answers, and Richard returns to his story:

> It blowed the roof off my daddy's house, and this old fiddle was laying up on a table—up in the upstairs bedroom. Well, it got wet, naturally. So I drove down there to see how my folks were after the storm. Their house was roofless. Downed trees were everywhere. And I went up there and found my old fiddle all laying all over the floor. It was strung up, and when water got on it, I think it went off like a rattrap.
>
> Well, I gather it up, and I put it in an old shoebox. And I brought it up here. That was way back yonder during the Depression time, and I didn't have any money to have it fixed. So I kept it. So one day, I said, "Why I don't see why I can't fix this."
>
> So I got me some sandpaper, went all over it, cleaned it all up. And they told me I had to have a certain kind of glue for a violin. Well my heart sank because I didn't have the money to have it fixed, so I went down to the five and ten cent store, and I bought a tube of liquid solder.

Richard keeps the crowd's attention rapt as the audience laughs at the humor in the story. Outside of his voice, the only sound is the grandfather's clock in the back of the church. The tick-tocks resound off the hardwood floor.

Knowing that repairing a violin requires a special glue so that the instrument can be taken apart, George cannot resist commenting, "I'll bet it's never been apart since!"[3]

Richard shows him the black fiddle, and says, "You can look down there, and you can see it."

Peering inside the f-holes, George responds, "Oh yeah, that'll hold it."

The audience laughs as all of the performers are clearly enjoying the story, and Richard continues, "And I put it back together with clamps, and it looked pretty bad. It was rough, scratched, and beat up. I played it. One day, I think to myself, 'that looks terrible.' So I got myself a wood filler, and I went all over it. Sanded it down, got me a three-dollar can of paint, and painted it black."

George says, "Sounds good."

Richard concludes his story, "So for three dollars and ten cents, I got it fixed!"

Laughing, Bob exclaims, "All right!"

Richard continues, adding to his description of his fiddle, "But I don't know how old it is. It was hanging up on the wall as far back as I can remember in the old house I was born in. It just hung there. My dad didn't play it. And after I got big enough to get around them woods they had square dances. It was the only means of entertainment we had: picnics and square dances. So I used to go around to the square dancing, and I heard them old boys play. I liked that. I went home, and I was trying to learn it by ear. I wasn't doing too good, and one day one fellow says, 'Say fellow, you've got to tune that fiddle before you play!'"

Richard's humor goes over very well as the audience laughs. Looking at his fiddle, he continues with a story about learning to play, "So I finally found out something about it and started playing along. And when I first started, my mother says, 'I can't stand that. That's terrible. You can get outside.' She made me go outside and sit on a stump. And one day she said, 'Now the better you play, the closer you can get to the house.'"

Responding to the laughter from the audience, George comments, "That'll teach him real quick, won't it!"

Richard winds down his story by concluding, "It was five years before I ever played a tune indoors."

The audience and workshop participants laugh, and Chubby affirms the psychological trauma of learning to play a difficult instrument. He adds, "I know what you're talking about, though, because Ma didn't send me to that corncrib to shuck corn when I was learning there!"

Hearing their common experiences, George contributes his story to the workshop:

This almost sounds like we've got the same script, but my dear little momma, a Georgia lady, just passed away here three or four years ago. I was born there by lamplight. It sounds like I'm telling an old story, but they didn't have electricity through that part of south Georgia, Tift County. It was the same bedroom where Mamma was born. That was back in the days to where it come time to have the baby, you'd go home to momma, you know.

So Granny Rutland, she started helping me, encouraging me to get started. I guess I was about seven or eight years of age.

Boy, I'd save up all my practicing for Saturday, and there's been many a time I'd go at it three and four hours, sometimes five and six.

I remember, now, little Momma very nicely saying "Son, it sure is pretty weather outside. Don't you think you ought to play outside?"[4]

"Our stories are similar," notes George. His broad smile acknowledges the crowd's laughter, and he uses the three stories about learning to play the instrument to conclude, "I guess it just has to be part of your bloodstream or bone marrow to love and play the fiddle. It's the closest thing to the human voice, and it can communicate where words sometimes fail us."

Picking up on George's recognition that there is deeper significance to the stories, Chubby contributes to the discussion:

You know, George, I was just thinking now. And this is all kidding aside. The love for music, I think, begins at a very small age. And if you love it, you just hang in there. I don't care how rough it gets or how good it gets, you just don't seem to want to give up. I really started part of my career right here in Jacksonville, Florida, back in the middle '30s. I played some of the very fine places, beer joints, for tips—no salary involved. I was driving a ten-cent taxi. Now if you've been around here that long, you know what I'm talking about. You could ride for a dime then. Now you can't even get in one for less than a dollar and a half.

George notes, "I remember the quarter haircuts." Richard acknowledges, "That's right."

Chubby continues: "And I was driving a ten-cent taxi in the daytime from five in the morning to five in the evening. And then at nine o'clock, I'd go to the beer joint, and I'd play for tips till closing time. There was no salary involved, but we got our lunch free. Back in them days, that helped out too. But I feel like I think I've paid my fare. That's where I started out, and I've loved it so good I couldn't quit. I didn't have sense enough to—I reckon. So that makes about fifty-eight years, I've been trying to make a living in this business."

There are nods and murmurs of appreciation in the audience. Bob follows the flow of discussion and asks the right question. "Chubby, can you tell us a little bit about how the 'Orange Blossom Special' came to be while you're talking about that era?"

Expecting the topic to come up, Chubby has his story ready: "Yes, I can.

That's one I'll never forget. The late Ervin Rouse. As a matter of fact, I was living out at 809 East Adams Street."

Chubby points his bow in the direction of the St. Johns River, and Richard comments that he knew Mr. Rouse. Chubby says to Richard, "You knew Ervin?" and turns to the audience.

> Well, he and I got to be pretty close friends, and one night he had been out. After we had got off, why we run up on each other and went to the old Union Station. At Park and Main, I believe it. It's a new building now. But at that time, it was Union Station. We went in and had some coffee. They didn't have no big oranges there at that time of the morning, so we just come up with a cup of coffee. And we were sitting there talking about the Orange Blossom Special. And on the way home, I never will forget how Ervin put it, he said, "Doc." He called everybody "Doc." That was his byword. He says, "Let's write a fiddle tune when we get to the house and call it 'The Orange Blossom Special.'"

> And we took our two fiddles out and sit on the side of the bed at about four o'clock in the morning at 809 East Adams Street. And, ladies and gentlemen—so help me—in about forty-five minutes we had the melody on that fiddle tune wrote.

> I told my wife a lot of times, I said, "Lady Luck didn't smile at me and Ervin: she laughed out loud when we wrote that one because it got to be the biggest fiddle tune that ever was written."

George, aware of the audience's presence, clarifies a detail in the story. "Chubby, for some in the audience that might still not know. Of course, I don't know when it ended, but the Orange Blossom Special was a special train. Wasn't it out of New York?"

Chubby answers, "It run from New York to Miami" as Richard nods his head and acknowledges George's comment.

George continues, "New York to Miami. And it, of course, made one of the stops here on the Seaboard." Chubby affirms George's memory, "The Seaboard, yeah." Reiterating, George comments, "Yeah, and it was known as the 'Orange Blossom Special.'"

Richard interjects, "I worked for the Seaboard. I knew the Orange Blossom Special."

Chubby is beginning to conclude his story once again, and he says:

> Well, that's how that "Orange Blossom Special" was born. Now I had nothing to do with getting the words. His brother, Gordon, and

his brother, Ervin, wrote the words on that. And they were the first ones ever to record it as far as I know. They put it out on this old Blue-bird label, which was a subsidiary of RCA at the time. And I heard through the grapevine. I don't doubt it, but somebody told me that the tune has been recorded by around one hundred different artists over the period of years.

And here's the beauty of it. But it's not so beautiful, but it happened. I gave Ervin my half—just like you'd share a cigarette. I never will forget it. He said, "Doc, let's go get that fiddle tune copyrighted." I said, "Ervin, I don't have time to fool with no fiddle tune, I've got to go check on my cab in a few minutes and go to work. If you can do a thing with it, it's all yours." He done something with it for him.

And I want to say that I'm very grateful. I'm not hurt one bit about it. But I figure this: I'm lucky enough to help write a fiddle tune as big as "The Orange Blossom Special." And it opened a lot of doors in the business for me—as you know.

George affirms his friend's healthy way of resolving any residual resentment, "Oh, why, I know so."

Chubby explains why the tune has helped his career, "I never made no money directly, but indirectly it's got me a lot of jobs. 'The Orange Blossom Special.' I'm just grateful that I was lucky enough to help write it."[5]

Bob, once again, asks the appropriate question, "Any chance we could hear a little bit of it?"

There is a murmur of affirmation mixed with anticipation from the audience. His smile revealing his gratitude, Chubby pauses, looks to Bob, and answers, "Yeah, it's very possible."

The applause is keyed beautifully as audience members know that they will hear a song that drew them to the folklife festival. Taking advantage of the setting that is established through the crowd's mood, Bob holds up a copy of a magazine and announces in his husky, southern-tinged voice, "Folks, before they get started, if you've seen this current issue of *Smithsonian* magazine, there's a big article about bluegrass. And there's a familiar-looking person there."[6]

There is more applause as the audience sees a photograph of Chubby Wise displayed at the front of the church. "Congratulations, Chubby," says Bob.

Acknowledging the compliment and the applause, Chubby counts off the tempo, "One, two, three, four." Jim Quine strums the familiar chords in the shuffle rhythm to kick off the "Orange Blossom Special."

Chubby plays the breakdown's opening notes and shuffle. He savors each long bowstroke, feeling for exactly the right amount of pressure as he bears down and slides into the tune's introduction. As he leaps into the breakdown and plays the familiar bluegrass standard at a bullet-train clip, the fiddler evokes the same sense of excitement that audiences had to have felt when he first played the tune with Bill Monroe on the Grand Old Opry a half century ago. The "Orange Blossom Special," when played by an innovator of bluegrass fiddling, is no warhorse. Hearing Chubby play, the cognoscenti of the fiddle world would forget that this tune is so overplayed by tyros that it is banned from most fiddle contests. A major contributor to bluegrass music is playing the "Orange Blossom Special" in live performance. His fiddling is astounding. Everyone hangs on to the melody line as Chubby tags the piece to bring it to a close. There is no question why Chubby's renditions of the tune have set standards for hot fiddling.

The applause settles, and George beams, "That takes the cake right there!" There is more applause. George completes his compliment, suggesting that Chubby's show-stopper has brought the workshop to an untimely demise. "It's been nice being with you," he quips with a grin.

Wanting to continue to play and knowing the protocol of performance, Chubby offers another tune for everyone to play. He says, "I think it's time to slow it down and do a waltz that all three of us knows. Now this is a brand new one. You folks have never heard this one. We have."

Chubby completes the tune's introduction, "One called 'Over the Waves.'"[7] Richard's eyes sparkle, and George looks over to Chubby and reveals that he knows the tune. Chubby laughs and exclaims, "Ah-ha. That's one of the old-timers. Key of G. How about that? You remember that one, I know."

George asks Chubby, "You want to start it off?" Chubby orchestrates the tune's arrangement, "Yeah, let's all do it together and then we'll take it one at a time. 'Over the Waves.'"

Although fast-paced tunes are often seen as showstoppers, playing slower tunes can be more challenging. Slight mistakes in timing and intonation can be glossed over in fast fiddle runs, but holding a note in a waltz requires smooth bowing, precise finger placement, and control over the pressure that a fiddler places on the bow.[8] Fiddlers work hard to turn the waltzes in their repertory into showcase pieces. To hear Chubby Wise play a waltz is to hear one of the genre's masters, and the twin fiddling played by George and Richard now adds more icing to the cake. All three musicians finish the tune and lay their fiddles down on their laps.

As the applause settles once again, George explains a bit about improvising his tasteful and elegant harmonies, "Don't ask us to do the same harmony again. That just spins off the top. I can't tell you what I do."

Chubby returns the appreciation that George has given him, "You must have done all right. That sounds good to me, George."

The audience's applause shows they appreciate George's playing. Bob shifts the workshop's content. His next question showcases George's virtuosity as a master of another style of fiddling that is derived, in part, from playing old-time hoedowns.

Turning to George, Bob asks, "One of the things that your Uncle, Georgia Slim, participated in was bringing some western-style fiddling back east. Can you tell us a little bit about that and maybe even play some?"[9]

George knows that he can tell a good story, so he prefaces his answer with a disclaimer before giving a more comprehensive overview of western swing fiddling. His resonant voice has the rich and gentle timbre of a gentleman born and raised in America's South as he tells his story:

> Well, I'll try not to get long-winded about it. That was back in the days in Georgia where they just had eleven years of high school. You'd get your high school diploma. Let's see—Slim was ten years older than me. I was born in 1926. So—well, goodness—he had his fiddle out and was going by the time he was about sixteen, seventeen years of age—up through North Carolina, tobacco markets and so forth. And they used the term that I never hear before: "busking." I guess it's an old English term to where they'd pass around a hat. Slim said whether it was a guitar or whatever, they would just pass it around, and if it was a nickel or a penny or a dime that helped them to keep a little body and soul together with food.[10] But anyhow, he met Harold Goodman. He was known as Cousin Harold Goodman, and some of you old-timers might know "When It's Lamp Lighting Time in the High Country"? Harold Goodman and his brother wrote that thing, and that was one of the big hits, years ago.
>
> Well, they wanted to break away from WSM, Grand Old Opry. No problem, but they just wanted to see something new. So they formed "The Saddle Mountain Roundup" and went west to Oklahoma. In fact, that's where Howdy and Slim met their wives.
>
> But they were with KBOO, a big station there. They were more, I'll say, "hard-driven." Wills was also on KBOO, and he was strictly western swing—even back then in the later '30s. But that's where it got started.
>
> World War II came along. Slim volunteered and came in. Howdy was in the Navy: Slim, Army Air Corps. He later got into bombardier training and was stationed right down here at MacDill Air Force Base.

Slim, after the war, reformed the band. Howard Forrester, his brother Joe, they added two more. They had five. It would vary from five to seven pieces. And luckily they got on with KRLD, a big 50,000-watt station there in Dallas. And they had an early morning radio show, and of course, that thing just went out all the way into New Mexico, all over Texas, Oklahoma.

So they kept very busy through the '40s, playing everything from schoolhouses to dances to rodeos. Gene Autry would come frequently to the Texas State Fair in Dallas.

They called it "Georgia Slim and the Texas Roundup." They had steel, bass, and all of them practically doubled on instruments. Slim and Howdy at one time played pretty good mandolin. All of them, vocals.

So anyhow that was the taste. They liked what they heard in the Texas-style fiddling which many of you know as well as I do. It's a little bit slower and more ornate style than your hard-driving bluegrass and the southeastern Appalachian style of fiddling.

But I think he and Howdy took the best part of both. And they were just not only blood relatives but dear friends of mine. I think we all see people like that. And, I don't mean to get on the podium or behind the pulpit, but we each have a season and a measured time. Just make use of it.

George completes his story, and Bob shifts the audience's attention to his side of the church by asking George to play a sample of western swing fiddling. George lights up at the chance to play a tune, and he and Chubby negotiate which one to play. George suggests "Don't Let Your Deal Go Down."

As they are coming up with a tune, a voice from the audience suggests, " 'Faded Love' would be a good one for you guys to play."

George affirms the request, "Yes. Oh, you read our minds."

The man making the suggestion answers, "Yes, sir."

George kicks off "Don't Let Your Deal Go Down" by playing a few bars of the melody line. Jim looks at me, raises his eyebrows, looks a bit puzzled, and then nods to me that he can figure out some chords to play to accompany a tune that he has never backed up. This tune is not in Richard's repertory, so he decides to sit out and just listen to George and Chubby play a sample of western swing.

They play a spirited swing version of the bluesy tune, and George and Chubby's jazz inflections and ornamentation give the song a sharp vibrancy. As they play, I need to change the tape to record the workshop. I take the moment to whisper to Bob that Richard has some good stories to tell about playing house parties. Bob lets me know that he is planning to bring him back into the workshop a bit more. I head back to my seat at the front of the audience, and I snap a photograph of the workshop participants.

As the applause settles, Chubby remembers the earlier request and offers his gratitude to a fan. He concludes, "I reckon we ought to do 'Faded Love' for that man."

George agrees. "Yes, yes," he adds. "Our good friend—I don't know whether Richard knows him or not, but Lord what a wonderful fellow: Johnny Gimble. He's a master at that."

Chubby pays a tribute to the fiddler whom he greatly admires, "Oh, he is the master of the recording studio. Like I told them just now, there's fine fiddling, there's great fiddling and then there's Johnny Gimble."[11] George confirms Chubby's praise, "Absolutely."

Chubby is eager to play the tune, "Let's do a little bit of that 'Faded Love' for him."

Richard knows this tune. He regards it as one of the greatest tunes ever written for the fiddle. "Faded Love" lends itself well to twin fiddling, and the way that he, George, and Chubby offer twin fiddling layered on twin fiddling reveals the beauty of one of Bob Wills' most popular tunes. The performance is gorgeous.

George acknowledges the audience's appreciation by commenting on the song. He notes, "That was probably one of the finest numbers to go beyond its bounds. You'll find a few tunes like that—that kind of bleed-over to bluegrass, country, folk, pop. It's been recorded by some of the greatest pop singers. That 'Faded Love,' it's one of my favorites. It's a chance to do some pretty, pretty, fiddle harmonies."

Chubby clarifies George's observation that fiddle tunes are transformed and revived over time.

> Of course, we were speaking of course of Uncle Bob. I call him Uncle Bob, Bob Wills. He was one of the all-time greats as far as the western swing dance bands. He had, I guess, the greatest dance bands that have ever been on stage. Bob was also a good writer. I'm from Florida, Lake City, over here. The old-timers, I'm sure, know a little place on the Suwannee River called "Old Town."
>
> There was an old gentleman back when I was a kid. In fact, he was one of the first fiddlers I ever heard. His name was "Sharon," and he wrote an old breakdown fiddle tune. And its name was "Sharon." Later on they called it "Cotton Bagging."[12]

George knows the common nineteenth-century fiddle tune. He acknowledges, "That's what my uncles called it, 'Cotton Bagging.'"

"Shear 'Em" is the first tune that Richard learned in Kissimmee Park. He tells Chubby and George, "I heard it called 'Shear 'Em.'"

Chubby asks him, "You know 'Sharon?'"

Richard answers, "Not many people know 'Shear 'Em.'"

Chubby picks up on Richard's cue, "That's right," he notes. He continues to illustrate how fiddle tunes are created and re-created over time: "But I want to stress the fact of how a fiddle tune can come together. And you'd almost declare that Uncle Bob Wills heard this and came up with this special tune that I'm thinking about—'Take Me Back to Tulsa.' I know everybody's heard that. I'll play it similar to the way Uncle Bob done it."

Chubby begins playing "Take Me Back to Tulsa." Richard picks up on the tune. Hearing how close it is to "Shear 'Em," he twins with Chubby. George listens, thinks about the tune, and adds some harmony lines to this hoedown piece that is rendered in a western swing style. Richard continues playing the B part of the tune as Chubby stops playing and comments, "Now listen to the old 'Sharon.'"

As Richard softly fiddles "Shear 'Em," Chubby pulls the fiddle from under his chin and places it on his lap. He asks, "Now, how much difference is there between them?" Richard tags the tune to end it.

Richard, George, Bob, and Jim laugh, and Chubby concludes his point, "That's the way fiddle tunes are born—right there."

George is intrigued with Chubby's demonstration. He makes a request of Chubby. "Do one more time of the 'Take Me Back to Tulsa' part of that."

George and Chubby play "Take Me Back to Tulsa." Richard plays "Shear 'Em." Listeners can hear that "Shear 'Em" has a few more shuffles whereas "Take Me Back to Tulsa" is played a bit more smoothly, and it has a jazzy feel. But Chubby's point is well taken. Each tune's melody line is essentially the same.

Chubby makes sure that the audience hears his point by asking, "It's right close to 'Sharon,' isn't it?" The applause and the nods from the listeners show that they recognize the connections Chubby, George, and Richard have so vividly demonstrated.

Bob takes advantage of the opportunity to talk about the context for the hoedown tunes. He makes a request. "Richard, I was wondering if you can tell us a little bit about fiddling for dances and so forth in the old days—both in Kissimmee and Jacksonville."

Richard pauses a moment and collects his thoughts. He begins his narrative, speaking quietly but expressively in his soft southern accent: "Well, really, square dancing and picnics were about the only thing we had for amusement.

They'd have a picnic, and everybody would get together in the community. That night, they'd dance. Somebody would have to play, and there was only one or two down there that could play a fiddle. Some of them couldn't do very much at it, but if it wasn't for the fiddle beater, why they wouldn't have any tempo. But anyhow, they'd dance. I'd go hear them old fiddlers you know, and I'd practice on this."

Richard lifts his instrument and shows it to the audience. He continues. "And finally I'd sit in there, in the corner, and I'd play too. But it stemmed from that. We didn't have much chance to learn tunes because we had no way to hear them unless somebody came through and played it. So we done it that way and then we sit up there almost the whole night playing. If you play some of them old-time fiddle tunes and if you put every note in there, you were going to work yourself to death. So you'd get them to dance, and you skip it, you see?"

Richard smiles at the audience's laughter. He recognizes that many of the members of the crowd understand his point that the country fiddler could strip down the tune's ornamentation and play a bare-bones melody line straight away to accompany the dancers.

Bob draws from his own experience in playing for old-time frolics by remarking to Richard, "When you're playing for a dance, you might play for ten or fifteen minutes without stopping."

Richard contrasts his own experience playing eighty years ago with Bob's experience playing in Gainesville, White Springs, and other musical hotspots both inside and outside of Florida. He interjects, "Oh sir, I've played for an hour."

George is interested in hearing Richard's story. He asks, "There was nobody to relieve you, was there?"

Richard continues, "No, nobody to relieve you. No, it was all stomping. You'd just have to stomp, you know. And about ten or eleven o'clock, they'd all have a drink, and they'd get more stomped." Richard knows that this detail will amuse the audience. He laughs as much as the members of the crowd.

George also knows a few of the details about this aspect of the dance. He shares his knowledge, by adding, "And it wasn't always Coca-Cola, was it?"

Richard picks up his story again: "No, there was no Coca-Cola. And then you'd have a scrap or two out there, and that made it even more interesting. But anyhow, it was the only fun we had, and we'd get out there in them woods. And I often wondered what it would sound like for the animals out there that heard all that going on out there. You actually could hear when you were going up where they were playing for a square dance. The first thing you could hear was the fiddler stomping his foot."

There is a silence in the old church as Richard pauses for a moment. The silence is broken by the crow of the rooster outside on the small lawn that separates the church from the museum's parking lot. Richard then stomps his foot to demonstrate the fiddler's tempo. He concludes, "The fiddler stomping his foot—you'd hear that before you could hear the music."

Chubby has played for these kinds of dances. He is quick to establish another connection with Richard. "Hey, you remember the old straw beaters, don't you?"

George affirms that he does, and Richard answers, "Yeah." George notes, "That's what they used to use for rhythm."

Interested in what Richard has experienced in central Florida, George now asks an interview question, "What would a band consist of back then in your parts in those early days? Just a fiddle and somebody beating straws?"

Richard answers, "Yeah. Just a fiddler—that was all we had—and somebody sitting there and beating the straws. We didn't have any accompaniment at all. But anyhow, it didn't make much difference. You could take two broom handles and dance by it."

Richard taps out a shuffle rhythm on his chair as Chubby exclaims, "That's right!" Chubby has seen dancers sashaying on the dance floor to the beat of two broomsticks on a hardwood floor. Richard further explains what he has been discussing. "You'd hit one twice and one once, and they'd got to dancing. They had that tempo, and they'd go to dancing. They didn't care. So if you was playing and you got tired, you just sawed it that way, and they didn't know the difference."

Chubby connects with Richard's story, "As long as you kept the timing, it didn't matter, did it?"

Bob asks, "Richard, have you got a nice old tune from back in those days that you could play us?"

Richard is noodling around with some fiddle lines that he knows. He plays through a tag, stops a moment, looks at Bob, and says, "Yeah."

He pulls his bow into a fast shuffle rhythm and plays an up-tempo version of "Yellow Gals." I have heard him play this version of "Buffalo Gals Won't You Come Out Tonight" many times. This rendition is the fastest that I have ever heard, and he hits every note perfectly.

As he nails the tag, Chubby lights up, "All right. That's fine!"

I reach over and pull two fiddle sticks from Richard's instrument case and hold them as Richard is playing. The applause settles, and Bob exclaims, "All right!" as I hand him the fiddle beaters from Richard's case. Bob takes them and says to me that he has never used them. He shows the straw beaters to the crowd.

"These are some of the fiddle sticks, or straws, that he was talking about. You beat them on a fiddle. I've never done it, or I would," Bob announces.

He hands the straw beaters to Richard, who takes them and then lays his fiddle across his lap. He explains, "Let's see. I've never done it much here, but you got sort of a rhythm going."

Balancing each light, wooden dowel lightly in his hands like a drummer holding two drumsticks, Richard demonstrates the technique by gently tapping on the strings near the bridge.

As Richard explained previously, a separate musician would tap out a rhythm while the fiddler was playing. At times, a fiddler would tap out the rhythms against his own instrument.

Chubby notes, "That's what we done, right there."

The scene is familiar to George, who comments, "Right, and they'd take and stand out of the fiddler's way where he wouldn't get in the way of his bowing. And I've seen them just use maybe one stick and tap it like that."

Chubby comments, "That's right," and he completes the discussion. The demonstration of beating straws provides perceptive members of the audience with a new insight into the etymology of the expression "fiddle sticks."[13]

There is a shift in the light-hearted tone that is created through the style of presentation when Chubby's testimony introduces another tune:

> I think it's safe to say I never ever do anything for anybody unless I do a hymn. I'll tell you—I'm grateful. I'm not ashamed of this a bit: I'm a born-again Christian. I love the Lord. About four years ago, He gave me the most precious thing a man could have. He gave me my life. There was three doctors. They told my wife, "It's just a matter of time for that man. There's no way for him to get well." But the good Lord had a different idea, and he spared me. And I'm just so grateful, I don't miss a chance to tell everybody about that. And I don't do anything anywhere, if I have a chance, to say a good word for our Lord and at least play one hymn. So if you-all don't mind, let's do "Amazing Grace."[14]

There is a low rustle of approval and a murmur of appreciation in the church. It comes mainly from behind where I am sitting near the chancel. Robert "Chubby" Wise picks up on the recognition of familiarity and offers, "It's one everyone knows and everyone loves. And I'll tell you what, if you could, join in and sing with us."

Chubby lets the musicians know that they will play the hymn in the key of G, and the three fiddlers, backed up on guitar, open up the well-known melody.

As they first play through the hymn, there is scattered and shy singing from the audience. Working through the melody again, Bob leads the audience members in singing the lyrics. Situated on the grounds of Jacksonville's Museum of Science and History, the Carpenter Gothic Church resounds with one of the hymns that was sung when the church was a consecrated house of worship years ago.

The communal singing of the sacred song comes to a close, and its sound is replaced with secular applause. George's words bring us back to the workshop setting, "Three old Florida boys. We get along real well, don't we."[15]

He looks to Bob and jokes, "Why haven't you had us up here before?"

Bob laughs and comments, "Really."

Chubby chimes in, "Let's just hope this won't be the last time!"[16]

Bob's "That's right" is almost inaudible over the applause from the crowd. As the clapping diminishes, Bob offers a suggestion to George: "While we're playing hymns, I was wondering if you might do your little trick fiddle thing with your bow hair." Chubby exclaims, "That's a good idea!"

George begins to retune his fiddle and explains, "Let's see if I can retune it." He then provides a good context for this form of trick fiddling, explaining how and why he has used it in music shows:

> Sometime when we might be playing a bluegrass show and the guitar would break a string—rather than just bringing things to a halt—I'd just use this as a little filler. But it's the truth—the background there. In Tift County in the parlor in the front room of Granny's home, there was an old-time pump organ. And I know you've seen them in the antique shops, with the little pedals on. I remember hearing her and my aunts and my mother. They'd get there at the relatively short little keyboard. Oh, to me, the thoughts of back then—Some of the prettiest music. Usually hymns were played on it. But anyhow, this is what I hear in trying to imitate the old-time pump organ.

George has finished retuning the fiddle, thereby allowing the four strings to play an open chord when they are all bowed without the left hand stopping any strings. George loosens the bow hairs by adjusting the screw of the frog that holds the horsehair in place. The hairs loosely dangle from the wooden stick as George adjusts the bow so that its hair can be draped over the fiddle's body.

George cannot resist making a pun about this technique, "And if you want to put a little humor in it, this is my 'broke bow.' My 'baroque bow'—for those of you that are into baroque music." A couple people in the audience get the joke. George works to recover by commenting, "That's not much humor—George, play the fiddle and don't try to be funny."

Fitting the loose hairs over the fiddle and then tightening up the bow hair so that he can keep the horsehair in contact with all four strings, George explains, "This allows us to get three and four part harmony, and I hope you can recognize the old-time hymn."

George plays a slow, even version of "What a Friend We Have in Jesus." George's unaccompanied fiddle rings true throughout the resonant walls that contain the church's interior space.

As he brings the hymn to a close, George explains how he used these types of tricks when playing for various music shows: "That always allowed the guitar picker or mandolin picker to get a new string on. If not, I'd just play it through twice. Sometimes, I'd even pay him a quarter if he'd just make like he couldn't get his string on. Chubby and Richard would be aware of the tricks. You couldn't get by just on music. Folks back then expected a show. Uncle Slim said he must have demolished three or four fiddles trying to learn to do backward somersaults while doing 'Pop Goes the Weasel.'"[17]

George expands on his commentary by providing his view on the importance of public folklore programming and cultural conservation: "The important thing that we're talking about today, and it could be said better. It applies to country music, fiddling, classical, jazz. The art of fiddling or violin playing is a perishable art. And it must be passed on from each generation. You can read all the books you want to about it, but unless you've got somebody to show you, or listen to, it will die."

Richard's nod shows that he agrees with George. Chubby's "That's right!" also supports George's concern with preserving the tradition of fiddling. All the musicians know that the feel for the music must be learned through an oral and aural tradition rather than from reading the printed page.

George continues, "I'm glad to see the resurgence of fiddling. It's come back. We just about lost it."[18]

Ever the courteous gentleman, George pauses to preface his brief lesson in music history. "Now, this is not a knock against this different kind of music. But during the '50s and '60s, we just about lost the fiddle with all the guitars in the rock era. But I'm happy to say—"

Chubby finishes George's point, "They're coming back. Yes. They are coming back. It will be a fiddle reunion again!"

The time for completing the workshop on schedule is ticking along. Bob Stone recognizes the time constraints and makes sure he is bringing up an important part of America's musical history. He asks Chubby Wise about his contributions to bluegrass fiddling, "Chubby, I was wondering if you can tell us about some of your early times with Bill Monroe. You've been called the first bluegrass fiddler, haven't you?"[19]

Chubby acknowledges the question, "Well, yes." He begins his story of how he replaced Howdy Forrester, the original fiddler in Bill Monroe's Blue Grass Boys.

> I went to work for Bill either in '42 or '43. I was in Gainesville at the time with a group called "Yulee's Hill-Billies" working out of WRUF. I heard Bill announce that Howdy was going into the Navy. That's how come I come to get the job.
> He said, "I got to have a fiddler." He said, "My fiddler's going to the Navy, Big Howdy."
> And I just caught a train and went to Nashville. And I walked in like a big dolt, and I said, "I'm from Florida and I play the fiddle and I want the job. I understand that you have it open."

Bob grins as he chuckles at Chubby's story. Chubby appreciates the scattered laughter from the crowd and continues:

> And I'll never forget it. Bill was a very unconcerned type of a fellow, you know. He was quick. He talked real fast—quick—there's just not any "yes or no" about it. He's just "that's it."
> So he said, "Do you know my stuff?"
> And, of course, I didn't know too much. I had heard Howdy play a couple of things. And Howdy always played them double-stops on "Footprints in the Snow." Oh, it just slayed me. And I told Bill, I said, "Oh yeah, yes sir, I know them." And I said, "How about 'Footprints in the Snow.' Let me play that one with you. I can play that one real good." So I did it. And he said, "Well, play me a breakdown." And I knew I would be able to play "Katy Hill." And he said, "You got your clothes with you?"
> And we were in the dressing room in Nashville at the Opry. I said, "No sir. They're at the hotel." And he said, "Well go get them. We're leaving in three hours." That's how I got my job with Bill Monroe. I was with him for about seven years, so I must have held out pretty well.

Bob knows that Chubby is credited with developing and refining the blues and jazz-inflected qualities that help to define bluegrass fiddling. He asks Chubby about this innovation: "Well, you kind of put 'the blues' into bluegrass, didn't you?"

Chubby answers, "Well, I'll have to say this in all sincerity. Monroe taught me to play bluegrass. I had never played bluegrass. Many hours we spent in those hotels and motels, and he said, 'Chubby, I want it this way.'"

"You take 'Footprints.'" Chubby plays the opening shuffle and the first melodic phrase of "Footprints in the Snow" and comments, "Them long, bluesy notes, he was the man that showed me how to do that. I played more or less country when I went to work for him."

Chubby concludes his discussion of his contributions to bluegrass music with a paean to Bill Monroe and his music: "Bill, he was a legend. They tell me I'm a legend, I guess because I'm old enough to be a legend now. I'll be seventy-eight on my next one. Like I say, I love to give credit where credit is due, and Bill did show me how to play bluegrass music. And I'll always have a love for bluegrass. There's something about it. I think it's just real country music, real country music. I think it's mountain, country music, if that's the way you want to express it. It's got a feeling all its own."

Richard takes advantage of the feeling of closure by offering an encomium to Chubby Wise: "I think Mr. Wise, here, has been a great inspiration to a lot of old-time fiddlers as well as country fiddlers because he had a way about it. And the way he played, you didn't have to see who is playing to know who played it. I don't know how to explain it. He has a touch, I guess, or just a way of making a fiddle talk. And he's been a great inspiration. I know it's been years that Mr. Wise and I have played close by. And this is the first time we've played together. But he's been an inspiration to me, and I even learned some of his tunes." [20]

Chubby looks over to Richard and acknowledges his appreciation: "Well, I'm glad to hear you say that. Well, I'm lucky I guess. I have learned every style along with the rest of them. It's like I've said, I've been playing so long, I'm afraid to change now."

Richard further develops his observation about Chubby's unique style of playing: "I've heard tapes of different fiddlers, and just as soon as he goes to playing, I can tell that's Chubby's part right there. There's something, I don't know what it is, but you know it. Everybody has a little technique of his own." George nods and Chubby adds, "Yes sir, they have their own style, yes sir."

Richard closes the discussion by personalizing his comments, "And no two people play some of these old tunes exactly alike. Some varies them a little bit. I know I do."

Bob winds down the workshop by announcing the times for the remaining afternoon and evening performances by George Custer with Mossy Lee and by Chubby Wise with Salt Run. Bob makes a final request to the fiddlers: "Do you have one last tune you want to do together?"

Chubby, "Yeah, let's go and do a little bit of 'Liberty.'"

George likes the tune and says, "All right." He jokes, "Somebody told me that's what every man is searching for. I didn't say that—my wife said that!"

George kicks off the tune by announcing, "That's a good old fiddle tune."

As they bring the hoedown tune to a lively close, the audience bursts into a final round of applause and then rises to give them a standing ovation. The workshop session comes to a formal close when Bob thanks the audience and musicians and invites them back for the evening performance.

4

"Your Word Was Your Bond"

~

An Anthology of Tall Tales

The words of a man's mouth are deep waters; the fountain of wisdom is a
gushing stream.

—Proverbs 18:4

Richard explains that his surname comes from his great-grandfather, remembered in his family as "Captain Seamans." Richard's father, Lewis,
was also a seafaring man. Living in southeastern Pennsylvania, Lewis Seaman
sailed along the intracoastal waterways and off-shore waters of the eastern seaboard.[1] Following one of his excursions as a charter captain in the Chesapeake
Bay, Lewis left his home community of Chester, Pennsylvania, and sailed into
Florida.

Lewis Seaman arrived in Kissimmee in the late 1890s. He first found work
with Kissimmee's founder, Hamilton Disston, the Pennsylvania entrepreneur
who purchased four million acres from the State of Florida in 1881 and cut a
canal system into Florida's central region of swamps, scrubland, and prairie.
Disston and other founders drained the wetlands and developed the land to support farms and fruit groves, thereby opening up areas in central and southern
Florida for further settlement. By the turn of the century, Richard's father was
hired by William McCool to work as a caretaker of "McCool's Grove," an orange
grove located in the new subdivision of Kissimmee Park on the eastern side of
Lake Tohopekaliga. Lewis married Lula Irene Sharpe in 1902, and they ran a
small farm while he tended the orange grove and supplemented his income by
working as a market hunter and sailboat captain on central Florida's lakes and

inland waterways. When Richard was born in 1904, the family had a daughter named Queenie Husky Johnson from Lula Irene's first marriage to Abner Johnson. The Seaman family history records that Queenie was named for a Seminole princess. She, Richard, and his younger sister, Anne Elizabeth Seaman, remained close throughout their lives.

An intriguing aspect of the occupational folklife of watermen is that even today business deals often are conducted by word of mouth. Towboat captains commonly explain that the majority of their deals in picking up and dropping barges along the rivers are brokered through verbal assent. This system of commerce is viable because the community of workers along America's rivers and inland waterways is a tight one. Captains recognize each other by simply acknowledging whose vessel is plying the water, and disreputable characters are soon exposed. Dishonest riverboat captains soon need to seek other means of gainful employment.

This social norm of maintaining honest business dealings is also a strong value within farming communities. The expectation of honesty in human relations among river workers and farmers reveals why honest speech was less a positive value and more a social demand in Richard's home community. Honesty was an integral component within the system of neighborly survival, and it was essential for holding his community together.[2] Explaining the importance of telling the truth in Kissimmee Park, Richard affirms that people were expected to remain true to their word because "your word was your bond in those days." He explains that lying meant more than prevarication. A dishonest person could lie by simply not being trustworthy. "If you said you were going to do something, then you did it," Richard asserts to explain how words were to be sealed with action. Telling a lie in word or deed would ruin a reputation, for chances were that the untruth would soon be exposed. Lying also violated the social contract that chartered the system of cooperation that families depended upon for their survival. Finally, a lie violated a commandment from God. Although there were no churches to attend in his home community, Richard was raised not to bear false witness because doing so would fall short of Divine expectations revealed in God's Word.

Richard Seaman believes that writing a history means that one must honestly engage the pursuit of telling a true story. He thinks of history in highly visual and objective terms. He makes both explicit and implicit abstractions about what he presents, but his theory of history is rooted in a rigorous science of the concrete. His sharp memory is authenticated by historical records. Period photographs of Kissimmee match his descriptions of orange groves, scrubland, Lake Tohopekaliga, the town, and the little community. Archival recordings and field notes fully support that the tunes in his repertory were all played in central Florida prior to the widespread introduction of mass media. Recordings of "Shear 'Em" and other tunes from the 1930s reveal that his own contemporary versions of the hoedowns match what was played decades ago.[3] His descriptions of daily life can be trusted as accurate presentations of Florida's social history.

In at least one case, his oral history challenges the written record. In *Palmetto Country*, Stetson Kennedy writes of the legend of Tappan Mann: "Polk County ranchers tell a bizarre story about Tappan Mann, who once needed $1,300 to swing a cattle deal. Mann obtained the money by mortgaging his home, herd, and ranch to a neighboring rancher. This rancher coveted Mann's property, and so offered to pay a cowboy to kill him. The cowboy 'reckoned as how' if the property was worth a $1,300 mortgage, it was worth the same amount to kill Mann. So he demanded and got $1,300 in advance to do the job. But instead of killing Mann, he gave him the money, and Mann used it to liquidate the mortgage."[4]

Richard explains that he has read the story, but he provides a slightly different version of the conspiracy:

> T. C. Mann had a son. His name was Tappan, Tappan Mann. Instead of saying "Tappan," they called him T. C. They tell you about a fellow who planned to give some fellow—I forget how much money now—to kill old man Tappan. He took the money, and instead of killing Tappan, he gave him the money.
>
> T. C. Mann.
>
> I didn't read the whole book, but I sat down there one day, long years ago, and read quite a bit of it.
>
> So I asked Tappan about that one time. I said, "I read about your daddy in that book *Palmetto Country*, about the money." And he said, "Yeah, but they were wrong about the amount of the money." They weren't wrong in the story about what happened, but the amount of money was different, he said, than what was in the book.
>
> T. C. Mann was my brother-in-law.[5]

In Richard's story, his firsthand exposure to T. C. Mann supports the argument that the oral historian can sometimes provide a more accurate history than what is enshrined in the written record. The actual event can be interpreted as the primary document, and Richard's firsthand verbal description makes Kennedy's written text a secondary source. Seaman's version asserts that writing history presupposes the need to rely on the accuracy of empirical descriptions, and he feels that he must bear witness to the truth and set the record straight when he discovers omissions and errors in Florida's received history. Richard is so conscientious in telling the truth that when he does not remember a detail, he is careful to admit gaps in his knowledge.

Despite the demand for telling the truth, the tall tale is a rich and vibrant genre in Florida's folklore. Telling fictional prose narratives for comic effect has been an amusing and fulfilling diversion for Richard throughout his life. He heard numerous tall tales in Kissimmee, and he notes that his workplace in Jacksonville was also a good site for swapping stories. Curiously, although some storytellers in America's Southland refer to narratives in the tall-tale genre as "lies," Richard never heard storytellers call them "lies" in his home community. He explains, "Although they are lies, they didn't want to admit it. They wanted to omit the lie if they could. They would call them 'tales.' But we used to hear some tall ones."

After we share a laugh, I note that there used to be liars' contests in Florida and ask him if he ever entered one. He replies, "No, I was afraid I'd win."

It is the truth. If Richard were to enter a liar's contest, he would do well. He is a fine storyteller. He speaks in a soft, evenly cadenced voice that is a delight to hear. His steady, unhurried way of speaking is reminiscent of the smooth bowing of a master fiddler. Richard includes just enough expressive emphasis to be convincingly droll, and he shows that storytellers do not need to be overly theatrical, even saccharinely cloy, to hold an audience's interest. Although the logocentric appeal of his stories can only be suggested through the written transcriptions, scholarship on ethnopoetics provides a different way to read the texts. Rather than simply presenting his stories as blocks of data, I am presenting them more as found poems rather than as interview transcriptions. Frequent indentations and the use of white space evoke his phrasing rhythmic qualities to provide a visual representation of the rational and aesthetic values that he uses in a storytelling performance.[6] The ethnopoetic style of presentation emphasizes distinctions between ways of speaking that are often in sharp contrast to the written word. It is designed to evoke in print the feel of the spoken word as the shift in style is designed to slow the pace of reading. The style's unconventional line spacing and use of white space ease the strain of reading blocky transcriptions, thereby focusing attention on the poetic qualities of everyday prose. Ethnopoetics highlights the elegance of extended parallel constructions in the spoken word as the logical constructions of grammar are matched with the sound of hearing a story. In reading Richard's tellings as found poems that unite poetry with narrative, the reader's voice resounds in the certainty that the performance of speaking is different from the secondary experience of reading written texts. Ethnopoetic renditions support the view that the live performance of Richard's stories is central to his artistic expression.

His tall tales and jokes pose a conundrum. A puzzling question emerges when one first considers that he expects his neighbors to tell the truth and that he honors the social contract of remaining true to one's word. Why does he tell tall tales about life in his home community during public presentations when he also places such a high value on speaking the truth? In sum, Richard values honesty as a way of speaking, but he also enjoys telling tall tales.

The value that Richard places on honesty in his storytelling is essential for understanding his tales. This value is complicit with research on tale telling that supports the idea that Richard Seaman's tall tales are artistic creations that in actuality allow him to talk about truth.[7] The stories' epistemological function becomes clear when we consider that he uses his stories to teach his listeners about Florida's history and culture. A nuanced reading reveals that the ostensibly simple stories have a subtle quality that belies the claim that they are not to be taken seriously. By considering the content and form of the stories in relation to Richard's assessment of the contexts in which he tells them, the stories reveal intriguing facets of what it means to tell the truth. In telling tall tales, Richard reveals the importance of talking about truth when telling of Florida's history. In listening to his stories, we learn how his tall tales reveal truths about Florida folklife, for these stories connect his own experiences with what he wishes his listeners to learn about Florida. His tales present salient commonplaces about Florida culture and provide a commentary on the pragmatics of truth-telling. When understood in this respect, it becomes clear why the term "lie" is not an accurate label for his tall tales.

The first evening that Richard and I met, we recorded over two dozen fiddle tunes in his repertory. After I packed up my equipment and chatted with Richard for a few minutes, Jack Piccalo volunteered Richard to tell me some tall tales. Richard told some fine stories, and I took great delight in hearing my first live performance of Florida folktales. After he had finished, I found out that he learned many of the stories in Kissimmee and that he also picked up a few of them after moving to Jacksonville in the 1920s. As I left that evening, I asked him if I could return the next day to tape-record an interview with him about his tunes and tales. He warmly agreed to meet me in the early afternoon.

Since those two August days in 1988, I have heard Richard tell his tall tales many times when he performs his fiddle tunes. Richard has told them from various stages at the Florida Folk Festival in White Springs. He has also performed them at local arts festivals in Jacksonville. He has told stories for fourth grade students as part of the Duval County Folklife in Education Program in Jacksonville's public schools. He has played tunes and told stories at fiddlers' conventions, at the annual gathering of the Florida Fiddlers Association, during blue-grass festivals at the Spirit of the Suwannee Campground in Live Oak, and on a public television show that was broadcast from south Florida.

My favorite renditions of his tales arrived in the mail after I had moved from Florida in 1994. Richard had recorded a tape filled with tall tales because he saw my interest in these stories.[8] They are especially valuable because they contribute to the historical record of Florida's traditional culture. This collection consists entirely of traditional folk narratives that can be linked to wider patterns of regional history by categorizing their traditional elements using tale-type and motif indexes. These stories are also important artistic resources for understanding the stage patter that embellishes his performances of fiddle tunes. Richard's repertoire of tales begins as he invites his listener to travel with him to Kissimmee Park.

Sister's Milk Cow

A long time ago, I went down to my sister's farm down there. She had a big farm down there. And I always liked to go down there—visit with her, enjoy the country life.

When I went down there this time, they was all upset, running around there like they didn't know just what to do.

And I said, "What in the world's wrong with you people?"

She said, "Well, I'll tell you."

"Our prize milk cow fell in that old abandoned well down there, and we can't get her out. There's no way to get her out.

"She's the best milk cow in the country, and we don't know what to do."

So I went down there and looked down there in the well, and I said, "Well, I don't think that's any problem. I'll get that old cow out of the well for you."

So I got me a ladder—climbed down into the well, petted the old cow a little bit, soothed her a little bit, made her feel sort of more at ease and comfortable. And I got me comfortable, and I sit down and begin to milk. I milked that cow—and I milked that cow, and I just keep on milking her. And I kept on milking some more. And you know, I floated that old cow right out of that well. There wasn't nothing to it.

In form and content, Richard's first story is a prototype for many of his tales.[9] The narrative begins with the tacit assumption that Richard is in his home community of Jacksonville. He then takes the listener on a trip downstate to rural central Florida. He describes details of daily life on his sister's farm, suggesting what his own life might have been like if he had chosen to stay in his parents' home community. The novice listener can learn details of the social history of farming and ranching in Florida. The small details of using ladders to climb into wells, milking a cow by hand, and soothing a scared bovine prior to milking are the same types of intriguing textures that good novelists use to establish a sense of place. William Faulkner takes the alert reader on a similar tour of the southern dogtrot house in his short novel *Spotted Horses* by accurately describing the interior space of a common architectural form in Mississippi.[10] In the same way, Richard hints at the layout of a Florida farmstead and then takes us deep into the prison house of the well that confines the Osceola County Fair's blue ribbon milk cow.

The story suggests that there is something seriously wrong with the usual order of life on the family farm. Whereas the family's prize-winning cow should be held in a pen appropriate to her esteemed status, the cow is entrapped and its life is threatened. Whereas the well should be a benign source for life-sustaining water, it is now a dungeon. Richard's family has tried to solve the problem, but they are unable to restore order to their farm. A problem is clearly established, and Richard's tale moves forward as he assesses the situation. His story's denouement emerges as he uses his common sense to improvise a practical and pragmatic solution. The solution reveals how Richard, and Bessie, float out of the well by mixing his mastery of basic skills of life on the farm with the ingenuity to see novel means for resolving difficult situations. In virtually every tale, solutions to different problems are discovered in a similar manner.

Not only is this pattern of creatively solving exigencies an important theme in his storytelling, but his stories also rely on fantasy to resolve problems, thereby transforming plausible accounts into tall tales. In this story, the fantasy spins solely from the Aarne-Thompson motif D2156.2: *Miraculous increasing of milk from one cow.*[11] This pattern of expanding plausible action beyond the realm of everyday experience is vital to virtually every story within his repertory. Richard's storytelling accomplishes this shift after he first establishes the commonplaces about life in his home community and then invites his listeners to take a flight of fancy by asking, "What if?" His details of everyday life must first create a believable portrait of rural folklife before he can develop his playful foray into the fantastical experience of living within an imaginary community. Each of his stories establishes Richard as an authority on an interesting aspect of Florida's history while he is also playing with the truth. Telling the truth by telling tall tales paradoxically builds his status as a storyteller as he blends realism with fantasy. Consequently, his ability to trick his listeners presupposes that he can convincingly tell the truth.

Raising Popcorn

This story is one of the most common tall tales in America. It is a component of Ernest Baughman's tale type 1920: *Contest in lying* and Baughman subtype 1920A: *Tall corn* is a more precise resource for classifying this iconic image of rural life. This text is even more sharply categorized as a story centered on the Aarne-Thompson motif X1633.1: *Weather so hot that corn pops in fields, animals freeze to death thinking it has snowed.* Vance Randolph documented the story in the Ozarks during the 1940s, and a variant of the story appears as a Paul Bunyan tale.[12] Its widespread, diverse history suggests that the story has remained a vital part of oral traditions over an extended period of time. Richard Dorson documented that African-American storytellers in Michigan told it during the 1950s,[13] and Richard Seaman remembers that it was told in central Florida by the 1920s.

> One time, I had a farm down there—close to my sister. And I raised popcorn: that was my chief crop. I raised popcorn for most all the nation. And it was a profitable business. I made pretty good—until I had an accident down there one time.
>
> I had to take popcorn to town at night because it got too hot in the daytime. I was afraid that it would blow up—that sun was so hot. And I'd take it down to town at night and sell it in the morning.
>
> So one morning, I overslept—got a late start, sort of "drunk up." And on the way, about halfway to town, the sun got hotter, hotter, hotter. And it got so doggone hot, to all of a sudden, that whole wagonload of popcorn blowed up—right there in the middle of the road.
>
> You never saw such a mess. And to top it all off—them two mules turned around and saw all that popcorn and thought it was snow and both of them froze to death.

This tale is a logical inversion of his first story. Rather than heroically saving the day on the farm, Richard's character creates the problem. Falling off schedule because of the negative consequences of a night of carousing, he tempts fate by marching off to town with his produce. There is a stark simplicity to the situation. The farmer is late. The sun is hot. His crop blows up. The whole situation not only scares but also freezes his mules. The self-effacing farmer tells about the potential for economic disaster that can befall anyone who ekes a living from the land.

A gullible listener would be caught by the irrational hyperbole of the living reality of Florida's heat. Floridians remark on the absurdity of vacationing in central Florida during the summer as it is in one of the hottest regions in one of America's hottest states. Florida natives find it strange that visitors pay to walk around on seething asphalt as they sweat their way through the long lines in theme parks and tourist attractions. I ask Richard how Floridians survived working in the fields when he young. He notes that they did not think about the heat prior to the widespread use of John Gorrie's invention of air conditioning. His family just seemed to be used to the heat, and they figured out ways to work outside in spite of Florida's scorching sun.

The form of a tall tale will sometimes allow for recursive structures that embed a second—or even third or fourth—story into the text.[14] This tale could end with the explosion of popcorn, but Richard often continues his story. The second catch revolves around the anthropomorphization of beasts of burden. Snow in central Florida is such a rarity that an animal valued for its ability to work in hot weather, the mule, falls in its traces, a victim of shock. Its partner soon follows suit. When we consider the common knowledge that is required to understand both stories, the tall tale is another surrealistic portrait about the farmer's daily reality that provides additional commentary on farming. Richard's representation of farming is not a celebration of joyously tending one's fields and flocks. He portrays it as an arduous task that requires twenty-four-hour attention each day. The story's absurdities also reveal that mules are not pets but commodified beasts of burden that are essential for operating a farm. If not cared for properly, valuable stock will die. If not tended conscientiously, a farmer's crop will go to waste.

Cutting a Pumpkin

In the first two stories, the listener is led to believe that Richard is a young man who either helps out on his sister's farm or maintains his own operation. In real life, Richard worked primarily on his parents' farm. This tall tale, Baughman 1920: *Contest in lying,* is sometimes told as subtype 1920B: *Big strawberries,* but Richard's version is adapted to local produce. The story is sometimes told in dialogue form as a lying contest between two prevaricators, but Richard's story carries a more innocent tone than that of the braggadocio associated with competing liars. The Aarne-Thompson motif F816: *Extraordinary vegetable* is a prominent component, and Thompson notes that the story is especially widespread in Irish folklore. Stetson Kennedy documents a version of the story that was told in rural Florida in his 1942 study *Palmetto Country.*[15] Richard's version of the story begins with his description of what life was like when he was a lad.

I lived with my dad and mother on a farm when I was young. We lived way out there in the country, and we could hunt all the time. And it was just a good place to live. And one of the neighbors sent one of the little boys over there one day. And he said, "Mr. Seaman, can my daddy borrow your cross-cut saw?"

My dad says, "Well, what do you want it for, son?"

He said, "Well, we want to cut a pumpkin."

My dad said, "Well, it will be sometime this afternoon, son, before you can get it because we're just halfway through with a sweet potato."

Once again, Richard's story begins with an accurate description of his daily life. His laconic style of telling the story adds to his description's plausibility. It is significant that Richard includes courtesy titles to develop his characters. Lewis Seaman is addressed by the youngster as "Mr. Seaman," and Mr. Seaman calls the neighbor's child "son." Farmlife demands a certain division of labor that is hierarchical. Just as the narrative established this facet of social relationships on the farm, the story also articulates relationships created through the system of neighborly survival. Borrowing tools from neighbors is an acceptable social norm, especially when harvesting the fruits of honest labor.

The hyperbole of talking about the richness of Florida's land provides an important detail about the state's agriculture. Florida has rich farmland, but much of Florida's soil is sandy. Travelers in northern Florida often fail to notice much more agriculture than the acres of planted pine trees bordering the interstates. As one travels into central Florida, and eventually into the peninsula's southern region, farmland becomes more visible. Deep in south Florida, the overall quality of the farmland improves. A huge area in this territory was once immersed by inland swamps and the Everglades River of Grass.[16] At the end of the nineteenth century, developers began draining this land largely through an ill-planned system of canals. This system is currently being dismantled because Miami and the surrounding megalopolis is becoming parched and the ecosystem that supports marine life is severely damaged. The initial plan to develop the swampland did, however, result in building up incredibly rich topsoil that is farmed year-round. Today, the rich soil between the Everglades and Lake Tohopekaliga supports numerous produce farms.

Tall Corn

This version of tale type 1960D: *The great vegetable* is another widespread folktale that develops an agrarian theme. Richard Dorson identifies a similar text told in the 1960s in Illinois as a variant of motif X1522.1: *Rich land: corn grows so fast that it pulls up its own roots.*[17] Zora Neale Hurston also presents a story in Florida's African-American tradition that applies the same motif to cucumbers.[18] Richard sometimes narrates this story by itself, but he also occasionally embeds it into a string of other tall tales about farming. When he strings together these individual tales, he is following the form of a lying contest by offering another tale to match or top a previous one in the style of tale type 1920: *Contest in lying.*

> I forgot to tell you, though, about when we planted corn. We had to plant that on the run. When you planted that corn and dropped a kernel of corn down and kicked the dirt over it, that ground was so rich that it would sprout and run up your britches leg before you'd get away from there.

All of these stories comment on the intrusions of humankind's culture on the natural environment. Nature provides opportunities for the farmer and rancher, but tending the crops requires human effort and ingenuity. Even in the absurdly logical exaggeration of the tall tale, the storyteller reminds the listener that there are ways to work through what nature has dispensed.[19] In everyday life, the farmer must make the best of novel situations through creative imagination, quick thinking, and physical labor. As in the stories that deal with trouble on the farm, most of the stories in this cluster end on an optimistic note.

Fishing with a Lizard

Farming requires constant attention, but farmboys also enjoy occasional free time when the work is done for the day. Richard explains that he spent part of his time fishing in central Florida's lakes and rivers. Fishing has supplied such important fodder for tall tales that the Baughman index gives fish stories their own tale type 1960D: *The great catch of fish.* The Aarne-Thompson index also includes commentary about the motifs X1150: *Lies about fishing* and X1153: *Fish caught by remarkable trick* by noting that these stories are especially common in Canadian, American, and English folklore.

> I used to love to go fishing down on the Kissimmee River. It was a nice, pleasurable thing to do. It was a beautiful place, and you could sit there and enjoy yourself—and catch fish, catch plenty of fish.
> I always fished with a lizard, and I could catch them that way. I'd take a lizard, and I'd cut a slit in his tail and put a strong fishing line through that—and then tie it so he couldn't get loose, and then I'd

throw it out into the middle of the river, and let him go. Then I'd tie the other end of the string to a cypress knee. Then I'd go, lay down, lean up against a tree, and go to sleep.

And what would happen—trout love lizards better than anything else in the world, and they can't resist them. And when that trout saw that lizard swimming out there, he'd just run out there and gobble him right up—smacked his lips and thought he had a good meal.

But what he didn't know was that—that lizard didn't stop, he crawled right on out, and kept going. Another trout saw him, and he gobbled him up. And the lizard done the same thing. He kept right on going—kept on swimming.

The next one saw him; he'd swallow him. The same thing would happen. That lizard, he wouldn't stop. And that process would go on for a period of time.

And then I'd wake up from a nap and walk out there—and pull in a whole string of fish, already strung.

Florida is world famous for its saltwater fishing offshore on the Atlantic side as well as closer in along the Florida Keys and Gulf Coast. Anglers also recognize the state for its freshwater fishing, and the St. Johns River is known especially for its bass fishing. Part of this story's appeal is the way Richard couples his description of fishing along an inland river with the repetition of a fanciful way of catching a string of fish. Richard and his lizard have perfected an efficient means for saving effort during an activity that is known for its leisurely pace.

One telling detail is that Richard says that he is catching trout. Sea trout thrive in Florida's saltwater, but the freshwater trout that is so prized in the sport of fly-fishing can not survive in Florida's warm freshwaters. The nearest places for Floridians to fish for freshwater trout are the cool streams flowing through the Smoky Mountains of northern Georgia, eastern Tennessee, and western North Carolina, and American trout are caught primarily in the nation's northern and western states. It is tempting to imagine that Richard is stretching his story when he speaks of catching trout in a Florida freshwater river. The truth is that he really is fishing for trout. The name "trout" in central Florida is sometimes used to describe the Florida largemouth bass (*Micropterus salmoides floridanus*), a species unrelated to freshwater trout. Its common name is "black bass," but it also is known by numerous sobriquets including "green bass," "bucketmouth," "Oswego bass," and "green trout." This prize game fish is valued by anglers as a voracious feeder and active fighter. Originally, it was native only to Florida, but it has been stocked in freshwaters in other southern states. It is a distinctive subspecies within the sunfish family, and it is a different variety of fish from the northern largemouth bass found in cooler waters. Attentive anglers know that the Florida bass has different coloration and a narrower head than the largemouth bass found north of Florida.

Calling the Florida largemouth bass a "trout" is a good example of a way in which a regional speech pattern is linked to a region's ecology. Richard's use of regional speech clues the attentive reader into a colloquialism in Florida, and it establishes a commonplace of shared knowledge between Richard and other people living in the state. Through his public performances of these types of stories, Richard displays his willingness to share his own insider's view of life in Florida. His telling of this story demonstrates that regional speech patterns are not solely the lexical items that demarcate boundaries by linguistic glosses. Instead, his use of regional speech is a vibrant part of his everyday culture, and its use is an unaffected mannerism of a native Floridian. Regional speech contains linguistic commonplaces that invite listeners to participate in the process of turning empty geographic space into the common places of shared memories and imagination. In this respect, telling tall tales about common places demonstrates that relating truths about a region connects people within their own communities. The stories also extend an invitation to outsiders who wish to enter his neighborhood.

Bird Dog

Richard physically and conceptually pairs hunting with fishing, and it is not surprising that his repertory of tales includes variants of Baughman's tale type 1920F: *Skillful hounds* as well as tale type 1891: *The great rabbit-catch*. Baughman notes that the story has variations and that Canadian folklore includes stories of massive catches of frogs that are similar to this type of hunting tale. In the following story, the hound dog is transformed into a bird dog, so the rabbits become quail. The story also includes numerous motifs from the Aarne-Thompson system, including X1124: *Hunter catches or kills game by ingenious or unorthodox method;* X1215: *Lies about dogs;* X1215.8: *Intelligent dog;* and X1250: *Lies about birds.*

> I had me a bird dog here a while back—the best bird dog I ever had. I wouldn't have sold that bird dog for anything in the world. I thought that was the best dog I'd ever seen or heard tell of. Nobody had one any better.
>
> We'd go out to shoot quail, and that bird dog had a method. He had a method all of his own. He'd run a whole covey of quail down a gopher hole, and he'd sit on that hole till I got there. And then when I

got there, I'd tell him I was ready. He'd raise up and let one quail out at a time. And I could shoot singles.

This story also contains an intriguing colloquialism. A gopher is a furry animal that burrows holes into western prairies and farmland. This mammal would not likely find a comfortable niche in Florida's ecosystems. The gopher hole in this text was made by the gopher tortoise, a protected species in Florida. The commonplace once again clues the attentive listener into the commonwealth of knowledge shared within the state's boundaries.

To understand the story, however, the listener needs to know a bit about hunting. Richard owned a bird dog, and he used him to flush out game birds in central Florida. Training and working with a bird dog requires considerable skill and practice, and it is not surprising that a good hunting dog is the subject of bragging rights by its owner.[20] The story celebrates the way that a hunter and a dog can work together. It is a poetic truth that is revealed in the exaggerated image of a dog releasing trapped quail as if they were single skeets released by target shooters. The implicit personification of the hunting dog gives the animal a cartoonish quality, and it also suggests that a trained hunting dog is capable of forming a close relationship with a human being. Richard's hunting dog will not be given complete human agency, but he provides the dog with a greater degree of anthropomorphism than he is willing to bestow on any other animal.

Hunting Dog and Fur Stretchers

Tall tales about hunting dogs are commonly associated with lying contests. One good story about a dog deserves another good story about a hunting dog. Richard offers another variant of tale type 1920F: *Skillful hound* to top his first one. It also includes Aarne-Thompson motif X1215.8: *Intelligent dog*.

> I also had a hunting dog one time that I had well trained, and I wouldn't have taken anything for him. I had him trained real good. He'd do just what I wanted to do.
>
> I used to hunt quite a bit, and I had all kinds of boards to put the hides on. When I would kill different animals, I'd stretch the hides on the boards. And I had a board for a rabbit. And I had a board to stretch a possum hide on. And I had a board to put a coon hide on and so forth. And the bigger the board, the bigger the animal he'd get.
>
> And if I wanted a rabbit, I'd put the rabbit board out by the back step after dark—and just leave it there. The next morning, there'd be a rabbit there. If I wanted a possum, set the possum board out there. And

the dog would look at it. The next morning, there'd be a possum there. If I wanted a coon, put the coon board out there. And the dog would look at it. The next morning, there'd be a coon laying there. That went on for a period of time.

And one day, my wife left an ironing board out there by mistake. She forgot to bring it in. And I've never seen that dog since.

The story narrates Baughman's motif X1215.8 (aa): *Master shows dog a skin-stretching board; the dog brings in a raccoon just the size of the board. Master's mother puts ironing board outside one day. The dog never returns.* Because classification systems can be highly subjective, this extensive motif could serve as a tale type. The story (or motif) describes the epitome of a good hound dog. The affection for the dog is in stark contrast to the visceral quality of skinning game. This distinction between "working dogs" and "game" shows that a dog's value depends on how well it can be trained. Even the best dogs, however, can only master accomplishments that are in the realm of canine possibilities, and as the dog becomes almost too human by beginning to take on the hunter's tasks, Richard loses his prize hound. The story's content playfully reveals essential details of everyday life in Richard's childhood community, and it reinforces relationships between humans, working animals, and game within the local taxonomy. Its content provides context to understand the hunting culture of his rural community, and the detail of leaving the ironing board on the porch serves as a mediator between the great outdoors and the domestic sphere of interior spaces.[21] Symbolically, the ironing board left on the porch supports the gendering of space into feminine interiors and masculine exteriors.[22]

At first gaze, his narratives often appear to be little more than ordinary speech. In many texts, his storytelling is as sparse as it is logical. In other stories, he masterfully uses a range of literary resources, including parallel construction, repetition, rhythm, alliteration, assonance, vivid description, metaphor, personification, and irony to craft elegant stories. When one looks at the form of his narratives, the subtle eloquence of Richard's storytelling aesthetic emerges as he blends the poetic quality of everyday speech with a finely honed sense of style. This particular story is a beautiful display of literary form.[23] The initial lines key the listener in on the appeal of listening for the story's artistry as he opens his telling by establishing the value of a finely trained hunting dog. He calls attention to the aesthetic appeal of watching dogs work as they track down game, flush out birds, hold a point, and retrieve game. He explains the qualities of a good hunting dog and describes how his dog has responded to his training. Stretching the truth by talking about the reality of stretching hides, Richard develops a series of parallel constructions that emphasize the poetry of his prose. He introduces each variety of game with the same phrase, and the pattern creates the expectation that his dog will track down these animals later on in the story. He breaks the pattern of incremental development when telling of stretching hides, but another line sets up his delivery of the expectation that he raised when he names his primary game as rabbit, opossum, and coon. The dog sets out hunting and returns in successive order with a rabbit, a possum, and a coon. This repetition not only helps Richard to remember the story, but it also provides a resource for building up the flow of his narrative's repetitive cadences. Expectations raised, the denouement is fulfilled as Richard articulates the circumstances that led to the loss of his dog. The binary relationships of problems and solutions and the threefold repetition are comfortable formal patterns that allow the listener to follow the story easily.

Fishing and the Fog

Repetition, parallel construction, and other formal patterns show up in many stories. This fishing tale is best classified as a combination of motifs X1150.1: *The great catch of fish* and X1651.3.1: *Fish swim in fog*. Rendering it ethnopoetically calls attention to the differences between verbal art and the written word. A verbatim transcription of this text would result in an awkward run-on sentence. Ethnopoetics emphasize differences between the aesthetic values associated with verbal art, for scoring the text in a highly visual rendition displays this tale as a found poem. By using "And" to mark the beginning of each sentence, Richard establishes a common expectation for the listener in a way appropriate to the spoken rather than the written word. Each line then follows a binary structure that moves the story forward either temporally or conceptually as the story's narrative flow shifts back and forth from encountering problems to finding solutions.

> Not very long ago, I went fishing on the St. Johns River. And we got down there and fished a while. And we got quite a few fish: the speckled perch was biting fine.
>
> And we hadn't been out there too long before the fog came in. And, well sir, it kept getting foggier and foggier and got to where you just couldn't hardly see. And finally it got down to where you couldn't see, and we were just hemmed in there. And finally, fog got so confounded thick you couldn't see nothing. You could fish overhead and catch fish.
>
> And I happened to look down in the boat, and we had quite a few in the boat. And I happened to look down there, and those we had in the boat had already swam out.

Rich Soil

Richard's characteristic storytelling technique of finding phrases to establish repetitive patterns in tall tales is evident in the following stories. A maze of narration builds binary relations and establishes problems and their attendant solutions in an embedded array of variants of Aarne-Thompon's tale type 1960D: *The great vegetable.* The first tale incorporates motifs X1455: *Lies about corn* and X1455.1: *Remarkable cornstalks.* His second story presents motif X1411.1: *Large watermelon.*

My sister had a farm down in the state, and it was the richest ground I ever saw. It would grow anything it was so rich. It would grow anything.

She planted a field of corn there, one time. And that corn growed so high that the moon had to detour by the way of Georgia every night to get over.

And also watermelons. She could not raise watermelons because the ground was so rich and the vines would grow so fast that it would wear the watermelons out dragging them across the ground. That's the truth if I ever told it! And she finally staked one down and saved it. She saved that watermelon.

Well, I don't know just how much it weighed. We had no scales big enough to weigh it, so we put it up on two sawhorses. We put it up on two sawhorses and screwed a faucet in it and had watermelon juice for two weeks!

And she found a little watermelon down in the field, and—somehow or another—it made it. It wasn't as big as the rest of them. It was a runt—what we called a "runt" down there. Just a small one. But we decided if we get enough people around, we'd get it up in the wagon, carry it up to the house. We thought we could do it because it wasn't as big as the rest of the watermelons. We finally got it up on the wagon. We got it up on that wagon, and it fell off and busted and drowned the mule.

The recursive properties that allow storytellers to top their own tall tales allow Richard to embed four tales into one long one. He begins with plausible statement of fact based on Bauman's motif X1532: *Rich soil produces remarkable crop.* Richard then expands on the different ways to grow crops quickly. He spins out four short stories to develop the consequences of quick-yield agriculture. His story ends with the demise of yet another Kissimmee mule as the horticultural motifs shift into a motif about livestock, motif X1242: *Lies about mules.*

Lightning Strikes

Richard generalizes some of his stories by referring to natural hazards that intrepid denizens of Florida continue to face. Motif F968: *Extraordinary lightning* is evident in a number of stories from Florida, and Stith Thompson notes its prevalence in Irish folklore.

> I was down there one time to my sister's farm when they had a thunderstorm. You never saw such a thunderstorm till you saw one in that neck of the woods. It really puts on a show. The wind blew so hard, and it thundered and lightninged.
>
> The wind blew so hard and fast that it literally blew a cast iron washpot out of my sister's yard so fast that the lightning struck at it three times and missed it—all three times.

This motif is common both in stories and in nature. Florida leads the nation in lighting strikes. Florida thunderstorms come up quickly, and the violence of a Florida lightning storm is truly terrifying—especially to anyone stuck out in open water or on unprotected land. In drawing from a commonwealth of shared experience, Richard's tall tale presents a portrait of Florida that is both accurate and fanciful. The state's lightning is so severe that his story defies the folk belief that lightning will not strike twice in the same place. In telling a story about lightning striking thrice, Richard uses folklore to transform the given experience of natural phenomena into a cultural creation. Because his text includes a warning about taking cover during a storm, reordering nature through storytelling can potentially thwart disasters created within the natural order.

Squirrel Hunting

Motifs dealing with thunder, lightning, and rain are prevalent in many southern tall tales. Vance Randolph's collection of tall tales from the Ozarks includes a version of tale types 1890: *The lucky shot* and tale type 1891: *The great rabbit-catch,* in which rabbits fall from the sky like rain.[24] Stith Thompson notes that the tale is historically common in America's Southeast and that it has been an important tale type in African-American folklore. In Richard's version, the shot results in a downpour of squirrels as the story develops motif X1124: *Hunter catches or kills game by ingenious or unorthodox method.* Richard also constructs the story around motif X1122.2: *Person shoots many animals with one shot,* and he adds a coda to develop motif X1121: *The great marksman's remarkable gun.*

> Several years ago, while I was down there, I thought I'd go squirrel hunting—while I was down to my sister's farm. So I got my old gun and started out—went down in the woods, and looked, looked, looked around. And after a while, I saw the biggest oak tree that I think I ever saw in my life. It was a great big old oak tree. I stood and looked up in that oak tree, and I never saw such a big oak tree in my life. And right in the top of it was the biggest squirrel nest I ever saw in my life. It was the biggest one I ever saw. It was a huge squirrel nest. So I up and shot right in the middle of it. And, you know, it rained squirrels out of the nest for fifteen minutes and drizzled the rest of the night.
>
> I was using my daddy's old shotgun—the best old shotgun I ever seen. They don't make them now like they used to, not like that anyhow. That was the strongest shooting old gun I ever saw or ever heard tell of. That gun could shoot nine miles and then start throwing rocks.

This hyperbole in the story relates to a wider pattern in telling tales. Keith Basso writes that Western Apaches use the idea of shooting an arrow as a metaphor for storytelling, a theme in American Indian folklore that N. Scott Momaday also brilliantly develops in his presentation of Kiowa folklore in *The Way to Rainy Mountain.*[25] The same relationship between firing a weapon and telling the truth is evident in the physical action of aiming a shotgun. Drawing a bead on a game animal requires that the hunter coordinate the idea of shooting with the physical action of pulling a trigger so that the shot cleanly hits its mark. In this respect, Richard's story shows a way to think about truth. Truth is not simply the pragmatic connection of an abstract idea with a physical phenomenon that exists in the objective world. Rather, the hunter must connect the abstract patterns of the subjective mind with the physical reality of what exists in the world. Subject and object are unified in shooting an arrow or a gun, for imagining the act of firing a gun must be accompanied by the pulsating reality of cocking back a shotgun's hammer and squeezing a trigger. In Richard's mind, simply thinking about what might be true must be tested out in experience.

Snake and Frog

Richard tells another story that develops the theme of outdoor life that he entitles "Snake and Frog." This particular tale is also known as "The Convivial

Snake," following Lowell Thomas's inclusion of the story in his 1931 anthology.[26] Thomas documents over two dozen variants of the story mainly from raconteurs of the southeastern states, and numerous fieldworkers have documented the story in Florida's oral tradition.[27] The story develops motif J426.2: *Snake wants to eat frog friend;* X1342: *Lies about frogs;* X1150: *Lies about fishing;* and X1153: *Fish caught by remarkable trick.*

> One day while I was fishing in the Kissimmee River, I was sitting on the bank on the river with my feet hanging off—under a big willow tree. It was shaded there. And I was just sitting there, fishing and enjoying myself. And once in a while, I'd catch a fish.
>
> And after a while, I heard an awful commotion, not far from where I was. And I heard an old frog hollering bloody murder. And I knew what had happened—a snake had caught him, a snake looking for a dinner. And he caught it too! So that old frog was hollering bloody murder, and I thought I'd have some fun with him. So I got up, cut me a limb off that willow tree with a fork at the end on it, and I went down there where they were. And I saw where he was. So I took that stick with the forked stick, and I jammed it over that snake's mouth and held him down tight while I pulled a frog out of his mouth. And that frog left there in a hurry. I mean, he left there going in two ways at one time.
>
> While I was holding the snake down with that there stick, I reached in my hip pocket and got a flask of white lightning—old moonshine. and I gave him a good drink of moonshine, poured his mouth plumb full, turned him loose. And he left out of there in a hurry. So I went back and sit down—went fishing, forgot all about that, and just about half-asleep, I felt something tapping me on the back. And I turned around—and looked. And there was that darn fool snake with another frog in his mouth.

This tale tacitly comments on truth-telling. Tall tales do not typically contain explicit warnings or moralizing, but Richard concludes his tale by castigating the snake as a "darn fool." In Richard's view, a fool may not "know any better," a damn fool knows better, but "does it anyway." On this story's literal level, calling the snake a "fool" provides an implicit warning against acting like a darn fool. This overt statement about foolishness is a definitive characteristic of the tall tale genre, for these tales' humor results from the storyteller's ability to fool the listeners. As in all his tall tales, Richard tells this story as if it were a true account of a personal experience, but he also has just enough twinkle into his eye to clue his listener into the truth that the story is fictional. Unlike some of the other tales, this particular narrative is entirely plausible until Richard delivers the last line. His storytelling aesthetic provides similar clues for listeners to detect lying, and his storytelling plays with ways to exaggerate common knowledge.

Duck Hunting

The following text is a variation of tale type 1890: *The lucky shot*. It contains motif X1122.2: *Person shoots many animals with one shot*. The curious element of this text is that despite the hunter's prowess, there is a surprise ending. Not all of Richard's adventures are successful.

> One time, not long after that, I was hunting down there on the Kissimmee Prairie. I was a' duck hunting, and I didn't have but one shell—just one shotgun shell. Of course, I knew that that's all I needed. One duck was all I wanted.
>
> So I got down there in the blind and set there a few minutes. And here come two ducks flying over, they flew right overhead, side by side. They were flying real close together—right directly overhead. So I thinks, "Well, I'll just shoot between them and get both of them." So as they went over, I drawed a bead right between the two and cut loose. They didn't fall though. I blew the left wing off the one and the right wing off the other. And they didn't fall—because they just butted their wing butts together and flew off like a P-38. And I didn't get no duck.

This playful tale contains serious messages about adult authority and the handling of weapons. Using sufficient details about outdoor sports to create plausible distortions on reality, Richard establishes his authority as an outdoorsman through these types of hunting stories. Youngsters learning to hunt must accept the authority of the mature hunter, for handling a firearm is serious business. Richard's own father used the sport of hunting to teach him to respect the expertise of adults when assuming the responsibility of handling a weapon that kills. Expertise with a weapon does not necessarily mean that an experienced hunter's intentions will be met with expected results, and perhaps this variant could be better termed "The Unlucky Shot." Opportunities to learn to handle a gun by hunting game in Florida's prairies are disappearing, and Richard is concerned about the new meanings of young people handling guns. Remarking on how it was common for any adult to correct any child in Kissimmee Park, Richard notes that many people are now afraid to set a child straight because "he's liable to pull out a gun and shoot you."

Bullfrogs on the Pond

Hunting and fishing stories sometimes are related to tall tales about unusual weather. Richard's story about bullfrogs on the pond can be identified by a number of motifs from the Aarne-Thompson system: X11303.3: *Frogs caught in frozen ice;* X1124: *Hunter catches or kills game by ingenious or unorthodox method;* X1342: *Lies about frogs;* X1606.1: *Lies about quick change in weather from warm to cold;* and X1623: *Lies about freezing.*

Down around my sister's farm, there was a pond there. Right below my sister's farm there was a big round pond. And I never saw so many bullfrogs in all my life around that pond. And they stayed there because it was a heaven for them—good refuge from the enemies. They could sit there, sing all night long. And there wasn't hardly room enough for them to sit side-by-side: there was so many of them around that old pond.

That winter, it come a sudden freeze. And that freeze come in so fast, so severe, that when that freeze passed over that pond, every frog around that pond jumped in the water to keep from freezing to death. And just as they were entering the water—that freeze was so severe, it came over so fast, that they froze just as they jumped in the water. It froze. Right there.

Well sir, I went out there and looked, and there was a pond of ice with froglegs sticking up all the way around—froze. So I just went home and got my lawn mower and went out there and mowed me up a good mess of froglegs.

This tale is another favorite. It is a quintessential tall tale that again shows characteristic patterns of Richard's storytelling. After first situating himself in a rural area near Kissimmee Park, Richard then invites the listener to enter into his physical environment. Continuing his description, Richard finds a detail that characterizes an aspect of southern living, such as the need to adapt to drastic changes in the weather. Some type of action soon follows, and the description begins to suggest the hyperbole that the savvy listener expects. The story's realism shifts as Richard provides his listener with a surreal image of life in rural Florida. The image is so strange that he could end his story at this point. But this story continues, and he tops the telling off with a great punchline.

The unexpected ending is a reminder that the best laid plans sometimes do go astray. He does not come out as the winner in all of his stories, but more often than not, his ingenuity pays off. In this respect, the story celebrates the value of resourceful thinking within strange situations. When encountering an iced-over pond that appears to be growing frozen froglegs, the most logical thing to do is to mow up a mess of this particularly southern delicacy. If one can expect the unexpected, then resourceful action usually delivers its just rewards.

Listening to the Mockingbird

In rural Florida, the bullfrog can provide a pleasant song during a summer's evening. Froglegs are also served on swampfest platters in Florida restaurants, and the meat—which tastes like fishy chicken—complements the native fare of fried gator tail, fried catfish, fried softshell turtle, and fried hush puppies, served with fried corn and fried okra, all to be washed down with refills of very sweet iced tea. In regard to the state's fauna, Florida wildlife is divided into two main categories: edible and inedible.[28] Subdivisions of inedible include trash fish, poisonous or unappetizing quarry, many trophy fish, and protected species. Domesticated animals fall into the categories of "pets" or "livestock." There is a certain degree of flexibility in the categories. Native Floridians have been known to attempt to make pets out of crows, crayfish, deer, and mockingbirds. The mockingbird is the official state bird and an emblem of southern identity in numerous literary works. This story develops motif X1250: *Lies about birds.*

> We used to have an old mockingbird down home. And everybody knew about the old mockingbird because he could sing the sweetest of any bird that I heard. And people from miles around would come around and hear that old bird sing. And his song was always so sweet that people just come and listen and enjoy him so much. There was always someone that would come and listen to that bird sing.
>
> But, you know, the State Board of Health made us shoot that old bird. It was a sad day for us. We had to do away with that old bird. We had to destroy him. But they claim that we had to get rid of him because he sang so sweet that everybody that heard him sing came down with sugar diabetes.

Farmers warn their children not to make pets out of livestock. It makes life easier when market-time and butchering season comes around. Children are also discouraged from attempting to domesticate wild animals although they are given more leeway to attempt to tame wild birds, raccoons, and a few other species. The dangers inherent in trying to tame wildlife are many. Wild animals bite ferociously. They usually run away from their tamers, leaving their erstwhile owners distraught. Moreover, a wild animal is difficult to train, and wild animals accustomed to living on farmland can do severe damage.

Contextualized with understandings about human and animal relationships, this story contains a poignant "coming of age" quality when it is compared to a novel by Marjorie Kinnan Rawlings. *The Yearling* is set in rural Florida, near Richard's home community.[29] Rawling's protagonist, Jody, had to learn that shooting his pet deer meant that he had abandoned the fanciful and egocentric world of the child. The author's point is that Jody had to surrender illusions from his childhood. As did Richard, he learned the important lesson that he does not control nature. The second truth he learned was that he cannot violate his community's norms without disrupting his family's life.[30] In perfect accord with Rawlings, Richard's tale reminds his listener of the harsh reality of accepting adult responsibility.

In taming what is wild, one may expect to pay a price. This norm is encoded in some laws. Contemporary Florida's citizens and visitors have to understand why the state has declared it illegal to feed numerous species of wildlife, especially key deer and alligators. A wild alligator is usually a shy animal, but when fed, the alligator loses its natural fear of people. Children playing along storm drains and holding ponds in housing developments do not realize a danger that is also faced by hikers who stray off footpaths to take a wet hike in the state's swamps. A hungry, aggressive Florida gator that associates people with eating food is a menace. When an alligator in Florida is declared a nuisance, the county's animal control officer will be dispatched to destroy the animal. Thus the maxim "a fed gator is a dead gator" is a pithy reminder that these reptiles are not meant to be tamed.

Honeybees

As Richard's story about the mockingbird suggests, nature's order dictates that not everything that is wild can be tamed. Distinguishing the wild from the tame involves experimentation, as cultural progress in agriculture and animal husbandry depends on finding the natural order of flora and fauna.[31] Growing up as a farmboy, Richard learned that using hybrid seeds, grafting fruit trees, and cross-breeding species can yield positive rewards. Variations on the theme of domestication are evident in a tall tale based on Baughman's tale type 1960M: *The great insect* and motif X1268: *Lies about bees*. The American honeybee also challenges neat dichotomies between wildlife and domestic animals, for America's wild bees came from domestic swarms just as domesticated swarms can go wild.

My sister used to raise honey, and she had lots of bees. And she raised honey, and everybody liked that honey. And she couldn't fill the demand, though, because she didn't have enough bees. And she was always behind with her orders because she just couldn't make enough money to satisfy all of her customers. People like that there orange blossom honey, and they came for miles around there for it. So she didn't know how to make it any more. She had all the bees she could put down there.

But she struck up on an idea that worked fine. Yes sir. You know what she done? She crossed them honeybees with lightning bugs. Yes siree. And they could work nights, so they made honey twenty-four hours a day.

This story adds to the many tales about bees and insects found in American folklore. It provides apt fodder for considering the importance of taming the wild in Florida's history. This story and similar variants are found throughout the United States, and Dorson provides a clever version of the motif in his collection of African-American tales from Michigan.[32] Richard localizes the story to Florida, one of the nation's leading honey producers. Two types of Florida honey, tupelo gold and orange blossom, are Florida delicacies. The orange blossom is also the state's official flower.

A Mosquito Problem

Another Florida icon is a prominent character in another story. This tall tale about mosquitoes is so common that it appears as its own tale type in the Aarne-Thompson index: 1960M2: *Large mosquitoes carry off men or animals.* Vance Randolph documented a version in Arkansas that is close to this exact text, and the story also shows up in numerous repertories across the United States and in Mexico. The text also includes motif X1286: *Remarkable mosquitoes.*

You know, the mosquitoes ain't bad now like they used to be. Mosquito control has got them pretty well thinned out. Below Kissimmee, down on Kissimmee Prairie—I went down there to my sister's one time. When I was staying with my sister there one night, the mosquitoes were so confounded bad—And I had mosquito nets all over the place. But they were so bad.

I woke up during the night, and two of them had crawled in there—under that mosquito net—and dragged me off the bed. And one of them says, "Should we eat him here, or take him outside?" And the other one spoke up and says, "Let's eat him in here because if we take him outside, the big ones will take him away from us."

This narrative is unique in Richard's own repertoire. It is the only story he tells in which animals speak and act as if they were human beings. These features indicate that this text could also be classified as an "animal tale," a vibrant genre within Florida's folklore. Throughout the state's history, tales within this genre have been told mainly by African-American and American Indian storytellers.[33] Richard does not know where he first heard the story, and it would be difficult to track down the story's origins. African-American folklore from Florida does include stories about mosquitoes, and a number of African-American animal tales feature talking insects.[34] This particular text's unique quality as an animal tale and its high degree of anthropomorphism suggest that the story could be a cultural contribution from African-American or American Indian storytellers.

Horse Race

When Richard was growing up, large portions of Florida were considered frontier country. This tale deals with dichotomy between what is wild and what has been tamed. The corpus of the story is centered on motif T589.7.1: *Simultaneous birth of domestic animal and child,* an ancient motif that is especially common in Irish folklore. The story also incorporates motif F989.17: *Marvelously swift horse* and motif X1241: *Lies about horses.*

Many years ago out on the Kissimmee Prairie, there was a family that lived out there all by themselves—this man and his wife and a horse. And the Indians was wild out in through there. And it was just isolated from the world, and you just had to do the best you could.

So this woman became pregnant. And when it come time for her to give birth to her child, she thought it would be a good idea to go to her neighbors—her closest neighbor—which is about fifteen miles away. So when the baby come, she'd have somebody to help her. So she saddled up the horse to ride, and the horse was pregnant. And the woman was pregnant. And she crawled up on that horse and started out to her neighbors. It wouldn't be long now. She knew it wouldn't be long before the baby would come.

So on the way, the Indians got after them. There was a band of Indians that seemed to come out from nowhere and took after them. So they and that horse, they tore out. They set out. They tore out. That was the darnedest race that you'd ever seen. That horse was really running for its life, and that woman was hanging on for her life.

Now during the race, that horse just had to give birth to that colt—right then, now, no waiting. So the horse laid down, gave birth to the colt. The woman laid down by it, gave birth to the child. And the Indians was still closing in on them. Well, the horse jumped up, and the woman jumped on his back. And they tore out. And that colt jumped up, and that baby jumped up on that colt, and they tore out. And, you know—We beat them!

Two Jokes

In addition to narrating tall tales in his performances, Richard also tells jokes. He uses these shorter stories as part of his stage patter, following the style of cornball humor used in some country music shows, bluegrass music stage patter, and television programs such as *Hee-Haw*. A common subject is marital tension: "Two weeks ago, my girlfriend put mud on her face to improve her looks. Well, it improved so much that she ain't took it off yet!" And: "My wife has always nothing to wear. And she's got three closets to keep it in!"

In the first joke, Richard prudently creates the character of a girlfriend to avoid impolite insinuations about his wife's appearance. The second joke spins on a stereotype about women's wardrobes. When he tells these jokes, his wife laughs at them. She teases Richard and calls him "a rascal," for his tone is more ornery than mean-spirited.

Preacher Story

For listeners afflicted with what the eminent cultural anthropologist Clifford Geertz calls the "moral hypochondria" of postmodern ethnographic writing,[35] Richard follows these potentially offensive texts with a caveat against steering one's way through the world with a sanctimoniously moralistic compass. This text falls within Aarne-Thompson tale types 1725–1874: *Jokes about parsons and religious orders,* and it presents motif K1956: *Sham wise man.* The story updates motif X443: *Parson's poor horsemanship.*

One day a preacher was driving from his home to his church, one early Sunday morning. And he happened to look in his rearview mirror of his car—that there was an old drunk driving right behind him. Well, that irritated the preacher, so he decided—he didn't like it, so he decided he would speed up a bit and leave him. So the drunk man, he speeded up too and followed right behind him—right behind the preacher. And that irritated the preacher a little more. So the preacher got driving faster. The drunk kept right in behind him, weaving back and forth back there.

It made the preacher real mad. So he floor-boarded it—floor-boarded that car, and tore out to get away from him. And while he was looking up in the rearview mirror to see what the drunk was doing, he failed to see a sharp curve in the road. He couldn't make that curve, so he went off the road, through the ditch, off through the woods, and he hit a stump and turned his car upside down. Both wheels—straight up.

So the old drunk jumped out and run over there—got down on his knees, looked out at the car. He said, "Are you all right sir?" The preacher says, "Yes, I'm all right. I've got the Good Lord riding with me." And the drunk said, "You'd better let him drive with me because the way you're driving, you're liable to kill him!"

Richard would agree that drunk driving is a serious subject and that Florida's crackdown on crime is needed. Richard would also agree with the novelist Milan Kundera when he writes that "humor can only exist when people are still capable of recognizing some border between the important and the unimportant." [36] Richard's willingness to edit his own storytelling demonstrates that he also would agree with Kundera's observation that "nowadays this border has become unrecognizable."

Tall Tales about the Weather

Richard's jokes tend to be short. A few of his tall tales are equally brief. When he tells these tales, he follows the pattern of adding one tall tale onto another to stretch out his telling. Both texts, thus, are components of tale type 1920: *Contest in lying.*

Last summer the weather was so dry. Everything just dried up. It was actually so dry that the fish was kicking up dust as they swum up the St. Johns River. And the sun was so hot. It was actually so hot that the river had to stop under the bridge to cool off.

Big Rattlesnake

This last tall tale is a version of tale type 1889M: *Snakebite causes object to swell,* and it incorporates motif X1242: *Lies about mules.* It is another excellent model of Richard's characteristic storytelling aesthetic. He begins with a veritable description of everyday life in Florida.[37] He develops the text smoothly and eloquently, using symmetrical verbal phrases and parallel constructions as the logic unfolds from realistic description into whimsically absurd images. He adds his own stylistic embellishments, but his modest style of narration remains true to the authenticity of the storytelling tradition in which he learned his tales. As Richard finally moves the tall tale into the heights of the absurd, he pauses to allow himself and his listener the chance to size up the situation. Leaving nothing to do but to create and exploit a potential advantage in a novel situation, Richard finds workable truths when faced with strangely bizarre situations.

> On my sister's farm, one time, I was out there working, and I saw a big rattlesnake. That was the biggest rattlesnake I ever saw in my life. And all I had to kill him with was a hoe. You know, I had a hoe in my hand. So I tried to chop his head off with that hoe. And he was a big snake, and he fought hard. And I was a' beating at him and a' hoeing at him and trying to kill him.
>
> And during the process, he bit the hoe handle. He almost bit it in half. And his venom was so strong and so powerful that after I got him killed and looked over there, that hoe handle started swelling. The hoe handle swelled up as big as a log. You never saw such a thing. The truth, if I ever told.
>
> So I got a log cart, and I carried that old log to the sawmill and had it sawed up into lumber. And I brought it back, and I built me a mule shed to put my mule in. Well, it worked all right, so I put my mule in it that night. I went out to the house and went to bed. The next morning, when I got up and went out there and looked, the swelling had all got out of that lumber. And that there mule shed had shrunk up and just literally shrunk my mule to death.

This story symbolizes a common outlook in many of his tall tales. He can use his wit to solve problems, but the results must be proven in experience. With luck, he can harvest the fruits of his innovative solutions to unanticipated problems. There are times, however, when luck is insufficient, and what he constructs will collapse. Viewing the obligation to tell the truth as foundational to establishing and maintaining social bonds, Richard admits defeat when he witnesses the collapse of what is merely a castle in Florida's sand.

Building this text to its conclusion, Richard breaks outside of the frame of narration and annotates the story as "the truth if I ever told it." This inversion of the Liar's Paradox is a clever use of verbal irony. The trope cleverly reverses the literal meaning of the original phrase, thereby reasserting the original Liar's Paradox, which in turn further destabilizes the tale's truth content. In this perlocutionary act, the way that Richard belies the literal meaning of the phrase articulates a key for interpreting the story. He is explicitly reminding his listeners that they are hearing a tall tale, but the metanarration implicitly asserts that he will also tell the truth in everyday speech. Calling attention to the genre thus marks off certain stories as "tall tales." This marking shows that he normally expects his listeners to believe what he is saying. It also reminds them of the importance of telling the truth. In dropping hints that storytellers can stretch the truth, Richard thereby asserts that learning the truth is also the listener's responsibility, and his stories encourage listeners to think critically about what he is willing to share about his life. The storyteller may reveal truth as well as untruth, but it is his audience's responsibility to discern a text for its true content.

By clearly framing his tall tales as fiction, Richard's seemingly simple stories provide a more complex treatise on truth-telling and his presentation of history. The distinctive features of the tall tale genre and the symbolism in the texts perfectly suit his goal of using untrue stories to share his vision of Florida's folklife. Each story's shift into the fantasy frame provides a vibrant resource for using fantasy to inspire curiosity about the history he presents. Through these stories, he establishes truths about the daily activities that form important components of his life experience. The stories accurately express cultural commonplaces that are essential to creating a sense of place out of Florida's vast spaces, and the truths about essential values emerge through the symbolism of salient features in the state's cultural landscapes. The idea of truth as the correspondence between subjective association and objective experience can be read from stories that deal with concordance and schisms between expectations and outcome.[38] The idea of truth as a cohesive linking of components within a system emerges in the rational, and occasionally surreal, logic that shows his worldview is impeccably reasonable. The idea of truth as a pragmatic resource for getting things done is evident in the practical solutions to the novel problems that he poses in his tales. The idea of truth as social accord with the use of language emerges when storyteller and audience make connections through his stories. The idea of truth as a way of being and disclosing the self emerges as he chooses to continue to tell stories. The idea of truth as the symbolic associations that reference important themes in social life becomes evident in the way that his stories present relationships between humans and the land, men and women, human life and animals, clergy and lay people, and a host of other intricate relationships. The idea of remaining true to an artistic system is clear in his mastery of the verbal techniques used by skilled storytellers as his performances hold an audience's attention.

The idea that his storytelling reflects a true historical continuity to an authentic narrative tradition is established by linking his texts to tall types and motives. These connections clearly show that his tales are rooted generally in the folklore of Ireland, Scotland, England, and America, and more specifically in the oral traditions of America's southern states, with strong influences from African-American and perhaps Native American culture. Finally, the idea of truth as a resource for maintaining social connections is evident not only when he avers that "your word was your bond," but it is also essential to his willingness to engage his contemporary listeners in his storytelling. By carefully and conscientiously establishing that his tall tales are not true, Richard reveals that his stories are not lies.

5

Uncle Josie's Farm

~

The Lord gave us these fiddles, and He expects us to play.
—Philip Tingle*

R ichard Seaman sets his tall tales in Kissimmee Park. His stories spin fantasies from the everyday history of his childhood in Osceola County. The truth of these tall tales provides listeners with plausible descriptions of daily life in rural central Florida. A sympathetic reading of his tales shows that his unpretentious style of storytelling resounds with truth. Richard forthrightly frames the tall tales as entertaining fictions, and the cultural commonplaces he alludes to vividly present Kissimmee Park as a place that becomes common to those who listen. But his storytelling makes it clear that he now lives outside of his boyhood community of Kissimmee Park. Richard moved to Jacksonville in 1923 when he was nineteen, after he visited the city to look for work. He soon returned to Kissimmee Park, staying there until an apprenticeship with a Jacksonville railroad line opened up for him in 1926. This opportunity prompted him to move once again from rural central Florida into Jacksonville, an urban area that grew to 130,000 people during Florida's boom of the 1920s.[1]

Richard recounts how his life history relates to his musical experiences. When he speaks of significant events in his life history, he often frames his life as a series of episodes. These personal experience narratives provide a context essential for furthering an understanding of his musicianship and his storytelling. Whereas the tall tales are derived from life experiences in Kissimmee Park and contextualize his hoedown tunes, his personal experience narratives relate actual events from his life history. They provide both texts and contexts for understanding continuities and changes in his fiddling as well as changes in fiddling in Florida. Richard begins his stories about his adult life by explaining that in 1921, when he was sixteen, his family moved from McCool's Grove. His father had purchased a six-acre tract of land and built a house a few miles away on the shore of Lake Tohopekaliga. Lewis Seaman had served during the Spanish-American War, and his military service made it more profitable for him to collect his military pension rather than to continue working as a caretaker in the orange groves. His father's ostensible retirement and Richard's own lack of employment options influenced him to leave his home community as he became an adult. Reflecting on societal improvements that open a wider range of occupations and professions for women, Richard explains that men also have more opportunities to forge a livelihood:

> You take a person nowadays—if he really wants something—if he really wants to, he can generally do it. He can generally find a way to do it. Out there, we had no way.
>
> I had to leave home to hunt work. I came up here. That's the reason I left home. I was nineteen years old when I left home, and I was twenty years old when I went to work for the Seaboard. Well, I was a deadweight on Dad and Mom, and I wasn't doing nothing. And I had no money. I'd get a few little jobs driving the sprayer in the orange groves, making a dollar or two. But you couldn't live off of that.
>
> I had to leave. I didn't want to leave. It wasn't that I didn't like the place. I liked the place down there. I liked everybody down there. But I had to leave. There was only two jobs down there. One of them was working with cattle, and the other was working in an orange grove. And I didn't like either one. There was nothing to it.

Richard grew up on a farm, worked the groves, and tried his hand at ranching. Today, Florida remains a leading beef producer, and the state's cattle industry has a colorful history that includes stories and songs of legendary cow hunters, range skirmishes, buried treasure and smuggling, and a history of supplying beef to Confederate troops during the Civil War.[2] Richard contributed to the industry's history.

> I wasn't a regular hand, but whenever they needed an extra hand, I'd go there. But I didn't like it a bit. It was too rough, dirty, and whenever a cow got in a bog or something like that, you had to go get him out. You had to tend the sick ones and stuff like that. Bad weather and

dry weather. Your pastures would dry up. You was constantly hunting new pastures. It was open range, but that didn't keep the grass from dying. Storms and stuff like that. Marking and branding is a dirty job. You go out there all day, you've penned all those cattle up there, and you've got to brand all those cows. If you're a cowboy, you get out there, and you've got to lasso them, grab them, and hold them down while the other fellow sticks a hot iron to him. When you get through, you smell like manure—and feel worse. Stink. Tired. I didn't like it.

Finding that trail riding was no pleasure, Richard looked for a cleaner, more secure job. With help from his family, he found one with the railroad, an industry that appealed to many Florida workers.[3] Richard found that he enjoyed working with the railroad, and he decided to stay in the city of Jacksonville:

> I've been here ever since. I made my living with the railroad. I was supposed to work four years to serve as an apprentice. I was laid off so many times in 1927, so it took five years to get my four years served. I was off so much. Then after I got out of my time and served my terms in an apprenticeship—that was in 'thirty-one—the Depression really hit. And we was out of work.
>
> I was out of work for five years until Roosevelt got elected, and things began to pick up: the WPAs and all that started. Finally, the railroad called me back, and that was in 'thirty-six. I started to work in 1926 as an apprentice to serve four years. I had to serve five to finish out my time and then in 1936, I was called back to work. All that time between then was not much.

Richard laughs about the misfortune of enduring a ten-year delay in his four-year plan to find employment. He gives me the sense that he wants to explain how he found means for gainful employment when he was out of work. When he was waiting for the railroad company to hire him, he discovered that he could play the fiddle to supplement his income from various jobs. To explain how he was able to find paying venues for playing his instrument, Richard tells of the fiddle's popularity during the 1920s:

> When I came to Jacksonville, there was fiddlers everywhere here then. Everywhere. It was a fiddler's capital. I think they had more fiddlers in Jacksonville than in any one town in Florida at that time. They claim they did—I don't know. But I know they were here. And I used to go and listen to them. And finally I got my courage up.

I took mine out and started playing a little bit. And I teamed up with an old boy that worked at the shop. He was a fireman, and he played the guitar. So I teamed up with him, and we played for quite a while. Dances and stuff like that. There wasn't much to do. But they used to have dances quite often around here. People would kick the furniture out the front room and say, "let's have a dance." Now, I haven't heard of a square dance in many, many years.[4]

As Richard notes, square dancing was not solely a rural activity. People across the nation gathered in homes in villages, small towns, and cities to dance to hoedowns. Many of the dancers and musicians were rural people who had migrated into the cities, and, as did Richard, they re-created their old favorite means of entertainment in new urban communities. In contrast to being rarely paid to fiddle for dances in Kissimmee Park, playing in Jacksonville often provided him with some spending money. City life also offered new performance venues:

You could go out on a Saturday night around town here, and some of the little country stores or little grocery stores on the outskirts of town—they had a lot of them before these chain stores come in—and they'd let you sit in there and play. And they'd feed you all the cold drinks and candy or beer, whatever you wanted—because that would draw trade in there. And we'd do that. Lots of times, we've done that. We'd just get together and go in and just start playing. We wouldn't have to announce it. Word would get around pretty quick in the community, and we'd have a storefront full of people, all in there listening to it. Of course, he'd make pretty good off that. There was a barbershop on McDuff where I got my hair trimmed. A fellow by the name of Wade Cruse was the barber there, and we'd sit in there on a Saturday night sometime, just sit there and play. And we'd have the barbershop full of people, stopped in there and listening.[5]

Richard notes that other business owners were quick to allow him to play his fiddle while Clyde Kirkland accompanied him on guitar. Their pay usually consisted of free beer, and they were sometimes paid cash by the storekeeper. When they would play at square dances, they played for long sets of dances, and the dancers would pass the hat and pay them each about two dollars a night. Richard explains that being compensated for his musicianship was a welcome bonus but that he was more interested in simply playing the music and in socializing with people at these events. He sought out other fiddle players, and he believes that he knew most of the fiddlers who played in public in the city. He also met a number of fiddlers from throughout Florida, Georgia, and Alabama by competing in fiddlers' contests: "They used to always be having a fiddlers' contest around town here off-and-on. But then maybe a hog-caller's contest at the same time. They'd all get in there and get quite a crowd there to hear it. So I'd always be in there. I never did get first prize. I got second prize one time. But I never got a first prize."

Richard shows me a yellowed program that provides a glimpse of what occurred on the contest stage seventy years ago. It is titled "Old Time Fiddler's Contest/Square Dance/Hog Caller's Contest." The competition's date is May 15, 1930, and the location is the Duval County Armory. The two-sided program lists the twenty-six fiddlers in the order of their appearance. Fifteen of the fiddlers are from Jacksonville. All of them are from northern Florida cities, including Palatka, St. Augustine, Ocala, White Springs, Lake City, and Pensacola. The second side of the program lists the four rules for the fiddle competition. The rules state that fiddlers can compete either with one accompanist or by themselves. They have to play two numbers. Each number is to be completed within three minutes, and the fiddler will be given a signal at the two minute and fifty second point to call attention to the time constraints. All fiddlers must use a regulation bow, and no trick fiddling or singing is permitted. The rules affirm that fiddlers will be judged "strictly on their fiddlin' ability." A final regulation stipulates that each fiddler must play old-time music and "nothing modern."[6]

The program shows that three elected officials were to judge the show that night: Taylor J. Harris, mayor of South Jacksonville, Martin J. William, mayor of Jacksonville Beach, and Henry W. Roberts, president of Local Musicians Union 444. Ten prizes would be awarded. First place is a prize of fifty dollars, second place thirty-five, third place twenty-five, fourth place fifteen, fifth place ten dollars, and there are awards of five dollars to those who finish sixth through tenth.

Richard explains that some contests featured a new fiddle as an additional prize for first place, and he adds that he won a new violin bow when he finished in second place during another event. Although he did not place in the money that particular evening, this contest was similar to other competitions. I see a familiar name on the program, and Richard explains that one of the competitors, Tom Acosta, also accompanied him on guitar. As we continue taping, Richard records where the contests were held: "Anywhere they could—like a school auditorium or a large hall or anywhere they could get a large audience. I don't remember being out in a park although we had played in the parks for picnics and stuff like that."

Richard explains that these contests would attract anywhere between eight and thirty fiddlers and that they could last for hours. A newspaper clipping about the event of May 15 records that about 1,000 people were in the audience and that E. O. "Fiddlin'" Purcell of Pensacola won first place that night.[7] W. H. Griffin took first place in the hog-calling contest. I remark that I have seen fiddle competitions in Florida but that I have never been to a hog-calling competition. Richard laughs:

> Well you don't hear it no more, but that used to be quite popular. It was a lot of fun, you know. Some of the awfulest calls you ever heard—that some of them people used to call hogs. And some of them put on a little extra to it. Whoever could call the best and call the loudest, he'd get the prize.

I ask, "Did they actually call hogs over?"

Richard explains, "No, there would be no hogs there. It was just a method of calling, you see?"

Curiosity piqued, I ask, "They'd just judge them on their best sound?"

He replies, "Yeah, the way they would call them, and some people would have an act of putting on to make their calls sound comical. It was just a lot of fun."

I ask him if he was ever in a hog-calling contest, and Richard laughs, "No, it was bad enough to get up there and try to play the fiddle than to get up there and call hogs."

Richard's decision to avoid this aspect of competition may or may not have been a prudent choice. I look over the yellowed piece of paper and find that hog-calling is not as lucrative a competitive venture as fiddling. The prize to be awarded to the champion hog caller is fifteen dollars, the second place finisher will win ten dollars, and third through eighth place prizes are two dollars and fifty cents each. If Richard had entered the competition that night, he would likely have won some type of prize as there are only seven registrants in the hog-calling part of the show. The program lists three unequivocal rules. Hog-callers must not use any instruments to make their calls, they can use only one minute to complete their performance, and the judges are to evaluate them on volume, originality of call, and musical tone.

A review of the program shows that local politicians and businesses provided this event with ample support. Six candidates or elected officials had contributed to the cash prizes, and the brochure features advertisements purchased by fifteen local businesses and two candidates for county solicitor. Finding familiar names on the program, I remember that Richard had mentioned playing with these two fiddlers when he came to Jacksonville. He tells me about hearing them playing in a hillbilly band and during fiddling events when he first came to Jacksonville:

> Tom Acosta and Jack Pitts had a band, and they was about the best-known band in this county when I come here. Everybody knew them, and it was hard for anybody to be in a fiddling contest because everyone knew them. And the newcomers, of course, would have to be pretty good if they come up to win a prize over them because they were so well known. They would get the vote.
>
> Tom Acosta, he worked for the railroad too. He worked in the car department. He was a carman. He repaired boxcars and stuff like that. Now he was a foreman, and he played the fiddle. Jack Pitts. Him and Jack Pitts played, and they called themselves "The Melody Makers." So him and Jack Pitts fell out, and I was playing around with a buddy of mine, Clyde Kirkland. When they broke up, Tom come and asked me to play for him.

As a "Melody Maker," Richard continued to play for square dances, at grocery stores, in barbershops, and on street corners. During this time, he met a number of people in the city. Remembering his courting days, Richard tells me that he courted a young woman named Annie Johns and that he also took out other women. Tom Acosta introduced him to one of his cousins, Daisy Turknett. She played the piano and sometimes accompanied Tom and Richard. Daisy and Richard were married on April 20, 1930.

It was after this time that Richard, Daisy, and Tom ventured onto the radio airwaves.[8] The Melody Makers played for a weekly show that was broadcast live on Saturdays from WJAX. The band played old-time fiddle tunes and did a comedy act mainly to advertise their musical gigs, and the half-hour show lasted for half a year. Looking at a few fan letters that Richard has saved in his fiddle case, I read notes that thank the musicians for their hoedown tunes and ask requests for a variety of songs.

Laughing while he recounts his radio days, Richard gives me the name of the program. "'Uncle Josie's Farm.' And we had to imitate horses and cows and dogs and chickens and roosters and play like we was in the barnyard."

"Whose idea was *that* to have you do the imitations?" I ask.

"It was Tom's. It was more his idea than anything else. He was a funny-talking kind of a fellow, and he was talking about 'Uncle Josie's Farm.' We'd have to crow like a rooster and cackle like a chicken and play us some old-time music!"

Richard pauses a moment to laugh, giving me an expression that beams bemusement coupled with a vague sense of chagrin. He continues to talk about his performances during the Golden Age of Radio:

> In those days, you'd just have one microphone, and we'd all stand around it. And the man operating it would give us a signal of what to do. There was one old microphone, a big old round thing with springs around it. And we would stand around it, and Daisy and her sister would sing once in a while. And they'd sing "Whispering Hope" or something like that as a duet, and it was really pretty. But I still got some old letters that we received from that.
>
> It was primitive in those days. WJAX was new. I don't remember just where it was. I swear I don't. It was uptown somewhere. They just had a sitting room, and in this other room there was a microphone. And when you performed, you went in there. You'd sit in the sitting room and wait for your turn before you went in. Tom knew everybody in town, and his brother was a city commissioner. They named the Acosta Bridge for Tom's brother. Tom talked kind of funny with "Uncle Josie's Farm." I don't know where he got the "Uncle Josie" from.

As Richard says "Uncle Josie's Farm," he drops into a gravelly voiced register and brings down the pitch of the word "farm." Richard's low drawl imitates the sound of Tom Acosta's accent that speaks of vocal timbres from America's Deep South. Watching Richard talk about Tom's vision of life on "Uncle Josie's Farm," I begin to imagine what might have been conveyed over Jacksonville's airwaves in the late 1920s and early 1930s. The city did not have slickly polished radio formats at this time, and Richard explains that sometimes it seemed as if everybody was attempting to host a program or become a radio star.[9] I ask him if he ever told tall tales on the show, and he replies that he tried telling the stories but that they did not seem to go over terribly well. He views the tall tales as working better for today's live audiences. These differences in audience reception demonstrated that his radio performances highlighted the differences between playing through mass media forms of communication and playing in venues that feature direct interaction with people.[10]

When Richard was playing as a Melody Maker, he had completed his apprenticeship but was unable to secure full-time employment in the railroad industry. Although humor now permeates his description of the lack of lucrative compensation for his musical ventures, his laugh hides deeper concerns. He enjoyed playing with Tom and Daisy, but he views this part of his life as a difficult time. When the Great Depression hit, Jacksonville's railroad industry was almost paralyzed, and Richard explains that he had to do almost anything that he could to earn a living. I ask if playing music helped him out when he was out of work:

> Yeah, sometimes it did. We finally got a job playing every week at the Francis Grill. That used to be a nightclub out on Lake City Road, and it was pretty rough out there. We'd get three dollars each. My wife would get three dollars for playing the piano, and I'd get three dollars for playing the fiddle. That was all the music they had. And that would be six dollars a week there.
>
> And then in Fernandina, Tom Acosta used to go up and take us along. And we played at Fernandina—the dance hall out there run on the ocean at Fernandina Beach. And we'd get three dollars apiece there. So that made us twelve dollars a week to buy food with, and we done pretty good for a while. But it wasn't a regular thing. That didn't last too long, but we made good of it while we had it. They sold near-beer and stuff like that. That was during Prohibition. But anyhow, it wasn't too hard to find the real stuff if you looked for it.

Remembering a story about an altercation at one of his gigs, I ask Richard about an event that transpired one evening. He describes what he saw in the nightclub and contrasts music in urban Jacksonville with music in Kissimmee Park.

> Francis Grill, that was a pretty bad place anyhow, and we was playing there one night. A friend of mine was calling. Of course, the caller didn't show up. Since the caller didn't show up, he volunteered to call for the evening. Well, later on, there was a man and his two sons came in there about two-thirds drunk and started a fight with this friend of mine who was calling. Well, he said he wasn't calling it right. So when the fight broke out, I went over there to get in it to try to help my buddy out, and somebody hit me just about the time I got up to where the piano was. Knocked me clean across the piano keys, and I rolled across off of them into my wife's lap. She was sitting there playing. That wound it up. That wound it up.
>
> It ain't like it used to be years ago when we first started out. People in the little, old country—like down home where I come from—why some of them would get a bit rowdy. But as a general rule, everybody knew everybody to the extent that they got along. Over here, like at Francis Grill where the fight broke out, you didn't know anybody in

there when you went in there. Everybody was a stranger coming in. And that way a little bit of whiskey would tear up the party.

Richard's story illustrates a major change in moving from a rural community to the city. The friendly and open qualities of house parties in Kissimmee Park are in contrast with the greater anonymity of urban venues. In the later years of the nineteenth century, Ferdinand Tönnies used the terms *Gemeinschaft* and *Gesellschaft* to distinguish between "a community of tradition" and a "society of law."[11] Richard's view of Kissimmee Park fits Tönnies' view of the little community as a system in which members emphasize collective social interaction over individualistic opportunism. Complicit with Tönnies' characterization of these communities, social life in Seaman's little community was regulated more by the bonds of the spoken word and the negotiation of time-honored patterns of tradition. Residents knew that the system of neighborly survival meant that weekend conflicts should be resolved by the time that disputants would return to daily work.[12] At the square dance frolics in his home community, Richard knew the other participants, and he knew that he would work with his neighbors throughout the week. He knew that he had to establish himself as trustworthy and that he had to learn to trust that his neighbors would help him when he was in need. When he moved to Jacksonville, Richard found neighborhood versions of the little community, but he also encountered a larger society in which urban residents were policed more by legal codes and law enforcement than by a concern with the consequences of one's actions on a community. Although fights would break out at dances in Kissimmee Park, Richard asserts that brawls were more common and more violent in Jacksonville's nightclubs because of the greater presence of anonymity.

Richard's story also shows that residents of Jacksonville still sought out entertainment despite the poverty of the depression. I was surprised that it was possible for musicians to support themselves economically during this time, and I ask Richard how members of the audience could compensate groups like the Melody Makers. His reply shows his resourcefulness in using his musical talents to help support himself and Daisy: "You didn't have any money to spend for one thing. And—not only that—you couldn't find nowhere to get it. But we did the best we could. We'd play sometimes on the street corners, sometime in the grocery store, or sometimes pass the hat around at a dance to make a few dollars that way. There was always somebody that was working enough that they could spend a little bit. But there was ninety percent of us that didn't have any job. We was just doing the best we could. It was sort of nip and tuck. You'd nip what you could get and tuck your belt in."

Richard's laugh shows his relief that this part of his life is behind him. He pauses in telling this part of his life story, and I recognize that he is recalling a place in his life when he was newly married, out of work, and faced with limited opportunities to earn his livelihood. He was also frustrated and angry over having to spend extra time to complete a four-year apprenticeship. Threatened with having to return to his parent's farm in Kissimmee and worried about the economic hardships imposed on himself and Daisy, he decided it was time to make a career change. Richard Keith Seaman became a moonshiner.

> After I served my time as a machinist, during that period in there, I got a job making moonshine in Thomas's Swamp. And I worked three days a week at the state road department, and the other four days, I'd go down there in that swamp. Get down there about three o'clock in the morning and get your fire started and bed it down. And get the coals—coke—burning so you wouldn't make any smoke. And time you got daylight, you'd have your still leveled out, and working good, and there's no smoke.
>
> And so I stayed there for, I guess, pretty near a year, and that helped me out. I bought some barrels and got an interest in the still, myself, and I was making some money then. But something got in, kept telling me to quit. So one day I thought I'd better do it. And I quit. And this fellow hired another boy, and it wasn't but about six weeks later before the still was raided. And he got a year and a day in Chillicothe, Ohio![13]

Richard laughs at the memory of his close call with the wheels of justice, and I congratulate him on his fortuitous decision to find other employment. I comment that north Florida was a major center for moonshine operations by asking, "Well, that was pretty common in Jacksonville, wasn't it?" He overlays his answer, "Yeah, yeah" on my unnecessary sentence fragment, "to run a still like that." "Yeah, people would make whiskey—get them a little still and make whiskey in their garage or something like that. Well, that house right across there." Richard pauses a moment and points out the window across Bridal Street, and I nod.

> That first house from this house—the white house over there. They sold whiskey there when I first moved here. That was a bootleg house. They could buy whiskey there. And they used to come there all during the night—cars picking up whiskey. They didn't make it there, but they sold it there.

"Did the police know anything about all that going on?" I ask, expecting to hear a tale of political intrigue.

"I think they did, but they didn't pay no attention to it—not unless somebody made a complaint," Richard flashes a wry smile and offers a conspiracy theory.

"The police—Hell, they liked whiskey too!"[14]

We both share a certain vicarious enjoyment at the subversion of Prohibition authority. I ask if he knew the police officers who imbibed, and Richard continues to substantiate his allegations of conspiracy within Jacksonville's corridors of power. "I knew two or three that the police didn't bother. That was one of them. If it was that open, the police knew it too, see? Well, they paid them off. Some of them cops, you'd give them a little something on the side and they'd look the other way."

My tape recorder's batteries are running out, so I stop the cassette. During our break, Annie returns from visiting her sister and enters the living room. She says hello and offers me a Coke, serving me a can of soft drink wrapped in a paper napkin. As I sip the Coke and insert four new alkaline batteries in my machine, Richard tells me that bootlegging was widespread in Duval County and the surrounding area during Prohibition. He explains that there has been a history of police corruption in the area and that Jacksonville was famous for its numbers rackets during the 1930s. Recorder on, Richard picks up his story:

> It was big business in some places, you know. People got rich off it. I knew a man that built him a nice brick house. He never hit a lick at the snake, but he built him a nice home. And the house is still standing. And he was well known. And he made it with liquor.
>
> A lot of times out in Nassau County—long years ago. We used to go out there, and it was still Prohibition. You could go out there and play, and if you wanted a drink, you'd go outside and feel around the bushes. And after a while, you'll feel a bottle somebody hid out there. Take a drink. Put it back down and go on. They'd have it hid all over the place. And after about ten or eleven o'clock, everybody would be tight. And I'd leave.[15]

By the mid-1930s, Richard and Daisy's life changed. In near desperation over the hardships of the Great Depression, they had to move back to Kissimmee where they moved in with Richard's parents for a short time. One day in 1936, Richard was called back to work in the machine shop at the Seaboard Air Line. I ask him what types of jobs he completed, and he provides an overview of his employment with the railroads. His story is especially interesting as he reveals a facet of the division of labor within the railroad industry's shift from steam into diesel-powered locomotion:

After I had finished serving my time and got back regular, I went out and was what you would call a "flunky." You worked on the floor. Every day the boss would give you a job—which engines to work on. Then later on after you worked there a while and get a little seniority, you had the privilege of bidding on a certain job. And if you bid on that job and got it—if you was the oldest bidder—why then that's your job. Nobody can touch it.

And after I got a little seniority, I bid in on what they called the "booster job." That was working on the boosters, that little engine that helped freight train engines get more power. I worked that for about a year and a half. I didn't care too much about that, and I bid in on what they called a "stoker job." That was an automatic mechanism that fed coal into the engine to relieve the fireman. That was on freight engines where they needed extra amounts of coal. They come up with a patent—a stoker, you'd put on them engines. It would automatically feed coal into the engine, and all the fireman had to do was operate it. I worked that for a while, and that was a pretty good job.

And finally I bid in on the welding job on our section—and got that. And I was welding for twelve years. Gas and acetylene welding. Then I got tired of that. I bid in on a machine job and run a lathe—a large turret lathe. I went from there to the air room, where I worked on airbrake equipment. Finally wound up as a bearing inspector for these diesels. We didn't have steam engines anymore. And I didn't like to work on the diesels myself, but I got a job as a bearing inspector. And I was on that until I retired.

That was a good job. It was a clean job. What I mean is you didn't have to crawl under them engines and burn yourself up with welding—or grease and all that grime. I had a little building, sit there—with all the bearings in there and equipment to test them with. And that was a good job.

But that was the job I had when I retired. And it was really a good job. I loved machinery and still do. I couldn't have found a job that I liked better to suit me. It was dirty—grease. And smelly sometimes—smoke. Air hammers all around you—going. But that's what I like. I wouldn't have done anything else. I was just like a kid with a toy. I enjoyed it.

I could run any of them and do anything that was supposed to be done on a steam engine. I wanted to try it—I'd get on the welding job, and it wasn't long before I had that under control. I could do any of that. Any of the machinery they had in the machine shop, I could run it. It made me feel like I was doing something.

Richard regards the railroad machine shop as a good place to work. He recollects that he enjoyed every day of work. Along with learning the machinery and completing the tasks, Richard explains that he appreciated the rich fellowship among the workers. The employment security and the solid pension were also attractive features. Another bonus to working with the industry was the strength of the railroad union. Richard was active in the International Association of Machinists, Number 257. He still carries his union card, and he keeps a brass plaque that commemorates his membership. He perceives labor relations as strong while he worked for the railroads. During his thirty-five years with the railroad, he saw only two strikes, one of which he regards as "silly." It was over a small technicality about water breaks. The other strike was more serious and involved a legitimate pay dispute. He notes that the problem was resolved relatively easily. In sum, although he appreciated the union's strength in labor activism, he views his union membership as more akin to belonging to a social organization than to a political interest group.

By the time that Richard gained full-time employment, he and Daisy had started a family. Richard, Daisy, and their two children, Daisy Jean and Richard Keith Jr., moved into a house in Jacksonville's Avondale neighborhood in October 1935. Richard recollects that he briefly rented the home for twelve dollars a month. When the owner decided to raise the rent by a factor of thirty-three percent, he was concerned about paying sixteen dollars for rent each month. He found that the owner was willing to sell the home at twenty dollars a month with four percent interest and no down payment. The Seamans accepted the offer because Richard's employment opportunities were improving. He explains that his job security improved by the end of the 1930s, and during World War II, he was able to work overtime as well as complete double shifts as a welder:

When the war was over, we began to level out. And I had the most money I'd had in a long time. There was nothing to buy much. Even at Christmas time you couldn't buy toys for kids. They were all pasteboard and stuff like that because they were saving the metal for combat use. So we had some war bonds; they weren't mature. I get to figuring here, and I figured I had maybe enough money to finish paying off the house. I don't know why, but I wanted to pay it off. Daisy went down and cashed in the war bonds. They weren't mature, but we got something. We counted the money we had saved up, and we lacked twenty dollars of having enough to pay the house off then. I said, "Now, dog."

The next day, I was at the shop, and I was talking to the foreman. Joe Parson was the foreman. I said, "If we had enough money to pay for my house—I lack twenty dollars of having enough."

He didn't say a damn word. He reached his hand in his pocket, pulled out his wallet, and says, "Here, go pay for your house."

I took it. I took that twenty dollars, and we went down. And I took a friend I knew that worked at the courthouse. And we paid that man off in cash. And when we come home, we didn't have a damn cent. But we had a home. The next payday, I paid Joe his twenty dollars back, and we started again. But we owned a home.

In concluding his story, Richard's voice displays a satisfaction that revives the comfortable feelings evoked by settling into homeownership. The sense of being uprooted from his Kissimmee Park community was replaced by the recognition that he had established solid connections in Jacksonville's Avondale neighborhood. Richard and Daisy opened their home to their friends, many of whom were musicians. Although the house was too small to host large square dances, music-making warmed the house:

When we moved here, they had a picket fence around each one of these houses. It's all rotted down and gone now. So we'd sit out there and play after dark. It'd get dark, and we'd play right on. And people would come out there. And one day, I woke up one morning and went out there. And my whole section of the fence was laying down. They were all perched up there on the fence, and the fence fell down. They didn't say nothing: they left. So I come along and took the rest down.

That night, they was sitting there on the fence, some were sitting on the ground. Some were sitting on the porch. We would all sit up there on the porch and play and have a big time.

It wasn't hard to get a bunch of people around in those days because there was no entertainment. Now they've got their television programs and all, and they can't leave that.

Not only did their front porch and yard host ample evenings filled with music making, but the Seamans filled their house with music when the children were growing up. Richard highly valued Daisy's musicianship. She could both play by ear and read music, and he recalls that she could listen to a tune one time and then play it on the piano. She played in a range of styles, but Richard heard her play mainly in a lively ragtime style. He explains that she and their daughter bought the sheet music of many tunes and that he learned numerous new songs by listening to Daisy and Jean play piano in their home.[16]

Daisy had a few rules that accompanied her housekeeping. She kept a linoleum rug in their living room because foot traffic would easily tear up fabric-based rugs. Despite this precaution, the use of heavy-duty floor coverings had to be regulated:

> Daisy wouldn't let the bass player set the knob of his player on that hard rug because it would leave little dents in it. She had a pie plate—a big old pie plate. It wasn't aluminum in those days. It was an old iron pie plate, and she'd bring it in here. And he had to set that bass fiddle on that so it wouldn't dent the rug. We'd all get happy in here, and after a while, she'd look over there, and he done drug his fiddle off the plate and onto the rug. She stopped the music right there. She put that knob back in that plate. She was strict.

By the 1950s, Richard decided to organize his own band. He could include Daisy when a piano was available, and his children, Jean and Keith, also contributed as vocalists. Richard showed Keith how to play guitar, and Keith learned to play it left-handed. Friends and coworkers made up the rest of the band, and they sometimes performed with a bass player, three other guitarists, and a mandolin player. They picked a name for the band, and the "South Land Trail Riders" toured through north Florida:

> We got together and organized a little band. It went along pretty good. We didn't really make no big name for ourselves, but we were known around quite a bit.
>
> In those days, you didn't make much. Money was tight. The tickets were sixty cents. That would be for a two-hour show, and we'd put on a show that would last for about two hours. Some of the clubs, they might give a picnic, and we'd play for them.
>
> If we didn't have a place to play, we'd put on a show ourselves. And we'd just sell tickets wherever we could get a hall big enough to hold a dance or whatever we was going to do. We played picnics, whenever anybody had a gathering. We never did play for a dance though. I

played for a lot of dances, but I played that with just two of us—fiddle and guitar. But we'd play for anything that required anybody wanting some music: they'd pay us to go play. We played at the beach when that big pier used to be down there and they had a big nightclub down there on it.

If the railroad had an excursion, we was right there with them. And if anybody had a gathering or picnics out or anything, why we were always in the bunch. We didn't make any real money with it. We played for schools. If they had an auditorium or anything in there, we'd get them to let us play there. Sometimes we made a little. Sometimes there weren't enough people there to pay for it. Actually, we didn't make anything at all. We didn't make enough to pay for the gas sometimes.

One particularly memorable concert was held at Lackawanna School, a public school located a few miles from their home. The performance was part of a carnival that was designed to raise funds for a new film projector. The admission was sixty cents, and the band earned forty percent of the sales. At the show's completion, the school had sufficient funds to buy the projector, and all the members of the band went home with a pocketful of change. This performance is memorable because it provided Richard with the chance to learn to emcee his events. He explains that this show helped him learn to present his music:

> We had the auditorium full. I was very green at it. Some little old girl come up there and took over emceeing, and I didn't know her at the time. She just sort of took over and run the show. I found out later on that she was from Nashville, Tennessee. She played with Ernie Tubb on 'Rainbow Ranch Girls.' She was one of them. And I knew that she knew what she was doing. She started us off pretty good. I didn't have any knowledge of what to do or say.

Richard enjoyed playing with the band, and long-time residents of Jacksonville speak of his family band with fond memories. His son became known as a strong guitar player, and the South Land Trail Riders put on good shows.[17] While Richard was playing with his family band, he also occasionally found other opportunities to play for dances and established a reputation as a strong fiddler. He gives an account of one particularly memorable night that took place a few years after the band had played their first concert:

One night we was up at the Boys' Club in Arlington, and we had a pretty good-sized crowd there. And we was trying to make a go of it, and it seemed like every damn thing went wrong that night. The guitar players, they was arguing. I don't know—everything just seemed to go wrong. And I thinks to myself, "What in the Hell? Am I just a butting block for all of this?"

So when we finished the show, I fired the whole damn business. I told them I was through. And then *I* quit. It wasn't worth it. If you're the head of the band, and there's somebody bellyaching all the time about the other one, and you're trying to get together, you get tired of it.

I don't know why it's that way. I got mad that night, and that's the last time I played.

Richard went home that night and put his fiddle up on the mantelpiece in his living room. The band broke up, and Richard stopped playing. There were only a few square dances held in the city by this time, and new forms of music were becoming popular in the nightclubs.[18] As time went on, it became hard for Richard to find anyone who knew how to play the fiddle, and there were few guitar players who knew how to back up an old-time musician in the city of Jacksonville. Richard concentrated on his work, and he became known as a fine mechanic in the machine shop. In 1971, he accepted that it was time to retire from the railroad. He speaks of the day that he had to turn in his retirement notice:

That was about the hardest thing I ever did—was to go in there and sign my rights away, to retire. It made me feel like I wasn't any good anymore—giving up and just quitting. But I had to retire. If I had worked any longer—

At that time you had to retire at seventy-five. If you didn't, if you worked on, you would lose some of your equity. And I think that I did the right thing.

I don't know why, but back yonder there were a lot of people needing work. And they didn't think it was right for a person who was eligible to retire to work on and keep somebody else from coming in and having a job. So when I left, that left another man in my job. So I'm glad I did, now. It was a good job.

I really didn't want to quit when I quit. I liked it there. After I retired, I went to work with Paschal's hardware store. It got so I'd just go crazy as Hell just sitting around here during the day.

Richard worked at Paschal and Shaw's Hardware Store for fifteen years before retiring once again in 1987. Working at the store, he helped to build shelves and manage the stock. He quickly acquired the reputation of being able to fix anything that was broken. The store was a short drive from his home, and he appreciated the chance to continue to work. Richard also opened a repair shop in his backyard garage where he fixed lawnmowers and small engines.

Richard's son, Keith, went on to become a plumber. Richard recounts with pride that Keith helped construct one of the largest buildings in the world, NASA's Vehicular Assembly Building at the Kennedy Space Center in Cape Canaveral. Keith continued to play guitar and perform in the area until his death shortly after he finished working on this building. Richard also sadly talks about the death of his daughter, Jean, who had died after a lengthy illness shortly after Richard lost his son.

My kids were gone, and there was nobody to play with. If you remember before the bluegrass festivals began to get popular around here, why you couldn't find nobody to play with. There was nobody I knew of that could play the guitar. Keith was the last guitar player I had, and when he died, why I didn't have anybody to play with. The fiddle sat right up there on that mantelpiece for thirty years, and I didn't have any feelings toward it at all.

6

Richard's Fiddle

~

And so I pat her neck, and plink
Her strings with loving hands,
And listening close, I sometimes think
She kind of understands.

                      —James Whitcomb Riley*

Hearing a fiddle tune for the first time, a novice listener hears rhythmic bow strokes that make it easy to find the beat. But a blustery flurry of notes may force the novitiate to strain to recognize the tune's melody. After initially marveling at hearing a virtuoso fiddler play, those who are unfamiliar with old-time fiddling tend to lose interest. Without knowing how to listen for each tune's uniqueness, tyro listeners are apt to remark that all fiddle tunes sound the same and move to another stage at a folklife festival. Live fiddle tunes are usually played for dances, and the concentration that a musician needs to maintain the patterns for hoedowns is often at odds with the listener's ability to listen to intricate fiddling. With practice and familiarity an aficionado of old-time fiddling learns to recognize the unique qualities of individual tunes. Eventually the listener develops an ear for appreciating intricate variations on established melodies. With time, some listeners decide to learn to play the instrument. While Richard believes that anyone can learn to play, he regards the instrument as difficult to master. He also believes that it is too easy to become intimidated by the idea of learning to play, for listeners sometimes overly mystify how a fiddler works out a tune. Richard uses concrete techniques that demystify the process, and an analysis of Richard's playing introduces one to ways to listen to a fiddle tune.

Learning how to listen to a tune is a first step in learning to play the fiddle. It is comparatively easy to learn to listen to a tune, but it can be intimidating to master the complex bowing techniques, accurate fingering patterns, and intricate embellishments that ornament the fixed form of a hoedown tune. Although it takes direct interaction with a fiddler to learn to play the instrument, it is possible to understand the characteristic patterns used in playing the fiddle by reading a description of how a fiddler plays.[1] Clueing in on ways of listening to fiddle tunes provides an understanding of the aesthetic standards that Richard embraces when he tucks his fiddle under his chin. In sum, understanding how Richard plays the fiddle requires the need to listen deeply to his tunes.[2]

A fiddle is a wonderful instrument. Its body's form is gorgeous. The color and texture of a finely crafted instrument add to the aesthetic appeal. Violin makers craft the instrument to make it fit comfortably into one's hand and body even though the playing position initially feels unnatural and awkward.[3] A fiddler will turn the instrument over and look at the back, gazing at it to see how the wood is matched and scanning the surface for fine patterns in the wood grain. Rich varnish and burls in the wood add to an instrument's character. The graceful f-holes that open up its body and the noble scroll that decorates the fiddle head are sufficiently rococo for the concert hall's stage, but the physical ornamentation seems perfectly unfitting when a fiddler jumps into "Sally Gooden." The violinist knows that Itzhak Perlman's Stradivarius could resound with Paganini's "Caprice No. 5 in A Minor." The fiddler knows that this same instrument could also play a spirited rendition of "Flop-Eared Mule." The major differences are that the fiddler may use heavier strings and would possibly carve down the bridge, flattening its arch a bit to make double-stops easier to note. Limited financial resources keep most fiddlers from owning fiddles that could also be museum pieces, and the famous violins are played by only the finest violinists and worked on only by the best luthiers. Because of the richness of the violin's legacy, the fiddler may display a mixture of both pride and self-effacement when playing on stage. Even when lying in a plush case, the instrument itself evokes shades of aristocracy tempered with whimsy. To answer the underlying question, the fiddle is the same instrument as the violin.

Richard owns three fiddles. He has recently purchased a high quality violin that he is pleased to allow me to play. Another of his fiddles is a copy of a Stradivarius that he rarely uses.[4] He received this instrument from the widow of a fellow musician, and he keeps it as a memento of their friendship. The main fiddle that Richard plays is one that he inherited from his father. This is the instrument that he painted black after he repaired it following its near-demise in the floodwaters of the 1926 hurricane that blew the roof off his parents' house.[5] In comparing the tone quality of these instruments, Richard provides significant aspects of his aesthetic standards as he shows that the art of playing is linked to understanding of the instrument. Although the Stradivarius copy is easy to play and produces a clear, loud tone, it sounds harsh and thin. Richard prefers the mellower quality of the fiddle that he glued together with epoxy and painted over with black enamel. This fiddle also is comfortable to note, and it resounds loudly when played with even a moderate pressure on the bow. The new fiddle is also a beautiful instrument, and its tone will become even richer as it is played over time.[6] The fiddle strings make it easier to play this instrument at loud volumes, and they will still provide a full tone when the instrument is played softly. All three instruments are easy to note, for the action—or the distance between the strings and the fingerboard—is relatively close.

Along with using heavier strings and adjusting the bridge to make the instrument easier to double-note, fiddlers modify their instruments in other ways. Richard remembers that there were some musicians in his home community who made their own fiddles, and he laughs when he remembers that a local fiddler used his wife's shoelace to restring a bow when the horsehair wore out one evening. One curious detail that Richard mentions involves how some fiddlers use rattlesnake rattles in their instruments, a practice that continues even today. "Some of them would put rattlesnake rattles in their fiddles. Some claim that was to improve the sound. Some claim that was to keep the insects out. I don't know why. But I never did put them in there. I couldn't see where it done any good."[7]

With or without the involuntary assistance of a rattlesnake, learning to play the fiddle can be a notoriously trying endeavor. Many fiddles slip out of tune easily, and fine-tuners on the tailpiece allow for minute adjustments that can be heard only by sensitive ears, or electronic tuners. A fiddle has no frets that block out precise intervals for accurately playing in tune. As the fiddler moves up the neck, closer to the instrument's body, accurate fingering becomes more difficult. The intervals between true and false notes become smaller, and a note that is misplayed in a higher register rings out its sourness more audibly than one played an octave lower. Learning to bow a fiddle accurately is challenging, and most novices find it difficult to smooth out the raspy sounds emanating from their instruments. In examining the techniques that Richard used both in learning to play his instrument and in continuing to hone his abilities as a musician, it becomes clear why playing the fiddle is a challenge. The range of variables make the instrument so versatile a skilled musician can play a violin in virtually any form of musical expression. These myriad variables that make the instrument richly expressive are also the same constraints that can make a violin a potential assault to the ear.

To ascertain the continuity of cultural expression over time, folklorists often ask musicians how they learned their tradition. It is a good question, but I prefer to ask folk musicians how they got their start. The question allows them to contextualize the tradition within their life stories, and it often provides interesting narratives. Richard has answered this question on numerous occasions, and this particular answer reveals essential elements of his musicianship. "Well, that started way back when I was a boy, going to old-time square dancing and gatherings where people made their own music, and I listened to other people play. And I started in that manner. And I was interested in playing too, so therefore I'd memorize some of the tunes that I'd hear and try to learn them on the fiddle. And then later on when I started playing, I began to play out with them and among them, and we would compare tunes and learn from one another. And I just sort of picked them up by ear and played them."

This text is characteristic of Richard's personal experience narratives, and it demonstrates how he uses stories to explain his musicianship. Situating the story in a specific place during his life, he then provides a precise description of the event's context. Richard speaks of an interest or motivation for trying something new and succinctly develops his answer. He ends the narrative by concluding with a statement to emphasize why the story answers the facet of my question that interests him. In this overview of learning to play the instrument, he drops in sufficient details to evoke the listener's curiosity about his music. Demystifying the knack of playing by ear, he asserts that it consists of learning the melody in his head and then figuring out how to play it with his hands. To complete learning a tune, he compares his playing with renditions by other fiddlers. His point that he plays by ear is important, for Richard does not read music. Even when learning tunes that are written down in sheet music or recorded on tape or CD, he acquires all his repertory from the aural tradition.

Richard's story invites more questions about his musical training, so I ask if he remembers the very first time that he heard fiddlers playing. He pauses, remembering an event that happened close to ninety years ago in Kissimmee Park. "The best I can remember, I went to an old farmhouse. The name was 'Barber.' Yeah. When they was dancing, I never seen it before. I didn't understand it: I was a little feller. I didn't exactly understand it. You know, a little old ignorant country boy—it had to soak in. And then finally, I didn't care too much for the dancing, but I liked to hear the old fiddle play. Yeah. I can faintly remember that. Really, I didn't know what it was about. I was young. But I remember that fiddle playing."

The memory is dreamlike. For a moment Richard's story carries us down to the place where the fiddlers play. He gives such a rich description of his home community of Kissimmee Park and has shown me vivid old photographs from his boyhood homeplace that it is easy to picture him sitting down to listen to old-time fiddlers at a Florida frolic. Richard vividly tells about the fiddle that he used when he was learning to play.

> The old fiddle hung up in the house. It belonged to Dad, and there was some strings on it. And I didn't know how to tune it. Dad tuned it different. But standard tuning—I didn't know how to tune it till Joe Barber, I think it was, come by there one day and showed me how to tune it. And then I finally worked out the scale myself.
>
> And I tried to learn when I heard a certain note where that finger went, and soon I got to where I could sort of maneuver that up. I began to bring the tune out.
>
> So he come by the house one day and helped me tune it, and he played a little bit. And later on he'd come by. I was able to play a little bit of "Shear 'Em," and he helped me with it.
>
> And it just come up that way.[8]

Richard clarifies that Ross Barber owned the house where he first heard fiddlers. He doubts whether Joe Barber was related to Ross Barber, explaining that Ross held most of the local dances at his home whereas Joe was a well-known fiddler in Kissimmee, a century ago.

Richard views playing by ear not so much as an esoteric natural talent but rather as a process of acquiring specific physical skills. To begin to learn the instrument, he explains that the fiddler cannot be afraid to make mistakes. Rather, the beginner should learn some scales and boldly work through phrases that begin to sound like a melody. It takes experimentation and practice to make the tune emerge. "If you work at it," Richard says, "it'll just come to you." After the novice fiddler has learned a few tunes, Richard suggests finding a group of fiddlers to play with, and he adds that it is essential to have the courage to just jump right in and try to play with better musicians. A fiddler develops a musical ear by learning to listen and then re-creating melody lines as the feel for the instrument becomes more familiar. His description of a square dance further clarifies this learning process as he embellishes his portrait of the context for dances.

> I didn't have a horse. If I went to the square dances, I had to use them feet. No sidewalks to walk on. Just walking through the woods. You'd have to go like the crow flies. You'd generally go straight through the woods because you couldn't walk around. It was too far to walk.

And you'd come home at night after you've been there, and that old wiregrass and stuff would be full of dew. It'd be wet from here down, wading through that old grass.

Richard smiles. He laughs as he shows me where he would be wet from his waist down to his feet. He continues:

I don't know why, but I liked to hear them fiddlers play. I didn't care about the dancing. I didn't care about that. But I'd go sit. I'd be sort of like a wallflower. I'd be sitting back there listening to the fiddler. And the only one who I can remember his name was 'Barber.' Joe Barber. There was another old man there, but I can't remember his name. Joe Barber, he was older than I was—quite a bit. I started playing when I was quite young. Trying, you know. Of course, I wasn't doing very much, but I was trying.

Richard pauses a moment and then describes how he would listen to the tunes at the dance and then walk home through the wiregrass and scrublands of central Florida. Another story extends his discussion of how he learned.

There'd be nobody with me. And practically all the way home, I wouldn't see anybody. And it'd be way into the night. I'd be walking along there, trying to remember that tune. And that whistling—it got to where if I could whistle it, I could play it. Of course, you don't play a fiddle—you don't just pick one up and go on and play it. It takes a long time to master it. So I'd work at it a little at a time, a little at a time.

Richard bends down, opens up his case and pulls out his brand new fiddle. He explains that his first tune was "Shear 'Em" and that it was the most popular tune in his area. He plays the tune for me, and it provides a break from the hour and a half of interviewing. When Richard finishes the tune, he explains that bluegrass fans often call the tune "Too Young to Marry," but he explains that there are some differences between the two tunes.

To play by ear, the fiddler has to develop the ability to follow and memorize a melody. Richard had to concentrate and listen deeply to learn a tune so that he could remember it while walking home. He also had the benefit of hearing tunes repeated scores of times as the fiddlers accompanied dancers, so he also picked up many of the tunes by simply hearing them repeated throughout a dance set and on numerous occasions. In this manner, he familiarized himself with the tunes in the same way that the dancers also learned to recognize favorite hoedowns. He views part of the reason that dancers primarily requested the old standards such as "Shear 'Em" is that they paid less attention to the music than did the musicians. Although square dancers would sometimes hum along with the melody of favorite tunes, many dancers were familiar with only a small part of the repertory of tunes played by a community's fiddlers. It was also common for fiddlers to know little more than a few dozen tunes. Dancers heard familiar melodies and listened for characteristic phrases, but their focus was on completing the dance figures as accurately as possible and staying in step with the beat.

What frequently happened historically continues to happen today as dancers, listeners, and fiddlers learn the tunes by a process that also requires little conscious thought.[9] Hearing the tunes repeated numerous times and moving the body in rhythm to the tunes' cadences, a dancer becomes familiar with the melody. Away from a dance and going about daily chores, it is surprising how often the melody of a fiddle tune simply pops unannounced into one's conscious mind, and Richard's routine of walking home from the dances reveals that he was accumulating a head full of old-time fiddle tunes. His learning task was simply to become familiar with the fiddle itself and then figure out how to make the sounds of the instrument match the melody he had learned. He emphasizes that he had to familiarize himself with the instrument's sound and learn the intervals between notes, a skill that he mastered by practicing scales and short musical phrases. This gridwork initially provided him with an understanding of musical elements and relationships, and it continues to allow him to piece together complete tunes by listening to other musicians.

Learning to play is not quite that easy. Richard emphasizes that he accomplished much of his initial learning on his own and that he had to experiment with the various sounds of the instrument. He did not master his fiddle tunes by taking lessons from teachers but rather taught himself the skills essential for learning the tunes. After trying out various techniques and developing strategies for learning and playing, he was then ready to benefit from other musicians' pointers. Eager to accept the tips from the area's fiddlers, Richard shows that learning is a creative act that requires attentive discipline. Develop the idea, and Richard's perspective is that education is primarily the student's responsibility. His position asserts that teachers should focus on "learning techniques" as an integral part of discovering effective teaching strategies.[10]

I find it curious that Lewis Seaman owned a fiddle but that Richard Seaman does not mention his father's playing as a major influence. He explains that his father was a fiddler but that he did not play in public. Richard connects his father's interest in the fiddle to his own musicianship.

My dad played the fiddle for a little bit—only just around the house. Just sort of a pastime, an amusement, I guess. But he never did play out anywhere. He just sort of picked up a few little tunes like I did. And that got me started. And then I got to playing. After I learned a little bit, I started playing for square dances too. That's a good way to learn because you get a set going. Well, you have to play sometime for forty-five minutes, and that gives you pretty good exercise and the ability to learn, when you play the tune over so many times.

Richard is amused that it did not take him long to be asked to accompany dancers. He laughs when he remembers that some fiddlers played at the dances but that they knew only one or two tunes and stayed only in one key. He explains that the square dancers were quick to accept beginning fiddlers. As long as a new fiddler could keep time, most dancers were not particularly concerned about the quality of the musicianship.

Richard first played with Joe Barber and other fiddlers, and the repetition of the tunes helped him to develop a feel for the instrument. Because a fiddler at an old-time frolic will play the same tune over and over again, Richard took advantage of the opportunity to practice. He would play the tunes until his fingers would go numb, and the repetition ingrained the tunes in his mind. Playing for dances also taught him to keep time evenly and accurately. Dragging or rushing the beat of a tune would throw the dancers and the caller off rhythm, and dropping too many notes would confuse the caller as well as the dancers who were trying to follow the tune. Even though the dancers' attention was focused on the caller as the featured performer, Richard had to perform in a way that met the community standards for fiddling. He understood that he had to help keep the dance together even though he was under less scrutiny than the caller. The comparatively lax standards imposed upon fiddlers provided him with room for practicing his tunes, and he finds it humorous that he could perform in public before he saw himself as a proficient musician. Nevertheless, Richard learned that it was easy to play at the dances because the dancers appreciated his mastery of lively, up-tempo tunes. His fiddle put people in the mood to dance. Their dancing, in turn, helped to make his timing solid.

He had to learn to keep time accurately and maintain the beat especially when playing as an unaccompanied musician. Some fiddlers develop their sense of rhythm by playing with back-up musicians who accompany them on guitar, banjo, or other instruments. Richard notes that in Kissimmee Park the only back-up came from accompanists who tapped out rhythms using fiddle beaters. He explains how straw beaters, or "fiddlesticks," were tapped out on the strings while the fiddler played. "They had two little sticks, about like you've seen these long matchsticks for barbecues. They'd have two little sticks whittled out. A person who did that, he would whittle him out little sticks to suit himself. Sandpaper them out. And he would carry them with him, and he'd sit up there and beat the bass string on the fiddle. And he'd use it as a drum while the fiddle was playing."[11]

I am intrigued that someone would stand in back of him and tap the sticks on the strings over the fiddle's body while he was playing. I ask, "Was it hard to play fiddle while someone was doing that?"

He laughs, "No. Just as long as you didn't hit him in the eye with the bow."

Richard notes that occasionally some of the men who tapped out rhythms with fiddle beaters were fellow fiddlers but that other fiddle-beating accompanists were not musicians. "They'd just sit there and beat on them strings all the time that the fiddler was playing for the dance. It didn't really add too much to the tune. It just gives a little, a little more, bounce to it. You know what I mean? So you could keep step to the music better. It didn't really add much to the music. It just had that little thumping sound."

Recordings of old-time fiddlers who are playing with fiddle beaters reveal that the tapping sound creates an effect somewhat similar to the rhythmic accompaniment of a banjo played in the clawhammer style. The beat helped a fiddler keep time, and the tapping provided a useful reference point for dancers attempting to find the beat.

His discussion of fiddle beaters includes an important aesthetic quality in playing hoedown tunes: bounce. Fiddlers use the term to describe an esoteric, yet palpably visceral, element of playing. To understand "bounce," imagine dancing to a live fiddle tune.[12] The effect of the tune's bounce will impel you to bend your knees on the downbeat and then drive your body upward on the upbeat. Bounce is created through the right hand's bowing technique. Holding the bow to the string and initiating a downbow with heavy pressure, the fiddler's downward slice usually follows the downbeats of a tune: that is, the downbow will usually correspond to the beats stepped off by the left foot.[13] As the fiddler runs out of room on the bow and begins an upbow, he or she often will lighten up on the bow's pressure, thereby producing a softer sound. A fiddler's bounce refers to how well this combination of hard and soft emphasis on bowing evokes the joyous desire to dance. This quality can be enhanced by ending the upbow with a quick and sharp stroke that punctuates the syncopated quality of a tune, and some fiddlers can create this same sense of bounce by first playing upbows and then a sharp downbow. Richard explains that many hoedown tunes are not especially complicated but that they have "something about them that makes you want to get up and move." That *something* is "bounce."

Bounce is established when Richard keys a tune with another technique that he mastered early on. His shuffle will sometimes kick off a tune with a characteristic pattern of a long quarter note followed by two eighth notes. The auditory effect can be visualized by thinking of a shuffle as consisting of one long downbow that uses most of the bow's length that is then followed by a quick upbow and another quick downbow which both use one-half the length of the bow.[14] The pattern is repeated with a long upbow and short downbow and another short upbow. Fiddlers will repeat the entire pattern, and they describe the motion of the bow strokes as similar to bouncing a ball. Richard plays this long-bow version of the shuffle to begin a tune, but he will also insert shuffle patterns into his tunes when playing to maintain the tune's sense of bounce. Having the ability to play a shuffle with the proper feel for bounce is a major distinctive feature of the old-time style.

Classically trained violinists are taught to keep the right wrist loose and flexible when coming to the end of an upbow or downbow. This flexibility allows the violin player to keep the bow on a plane that is parallel to the bridge, thereby keeping the bowing accurate. A supple wrist can help a fiddler smooth out a shuffle to create a sound quality that some describe as "liquid."[15] As do many old-time fiddlers, Richard keeps his bowing wrist straight. Consequently, he pulls the bow more with the muscles of his forearm than with his upper arm and shoulder. He still plays with a graceful fluidity, and his right arm position makes it comfortable for him to play shuffles by sawing a series of quick strokes using the upper two-thirds of his bow. The rhythm is the same as other shuffles, but the short bow strokes make it easy for him to throw in this variation of a shuffle to ornament a tune and enhance its bounce.

This technique is one element of a style described as "short-bow," an old-time style that is seen as characteristic of fiddling in America's South. A short-bow player is likely to use only small sections of the bow and play the instrument with quick, jabbing strokes.[16] It is quite common for short-bow players to hold the bow a few inches up from the frog that sits at the end of the bow, a technique that would make Isaac Stern cringe. A long-bow player, on the other hand, will use more of the bow's horsehair and is more likely to grip the bow close to the end, similar to the way a classical violinist holds it to achieve proper technique. In Florida, there is considerable confusion about whether long-bow or short-bow was the predominant early style. Chubby Wise, for example, first learned to play hoedowns in central Florida, and his long-bow style was likely more influenced by western swing and popular tunes of the late 1930s than by Florida's early hoedown traditions. Furthermore, he credits Bill Monroe with refining his long-bow style when he learned to play bluegrass music.[17] Other fiddlers note that fiddling in Florida shows characteristics of both long-bow and short-bow styles.[18] Richard explains that few fiddlers were concerned about characterizing their style as either long-bow or short-bow. His bowing style predominantly employs long strokes, but he explains that he "bows it the best way to get out of it" and will sometimes use short-bow patterns in these tunes.

Mastering complex bowing patterns is a challenge when playing the violin. An orchestral score is marked by signs that dictate upbows and downbows, and the violinist has little freedom to pull his or her bow down while all the other musicians are pushing their bows up. The unity of violin bows sliding up and down in perfect precision in an orchestra's string section is one of the great visual treats that accompanies the glorious sound of a symphony orchestra. A fiddlers' convention, however, does not display quite this same type of orchestrated musical and visual unison. When fiddlers play together, the visual mishmash of bows sliding down while others are shooting up creates a unified effect of organized chaos. Although there are regionally specific patterns of bowing that help to make one style distinct from another, old-time fiddlers have great freedom to find their own comfortable ways of sawing out a tune. This freedom to find one's own way of playing the instrument is a major part of the fiddle's appeal, especially for erstwhile violinists.

As Richard was learning techniques to maintain solid rhythms, keep steady time, and bow out a tune, he was also developing a sophisticated ear. Gaining the ability to keep time and put sufficient bounce into a tune, Richard also was learning to remember the melodies of tunes. There are subtle qualities to each melody line, and Richard came to recognize different variations of tunes throughout Florida and the Deep South. As I remarked on my difficulties in learning to back up fiddlers with the guitar, Richard explains the challenge of playing good backup. "Every old-time fiddler has a little different technique and time. He breaks time and plays different notes a little bit, and it takes a guitar player a while to play with him. And then, he'll go play with another one, he'll be a little lost. You'll notice you've heard a lot of people play some of the old tunes that we've been playing, and a lot of them play every one a little different in some way. It's the same tune, but it's a little different."[19]

Because each tune is played differently by various fiddlers, how can Richard recognize and play tunes by simply hearing them? Two major faculties help him out. Richard knows how to break a tune down to its component parts, and he knows his instrument. Although the Florida fiddle tradition includes tunes played in a variety of tunings, he plays exclusively in the standard tuning of G D A E (lowest to highest string).[20] As do many old-time fiddlers, he plays almost solely in the first position—the section of the neck that can be comfortably noted by the left hand when it is held down the neck, close to the peg box and scroll. This position allows him to play open, or unstopped, strings. Playing only in the first position makes it easier for him to find the notes to unfamiliar tunes, and it also means that he plays within a range of slightly more than two octaves. The limited range also makes it relatively easy for him to find the notes of the scale that comprise the tunes' melodies. Richard also plays mainly in *D, G, A,* and *C,* the keys that many old-time fiddlers commonly use.[21]

Learning to play by ear is challenging, but fiddlers learn this skill by listening for characteristic patterns, musical phrases, and licks that help them discover other musicians' techniques. The hoedown tunes are comprised of a myriad of established formal patterns that musicians learn to recognize. Fiddlers listen for these patterns and then try to replicate them on their own instruments when they learn new tunes. Knowing how to listen for the formal qualities in the music is thus the major step in learning to play.[22] Richard breaks this process down into clear steps. He first listens to an entire tune to gain a sense of how the whole piece sounds. He then listens for ways that the tune features repetition and variations according to established forms. To understand how he listens for these characteristic patterns and forms, it is useful to examine the first tune that he learned to play, "Shear 'Em." Richard usually plays this version of the entire tune.[23]

Characteristic of the majority of hoedown tunes, this tune's form consists of two parts. The first part is logically called the "A-part" and the second the "B-part."[24] Richard knows one tune, "Maple Sugar," that has a "C-part," and a few other tunes even feature a "D-part." The A-part of "Shear 'Em" is comprised of a pickup note and sixteen complete bars of music to form one complete musical strain.[25] Much of this part is composed of short phrases, each four measures in length. The first phrase establishes the strain's basic melody line, and the second phrase of four measures develops and complements it. The third phrase begins at the ninth full measure into the tune, and it is a variation of the first phrase. The fourth phrase begins with the pickup notes that lead into the thirteenth full measure, and it is a variation of the second phrase. When he learned this tune, Richard first listened for these specific phrases to discover the melody. In "Shear 'Em," it usually consists of the highest note in a chord or drone. After discovering how to play the first phrase on his instrument, he then learned the second and added it to the first. To complete learning the A-part, he discovered how the third and fourth phrases vary from the first and second, and he was able to learn the variations to each of these remaining phrases. He mastered the A-part when he could repeat this entire section twice to play the entire strain.

Similar patterns of repetition and variation also show up in the B-part, which can also be broken down into musical phrases. The B-part of "Shear 'Em" also displays patterns of continuity and variation similar to what is found in the A-part. The first phrase of four measures sets out a melody line that is varied

Shear 'Em

throughout this strain. A second phrase of four bars is also echoed in the last four measures of this tune's strain. The last two measures of this second phrase are essentially identical to the last two bars of the fourth phrase. Richard learned each of these phrases and then added them together to memorize this second strain, which he also repeated twice to play the B-part in its entirety. After playing the second repeated phrase of the B-part, the fiddler then returned to the A-part. When Richard learned to repeat both the A-part and the B-part through one time, then he could move from hearing the bare bones of the tune in his head to playing it on his instrument. Listeners will also notice that phrases used in the A-part are also developed in the B-part, for the last two measures of phrases two and four in both strains carry the same melody. Recognizing these types of variations on musical phrases is essential to forming building blocks that allow him to figure out how to play a tune. The task of learning a melody is thus a process of listening for continuity and variation in these types of musical phrases.[26]

After learning the melody lines for both parts, Richard then began to practice the hoedown. He discovered and repeated the fingering and bowing patterns that worked most efficiently, thereby smoothing out his tune with each repetition. A hoedown tune is formally structured with a recursive property that allows the fiddler to extend it ad infinitum even though this same tune might last less than a half minute when played through only one time. After learning the tune, Richard repeated it over and over to practice for square dances. Playing a new tune at a house party also provided him with opportunities to practice because he had to repeat the melody dozens of times to complete a square dance set. Because his fiddle was the solo instrument used in dances, Richard mainly played the hoedown's melody at house parties. Although bluegrass fiddlers improvise, play intricate harmonies, and back up other instrumentalists when they play solos, these characteristics rarely show up when an old-time fiddler plays a hoedown, and the focus on melody thus is another distinctive feature of old-time fiddling.

Learning the melody line is the essential technique for learning to play a new tune, but a fiddler will rarely play in solely a simplified fashion. After learning the melody through repetitive practice and live performances, he was then ready to move to the next step in mastering a tune by embellishing the melody's simple lines. Dressing up a tune involves the use of ornamentation. Julie Youmans describes the range of techniques that fiddlers use to "warm the cold notes of a tune."[27] Most of these techniques are fairly simple to describe, and they are not particularly complicated to learn. Youmans explains that the challenge of using ornamentation is to discover tasteful ways to use these techniques to enhance a melody's quality. Devoid of ornament, a tune sounds primitive and plain. When ornamentation is overused, a tune sounds confused and gaudy. The main ornamental techniques that Richard uses are slides, vibrato, shuffles, drones, double-stops, triplets, slurs, detaché bowing, and plucking the strings with the fingers of his left hand.

Richard slides up into a note by pressing a string and then slipping his finger up the neck to raise the note's pitch. A good example of a slide is evident in the first measure of the second phrase in the B-part of "Shear 'Em." He can also reverse the process to slide off a note although he seldom uses this technique. Vibrato involves stopping a note and then wiggling the finger against the string as it is bowed to create the wavering tone that adds color to long notes. He uses the technique sparingly as an embellishment for slow passages in his waltzes and parlor songs, but he occasionally uses vibrato on a few hoedowns.

As do most fiddlers, Richard often uses shuffle patterns to introduce a hoedown, but "Shear 'Em," like many tunes, features shuffle bowing throughout the entire piece. The A-part, in this tune, is built almost entirely by combining shuffles with double-stops and drones. A drone is a second note that is played with a string left open whereas a double-stop consists of two notes that are stopped, or noted by the fingers at the same time. Both of these important ornaments showcase Richard's ability to play two notes at the same time. "Shear 'Em" is filled with drones and a number of doubles-stops, and this technique is essential to the sound of old-time fiddling. It provides the fiddle with a louder volume, and the two-note chord fleshes out the thinner sound of a single note. Droning a note will not necessarily produce a chord, and it can create dissonance when it breaks from the usual harmonic interval of a musical third. When Richard uses this effect, he will either play a quick musical phrase to resolve the dissonance or walk up the musical passage to note another string to play a harmonious chord to create the same bagpipe-like effect.

Richard also can turn a quarter note into a triplet by running down or up the scale into it as he does in the second full measure of "Shear 'Em." A slur is played by running two or more notes smoothly together while playing with one bow stroke, and Richard usually employs this technique when playing triplets, but he also slurs notes to smooth out long phrases as in the last major run of the final two measures of "Shear 'Em." Detaché bowing involves lifting the bow from the strings and then smoothly placing it back down to engage the strings once again. The technique allows a fiddler to make certain notes ring out clearly, and it calls attention to the musical phrases that comprise the melody's main line. Richard adjusts his bowing techniques to personalize a tune, but a final technique involves playing the fiddle without the bow. He uses a pizzicato technique with his left hand when he notes a string with his ring finger and then snaps it off to pluck the note. As do many fiddlers, Richard features this technique to make a "pop" in the play party tune "Pop Goes the Weasel." He also uses the pull-off technique in the tune "Yellow Gals" to add a syncopated note after the phrase "Won't you come out tonight."

Playing a waltz involves techniques similar to fiddling out a hoedown. Richard created his original composition, the "Annie Seaman Waltz," by tastefully putting together musical phrases common to a number of country waltzes.[28] Although most waltzes also feature an A-part and a B-part, this tune consists of only one musical strain. Richard, however, will sometimes end this tune with different variations.

Annie Seaman Waltz

Richard often plays this waltz in a fairly plain style, but he will add double-stops and drones to notes that he holds longer, such as the G in the third measure. He also uses chromatic walk-up as in the sixth measure, sometimes droning the higher or lower string when he feels the technique is appropriate. Because waltzes are played more slowly than hoedowns, the use of shuffle bowing is not as prominent. The "Annie Seaman Waltz" includes quiet and subtle shuffle-like patterns, typically in phrases that involve a dotted quarter note followed by two or three eighth notes. The main technique for ornamenting the waltzes, however, is his alternation of bow pressure. He typically exerts heavy downward pressure on the first beat of each measure and then eases off the bow to lighten the sound on the second and third beats, thereby giving a lilty feel to the waltz. On some passages, he lightens up the bow's pressure and sometimes lifts it from the strings to further accentuate the lilt of selected phrases. In the "Annie Seaman Waltz," he typically uses this detaché technique when walking up or down into a longer note as in the sixth, fourteenth, and twenty-second measures. He also frequently uses the technique to punctuate the end of the waltz as in this tune's final three measures.

As Richard developed his musical prowess, he learned to recognize how other players were using these techniques. Learning various ornamental devices and other techniques as he was honing his own ability, Richard began to dress up his playing by figuring out tasteful and interesting versions of the tunes. In this respect, part of the appeal of playing the fiddle is working out the tension between playing a tune so that other fiddlers can recognize its melody and playing an established piece with a freshness that reveals the fiddler's own musical creativity. Richard was able to learn and adapt and modify how other fiddlers used various ornaments in their playing to create his own style. He does not think of the instrument as particularly difficult to learn, but he assures the beginner that learning to play will require time, practice, and patience.

Analysis of the techniques that Richard uses when fiddling provides an understanding of aesthetic standards that he strives for when playing old-time music. Today, he continues to play with spirit and smoothness, and recordings of him from the late 1940s show that he was a good fiddler. The early recordings especially showcase the power of his bowing and his ability to play hoedowns and rags at fast tempos. They also display the accuracy and evenness of his bowing, coupled with a steady speed and well-controlled pressure that allow him to keep time and inflect his tunes with the right amount of bounce. The smoothness of his bowing and the accuracy of his left hand's noting gives each tune a smooth, polished quality. Richard does not like to hear "jerky" fiddling, and he puts together a tune so that it sounds seamless. He knows that a good fiddler must also play so that the notes are true. Listeners expect to hear accurate notes, and they tend to notice the quality of a player's intonation only when the notes are sour. The use of ornamentation intrigues Richard, and he enjoys playing small variations as he repeats the tunes. When listening to other fiddlers, Richard appreciates their abilities to play a wide range of tunes in numerous keys, and he applauds fiddlers who make music that sounds effortless and natural.

In discussing how he plays the fiddle, Richard shows that learning techniques for playing the instrument and mastering the aesthetic qualities of the music are fused. The aesthetic quality of his old-time fiddle tunes is not the effect of his playing. Rather it is the quality of mastering the precise techniques that are required in playing the instrument. High-quality musicianship strives toward creating the perfect rendition, and Richard believes that there are better and worse versions of tunes.

Open to the beauty of an array of musical styles, Richard Seaman also has definite ideas about what constitutes quality in musical expression. He performs his music in public to foster an appreciation for the quality of old-time fiddle tunes, and he uses his stories to make his tunes ring true to their historical context. Just as his theory of history demands that historians speak the truth, his theory of musicianship asserts that a good fiddler must not play false notes. Dropping a note or not finding a note's accurate intonation clearly separates the fine fiddler from the novice. A good fiddler plays smoothly and shows a mastery of a repertory of fine tunes. A good fiddler plays tunes that other musicians would recognize and appreciate as belonging to communities of musicians. Mastering a corpus of common tunes, a good fiddler also shows mastery of the instrument by laying open his own personal sense of aesthetics in a performance. A good fiddler knows how to keep time to set the dancers going all night long. The quality of a tune is not merely a subjective preference that strikes the fancy of an individual's taste.[29] Rather it is a value that a musician works hard to reveal by mastering musical forms and techniques. If a tune is played right, then it is of high quality, and its quality can be recognized by others. If you listen to the instrument, Richard asserts "it will talk back to you" as you learn to play its tunes.[30] Learning to master the instrument, Richard asserts, is a process of learning to listen.

1. Jack Piccalo and Richard Seaman, August 1988. Photo by Gregory Hansen.

2. The Seaman family home, Kissimmee Park, Florida, circa 1905. Courtesy of Richard Seaman.

3. Richard Seaman with his sister, Anne, circa 1908. Courtesy of Richard Seaman.

4. Richard Seaman. Courtesy of Richard Seaman.

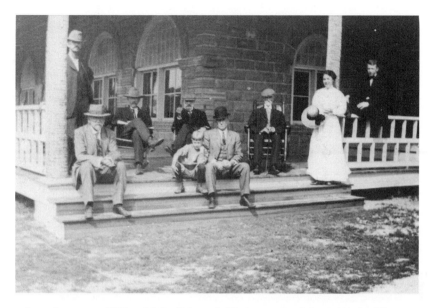

5. Surveying team at William McCool's home in Kissimmee. Lewis Seaman and William McCool, Sr., are on the left, and McCool's daughter, Jean, on the right. Courtesy of Richard Seaman.

6. Loading fruit onto a barge on Lake Tohopekaliga; Lewis Seaman is on right. Courtesy of Richard Seaman.

7. Lewis Seaman. Courtesy of Richard Seaman.

8. Neighbor nicknamed "Old Man Freeman" with jump shovel plow and the Seaman family's mules, Jack and Jim, in their cabbage patch. Courtesy of Richard Seaman.

9. Kissimmee Park hunting party. *Left to right:* Lewis Seaman, unidentified hunter, Billy McCool, and Luther Warren. Courtesy of Richard Seaman.

10. Richard Seaman. Courtesy of Richard Seaman.

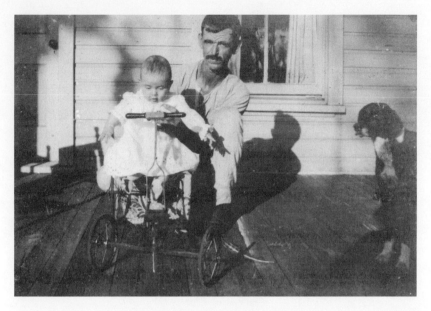

11. Anne Seaman and Lewis Seaman, circa 1908. Courtesy of Richard Seaman.

12. Richard Seaman, circa 1940. Courtesy of Richard Seaman.

13. Richard's fiddle. Photograph by Gregory Hansen.

14. Gregory Hansen and Richard Seaman playing for students in Jacksonville, November 1990. Courtesy of the Florida Folklife Program/Florida Department of State.

15. Demonstration of use of fiddle beaters, or straws, in Jacksonville's school system. Photograph by Gregory Hansen.

16. Miss Anderson. Courtesy of Richard Seaman.

17. Richard Seaman, summer of 2000. Photograph by Gregory Hansen.

18. Richard and Annie Seaman, summer of 2000. Photograph by Gregory Hansen.

7

Core Repertory

~

It's not just the melody or words that make old-time music what it is. It's the memories that go with the music. It paints a picture in your heart.

—Windy Whitford*

W hen fiddlers gather together to play, they are likely to strike up a conversation about the tunes in their repertories. As their conversation transforms into a musical performance, comparisons of individual variations of tunes become a major point of shared interest. Fiddlers understand what Matthew Guntharp discovered when learning the fiddler's ways: a fiddler's tunes reflect the musician's background, skill, and musical taste.[1] Fiddlers create their own musical histories by learning and playing the individual tunes that comprise their repertories. In this respect, a fiddler's repertory is especially intriguing because tunes encapsulate significant episodes in the musician's life history. Richard Seaman's repertory provides these types of clues, and a view of his repertory develops a portrait of the changing contexts of his musicianship. Comparing and contrasting these various contexts reveal how his life history provides an essential resource for understanding changes in a region's social history.[2] Examining these changes shows how he continually adapts his musicianship to shifts in Florida's social life. These changes support his view that fiddling originally was more integrated into a communally oriented social network as compared to the more individualistic social organization of Florida's urban culture.

A repertory is an inventory of songs. Richard keeps this inventory by writing his tunes' names on scraps of paper that lie in the bottom of his fiddle case, where he also preserves the titles of his tall tales. He remembers how to play a tune by thinking of its name, and because he does not read music he would find a tunebook to be of limited value.[3] This written inventory is a mnemonic device for remembering the tunes that he knows, and it also satisfies his curiosity about the number of tunes that he has learned. These scraps of papers make it easy for the folklorist to document his repertory. The difficulty is that Richard also plays other tunes whose titles he has not written down. He thinks that he has learned to play about a hundred different tunes. Audio and video recordings document that he continues to play at least seventy of them.

His fiddle tunes are catchy. When we listen to the tunes, it is striking how so many of the songs have a comfortable, even intimate, quality that makes them easy to remember. They have vibrant melody lines and a warm feel that makes them stay with the musician. It is not uncommon for old-time musicians to find themselves whistling tunes when they go about their daily tasks at work. There is beauty in each tune in Richard's repertory, and even tunes that are easy to ignore display a friendly quality about them. Grace virtually any fiddle tune with sufficient time, listen to how it is played by different musicians, hear it played through different instruments, and it becomes hard to dismiss even one as a clinker. When Richard is asked which one of his tunes is his favorite, he will usually respond, "the one that I just played."

A hoedown's melody is easy to remember, in part, because the tune is structured through patterns of formal repetition. This repetition helps make a tune memorable both when one is simply listening to a fiddler and when one wishes to learn a new tune. As Richard reveals in his description of learning his instrument, playing by ear is easier if the tune has a singable melody. If a fiddle tune strikes resonant chords within the musician, then the fiddler can learn it and eventually hand it down to a new generation of players.[4] If a tune is difficult for many fiddlers to remember, then it is apt to fall out of favor. A tune that violates the community's aesthetic and becomes snagged in the filters that separate catchy melodies from ungainly assemblages of musical phrases might appear in a repertory as a quirky novelty song. More likely, an unpopular tune is apt to be preserved only as a curious note in a tunebook or as an old field recording, sitting neglected in an archive.

Folklorists have documented and preserved thousands of old-time fiddle tunes in America, and fiddlers access their collections to add new tunes to their repertories. Finding out what tunes are preserved and why they maintain their appeal is an important area of study.[5] It is also intriguing to consider why some tunes are forgotten so that the researcher could understand how other tunes are remembered. As Richard Seaman, Chubby Wise, and George Custer all avowed in their workshop, fiddle tunes must be learned within an aural tradition. A fiddler cannot master the feel of playing a hoedown or a waltz simply by reading notes from a written score. The tunes are passed along by tradition, and this process includes mechanisms for dropping tunes from a repertory. Fiddlers rely on a community aesthetic that allows their tunes to survive, and this aesthetic system thrives because generations of fiddlers continue to appreciate and learn good tunes. Cold, unfriendly, and forgettable melodies are unlikely to stand the test of time in this combined process of oral and aural transmission. Temporal continuity preserves tunes. It also allows fiddlers to drop forgettable melodies into history's dustbin.

Because a tune's existence depends on whether it is accepted within both a personal and a community aesthetic, a particular tune's continuity over time shows that fiddlers continually preserve and hone the quality of their repertories. Fiddlers create new variations of old tunes, and many old-time musicians learn variations on tunes from each other. In this respect, the aural tradition of fiddling allows them to improve their tunes and expand upon their repertories. In his folklore scholarship, Alan Dundes explains that numerous other oral traditions include artistic resources that allow artists to improve the quality of their artistic expression. Dundes and other folklorists argue that the process of learning, sustaining, and teaching folklife is too often seen as a system in which the quality of various artistic forms becomes debased and degraded over time.[6] Instead, they argue that folk traditions often improve over time.

Thus, a fiddler's repertory is not a reified, static abstraction that exists outside a musician's mind. It is an anthology of tunes that a fiddler chooses to learn, perfect, and polish. Most fiddlers will not include new tunes in their repertories until they feel that they have mastered them. In this sense, a repertory is a showcase for fiddlers to display their tunes. Because fiddlers can always add another tune to their collection, a repertory is a dynamic, creative resource for artistic expression. When one regards the amassing of a repertory as a creative activity, this perspective yields a more nuanced reading of Guntharp's subtly trenchant observation that understanding a fiddler's repertory is essential for discovering how fiddle tunes link items in an artist's repertory to history. We gain a broader view of social history by examining why Richard made shifts in his repertory in response to the expectations, desires, and demands of his audiences.[7] Understanding the motives for these changes in relation to wider social concerns links aspects of his life history to significant facets of Florida's social history.

Richard's tunes index shifts in the social contexts for musical performances. The mechanism for understanding how a repertory shifts over time is articulated by a pioneering scholar of instrumental folk music in America, Samuel Preston Bayard. He compiled an early and comprehensive collection of fiddle and fife tunes from western Pennsylvania, and his musical ear was so fine that he was able to transcribe these tunes without the use of a tape recorder.[8] He would simply listen to them as they were played and write them down. In comparing individual repertories, Bayard found that they changed according to a generalizable pattern. Rather than viewing repertories as static entities, he writes of the "progressive displacement of older tunes alongside the adoption or evolution of newer ones" and explains how his process fosters a more accurate understanding of fiddling.[9] This continual pattern of change is a major aspect of Richard's repertory. Throughout his life Richard has preserved older tunes, but he has continually added new tunes and dropped older ones. Finding out how these types of changes in his repertory are related to the performance contexts for playing music is key to understanding changes in Florida's social history.

Establishing which tunes he learned in various time spans is essential for understanding why his earliest tunes are especially significant to Florida history. Along with adding and dropping, Richard also has kept a selection of tunes that he began learning around the year 1914 and that he had amassed by the early 1920s. He learned all of these tunes directly from other fiddlers. There are no commercial recordings of fiddle tunes from this era, for the first widely disseminated recording of an old-time fiddler was not made until Eck Robertson recorded "Sallie Gooden" in 1922 for the Victor recording company.[10] Additional fiddle tunes were recorded by the 1930s, but Richard had learned a corpus of approximately two dozen tunes before fiddle tunes were ever set down on wax cylinders. The tunes that he plays from his youth in Kissimmee Park are vital folk expressions learned through the oral tradition, and listening to his tunes in the twenty-first century brings the listener back to hearing what fiddlers in Florida played in the nineteenth century. The aural continuity could go back even farther, for he performs in a genre that stretches back in time to America's Colonial period.

Attending dances and learning directly from fiddlers, Richard first learned the most popular tune in the area: the hoedown called "Shear 'Em." He continues to play this tune, kicking it off with a powerful shuffle that he bows over a double-stop formed by noting a G on his D-string and a B on his A-string. Archival recordings of fiddlers from the area that were made during the 1930s WPA project document that "Shear 'Em" was a common tune in Florida.[11] The same documentation also verifies that the following tunes played by Richard were also commonly performed at hoedowns during the 1920s:

Mississippi Sawyer—Key of D
Flop-Eared Mule—Key of D
Sally Gooden—Key of D

I Don't Love Nobody—Key of G
Whistling Rufus—Key of D
Stoney Point—Key of D
Down Yonder—Key of D
Marching through Georgia—Key of D
Watermelon on the Vine—Key of D
Pop Goes the Weasel—Key of G
Skip to My Lou—Key of D
Cindy—Key of D
Dance All Night with a Bottle in My Hand—Key of D
Old Hen Cackled—Key of D
Old Joe Clark—Key of D
Soldier's Joy—Key of D
Yellow Gals—Key of A
Irish Washerwoman—Key of D
Rag-time Annie—Keys of D and A
Ida Red—Key of D
Dixie—Key of D

Richard remembers that he also played at least three other tunes that he learned from Kissimmee Park's fiddlers, but he has forgotten the fiddle lines to the tunes "Rabbit in a Pea Patch," "Sally Ann," and "Cotton-Eyed Joe." There were other tunes played in the area that Richard never learned. He notes that other fiddlers played a few others, including "Paddy on the Turnpike," "Billy in the Low-ground," and "Katy Hill."

In sharing his knowledge of tunes, Richard has given us a description of the common ones shared in his home community. His memory is supported by written documentation that verifies that these tunes were known by other fiddlers in his region in Florida. Folklorists studying fiddle tunes refer to this storehouse of cultural commonplaces as a fiddler's "core repertory."[12] Linda Danielson asserts the importance of examining a core repertory by showing that it provides a means to establish regional characteristics of particular fiddle traditions. In perusing Richard's share of tunes and the wider community's core repertory, it becomes clear that the fiddle style of his area reflects a wider tradition of American tunes with a particular emphasis on old-time music of the Upland and Deep South.[13] There are no tunes unique to Florida in his core repertory, and his repertory supports the claim that the state lacks a regionally distinctive style of fiddling. Although fiddlers were important musicians in Florida by the turn of the eighteenth century,[14] the massive migration of settlers into

Florida following the Civil War marks the primary establishment of the state's current fiddling tradition. Consequently, old-time fiddling in Florida features a range of styles and genres that are relatively recent imports.

Setting out in search of authentic old-time fiddling in Florida, I find in Richard's core repertory a remarkable selection of the actual fiddle tunes that were performed a hundred years ago in the state. Although some of these tunes were composed and written down for various occasions, the majority of them were learned outside of any media influences and passed along through oral traditions. Finding and documenting the musical tradition provide a significant resource to fill in major gaps in the written documentation of a region's social history. In sharing his repertory, Richard gives the historian an authentic record of a significant aspect of Florida's social history. Richard's tunes are authentic old-time tunes, and his own authenticity as an old-time musician is established, in part, by his ability to perform a variety of fiddle tunes according to standards set within the community of fiddlers and dancers. The importance of his knowledge of the area's core repertory thus lies not solely in its contribution to the historical record. The tunes also provide him with resources for honing his ability to perform as a musician. "Authenticity," in Richard Seaman's view of fiddling, is not merely a trope used to establish and sustain a romanticized view of a past tradition. Rather, the word names aesthetic values that he shares with other fiddlers. In Kissimmee Park, Richard could not make an authentic claim to be a fiddler until he had acquired the ability to accompany dancers. Learning to play hoedown tunes in an authentic style continues to provide him with the chance to offer his talent to his community.

As Richard moved from central Florida to Jacksonville, he continued to play the tunes that he learned in Kissimmee Park. He also added new hoedowns to his repertory. Learning from other fiddlers, radio shows, records, and tapes, Richard picked up more than a dozen more fiddle tunes. These consist of hoedowns, rags, tunes from minstrel shows, and songs from Tin Pan Alley:

Alabama Jubilee—Key of C
Bully of the Town—Key of D
Golden Slippers—Key of G
Big John in the Barroom—Key of D
Liberty—Key of D
Rubber Dolly—Key of D
Fourteen Days in Georgia—Key of G
Maple Sugar—Keys of A and E
Chicken Reel—Key of D

Girl I Left Behind—Key of D
Arkansas Traveler—Key of D
Up Jumped Trouble—Keys of D and A
Trouble Amongst the Yearlings—Key of D
Osceola's Rag—Key of D
At a Georgia Camp Meeting—Key of G

He also has recently added four more tunes to his repertory:

The New Five Cent—Key of D
Bill Cheathem—Key of A
Whistling Rufus—Key of D
Bile Them Cabbage Down—Key of D

Although tunes like "At a Georgia Camp Meeting" and "Bully of the Town" are derived from Tin Pan Alley renditions, Richard considers these pieces to be old-time fiddle tunes. They sound like hoedown tunes, and he has played all of them for square dances. He learned most of them from other fiddlers, although he credits a tape that he purchased from Chubby Wise as his source for "Maple Sugar," a fine old-time tune that changes key in its three parts. Richard continued to play these tunes for square dances in Jacksonville until the 1950s, and he also recalls playing some of them on return visits to Kissimmee. He found it easy to add these tunes to his repertory, and he notes that dancers quickly accepted these tunes.

The ease with which Richard added these tunes to his repertory supports the idea that authenticity is an important aesthetic standard in a community and not merely a scholarly construct. A tune is an authentic old-time tune if it fits the distinctive features of tunes within the same genre. In her folklore scholarship, Sandra Dolby provides a useful means for understanding the specific criteria that comprise Richard's idea of genre.[15] She asserts that a text must be understood within its contexts and notes that specific genres emerge when one examines an artist's entire repertory of creative expression for similarities in style, form, function, and content.[16] When one compares tunes to discover genres, the literary construct of genre becomes a useful resource for musical analysis. Examining fiddle tunes in relation to these features provides criteria for conceptualizing a tune as a hoedown. Stylistically, the dozen tunes that he added to his repertory all sound similar to the tunes in his core repertory. He plays them using the same techniques followed by other old-time fiddlers. The form of each of these tunes is similar, featuring the formal and ornamental features that characterize hoedown tunes. The function of the tunes is fairly easy to ascertain. Richard could use any of them to accompany square dancers, and he continues to play them for his own enjoyment. These particular tunes are also distinct from other tunes that Richard later added to his repertory.

An important part of the tunes' cultural content is that they are all dance pieces. The specific content of each tune is difficult to ascertain, but each is primarily an instrumental piece. If lyrics are sung to any of them, additional similarities in content emerge as the tunes typically present facets of everyday rural life. Richard typically will sing only snippets of verse, often as "jig-couplets," and he only sings these verses in private. After he has completed the following tunes, he will playfully recite the following lyrics:

"Bile them Cabbage Down"
Boil them cabbage down,
Turn those hoecakes around,
The only tune that I can sing,
Is boil them cabbage down.

"Cindy"
I had a girl that lived Down South,
She was so sweet,
The bees was all around her mouth.
Get along home, Cindy,
Get along home, I say.
Get along home, Cindy,
I'll marry you someday.

I went to see my gal,
She met me at the door,
Shoes and stockings in her hand,
And her feet all over the floor.

Get along home, Cindy,
Get along home, I say.
Get along home, Cindy,
I'll marry you someday.

"Old Hen Cackled"
Old hen cackled,

She cackled in the lot,
The second time she cackled,
She cackled in the pot.

"Sally Gooden"
Up on the hill side seen Sally coming,
Thought to my self, I'd kill myself a running.

Blackberry pie and huckleberry pudding,
Give it all away to see Sally Gooden.

He sings another rhyme to both "Sally Gooden" and "Cindy."

Some got drunk,
And some got boozy,
I went home with black-eyed Susie.

"Shear 'Em"
Makes no difference how you shear 'em,
Makes no difference how or when,
Makes no difference how you shear 'em,
Just shear 'em boys, shear 'm.

Similarities in style, form, function, and content all reveal that genre is part of a system that Richard has mastered when learning and adding new pieces to his repertory. This system allows him to classify the tunes, and it is shared in varying degrees with his listeners. As Briggs and Bauman explain, the artist uses genre as a device to establish an interpretive frame for a performance.[17] The fiddler connects to the audience through the interpretive key that he establishes by mastering tunes that characterize a particular genre. The distinctive characteristics implicit in a genre allow audience members to understand and appreciate both the old and new fiddle tunes. In concrete terms, the new tunes that Richard learned in Jacksonville were accepted by Kissimmee Park dancers because they followed the established formal and stylistic properties of older tunes within the hoedown genre. In this respect, Richard Seaman uses genre to arbitrate an artistic system shared to varying degrees between the performer and the audience. His use of genre connects the performer with the listener, and it is an essential artistic resource for creating and sustaining a repertory within the community.[18] Richard added the new old-time tunes to his repertory after he had met other fiddlers in Jacksonville. Woven together from strands of tradition, these tunes follow the form of hoedown tunes, fit into a canon of tunes recognized by other fiddlers as "old-time," and were handed down directly from other musicians who passed them down over time.[19] His mastery of a community aesthetic further expands his repertory of old-time music while maintaining distinct standards of authenticity.

Along with learning new tunes in Jacksonville, Richard also learned to play in new genres. He explains that the waltz was not danced in his home community of Kissimmee Park and that he learned to play these tunes for couple dances only after moving to the city. Over the years, he added the following waltzes to his repertory:

Don't Be Angry with Me Darling—Key of D
Waltz You Saved for Me—Key of D
Tennessee Waltz—Key of D
Kentucky Waltz—Key of D
Westphalia Waltz—Keys of D or G
Annie Seaman Waltz—Key of G or D
Wednesday Night Waltz—Key of D

These waltzes constitute a new genre. They are all in the familiar three-quarter time that sets them apart from the reels, jigs, and other tunes in his repertory of old-time hoedowns. The three-quarter meter of the waltz is similar to characteristic patterns of triplets that Richard plays in many of his hoedowns. The waltzes also feature a rhythm similar to patterns characteristic of jigs such as "Irish Washerwoman," as both the waltzes and jigs prominently features patterns of three notes played within larger sets of two. As he does with his hoedowns, Richard slightly syncopates these tunes by providing them with an enchanting lilt by changing the lengths of notes and varying his bow pressure and speed. Whether the waltzes belong in his core repertory is a topic open for debate. On one hand, Richard did not play them when he learned the hoedowns in his core repertory, and he picked up the tunes from fiddlers outside of central Florida as well as from media sources. On the other hand, fiddlers consider the waltz to be a genre of old-time music, and all of these waltzes are known colloquially as "country waltzes." Furthermore, these waltzes are part of the repertory of many old-time fiddlers, and they consider them important to their artistry. In dances throughout Florida, a waltz is now played as a traditional last dance, and it is an accepted, even expected, part of contemporary old-time music.[20]

The waltz genre expands Richard's repertory, and it is useful to follow Samuel Bayard's direction and consider how the changes in a fiddler's repertory provide a way to understand social changes in Florida. The relationship between social structure and the shifting popularity of genres becomes evident when the hoedown is contrasted with the waltz. A hoedown demands that dancers change partners and work their way around the dance figure. The waltz is a couple dance. Dancers at a hoedown are forced to mix comfortably with other dancers as part of the formal structure of the event. A dancer performing a waltz has to excuse himself politely and ask to cut in on another couple. Changing partners is a bold act, rarely used by couples dancing a waltz, but cutting in is the norm in a square dance. The couple attending a square dance has to expect to mix and mingle with other couples. The couple dancing a waltz can enjoy the opportunity to stay together throughout the night. A single dancer may go to a square dance and easily find an array of willing partners. A single dancer attending a waltz would probably have a more difficult time finding a partner. Although regarded as a country waltz, a tune such as "Don't Be Angry with Me Darling" is far better suited to a nightclub in the city where a man could go to take his lady out for a night on the town. It is difficult to ascertain why waltzes were not a part of the old Kissimmee Park dances, but when Richard moved to Jacksonville, he found that the social structure was different. He learned to play tunes in a different genre because the center of community life was far removed from his experiences in rural central Florida. Although he and other newcomers to Jacksonville continued to dance hoedowns, the popularity of the waltz by the 1930s reveals that the city had a different social order than Richard's rural community.[21] A couple was more isolated at a dance in the city because they were less likely to know their fellow dancers. Dancers had reservations about changing partners in public.

With the change in social structure came a change in the way that people heard Richard as a fiddler. Whereas Richard explains that the hoedown fiddler was almost drowned out by the stomping of square dancers' feet at a house party, he notes that a fiddler is a more audible presence at a waltz. The quiet softness of dancing a waltz makes the instrument easier to hear. The waltz is a musical genre that allows for virtuoso performances as it showcases the smoothness of a fiddler's bowing, the accuracy of the musician's intonation, and the tastefulness of the player's use of vibrato, double-stops, detaché bowing, and other ornaments. The fiddler accompanying square dancers at a house party was more a participant than a featured performer, whereas the fiddler playing a waltz became more a center of attention. When Richard began playing waltzes, he discovered that playing them honed his musicianship and augmented his sense of himself as a musician.[22]

Richard learned many of the waltzes directly from other fiddlers, but he also learned the "Westphalia Waltz" from the tape that he bought from Chubby

Wise. He learned other waltzes by listening to Daisy play them on piano from sheet music, a common practice that fiddlers use when developing their repertories.[23] Daisy also played a selection of cowboy songs and sentimental parlor tunes, which Richard also learned to play by ear. These include:

The Old Spinning Wheel
Won't You Come Home Bill Bailey
Molly Darling
When You and I Were Young Maggie
In the Good Old Summertime
Mockingbird Hill
Listen to the Mockingbird
When the Work's All Done this Fall
Red River Valley
Red Wing
Aunt Dina's Quilting Party

Richard still has the sheet music that Daisy and their daughter, Jean, read from when they played these songs. The parlor songs evoke a sense of nostalgia, with the old spinning wheel emerging as a decorative icon of rural life rather than a utilitarian feature of everyday domestic activities. The tunes were written for performance in a Victorian parlor, and it is easy to envision a young lady in resplendent white dress playing "Won't You Come Home Bill Bailey" at an afternoon tea following her piano recital. In the highly civilized space of the parlor, young musicians were evoking memories of an earthier place. The parlor songs work on the fiddle, but they sound different from Richard's fiddle tunes.[24] They have pretty melodies, but the new songs emphasize the talent of an individual musician who was performing for an audience listening attentively in a sitting room. In a variety of ways, the new tunes from popular sheet music were influencing how Richard was hearing music.

Along with the arrival of printed sheet music, new forms of media were also appearing. Richard listened to his wife and daughter play tunes from sheet music, and he also began listening to the radio and hearing recordings.[25] He picked up more tunes during the Golden Age of Radio:

Faded Love
San Antonio Rose
Washington and Lee Swing
Silver Bell
Amazing Grace

How Great Thou Art
In the Garden
I'll Fly Away
Life Is Like a Mountain Railway

The new media carried new messages. The scale for the social context of music-making was changing with the new media's increasing popularity.[26] Richard shifted from playing mainly for live dances into a broader sense of musical performance. The popularity of the written parlor song is a crucial component of this shift. Audience members no longer participated in musical performances by cutting figures at the house party or barn dance. Instead, the parlor tunes cultivated more genteel musical tastes in its audiences. They had to listen politely while seated in the uncomfortable chairs and overstuffed settees of the Victorian parlor. Furthermore, the media took music-making farther away from the cohesive social setting of the square dance and the live venue of the parlor as radio shows and records moved the creation of music out of the home and into the studio. Broadcast over the airwaves, or contained and distributed in cardboard boxes, musical performances no longer required that the audience had to be physically present with the music makers.

S. P. Bayard's call for analyzing why some items and genres fall from a repertory and are replaced by new pieces becomes especially important in understanding how Richard's repertory had changed by the end of World War II. As did other fiddlers, Richard attempted to play his hoedown tunes on the radio.[27] But the repetitious quality of a fiddle tune and its status as instrumental music were not well suited to the mass media. The same qualities that made the genre vibrant, familiar, and easy to follow at a dance made the fiddle tune monotonous and lacking in commercial potential when broadcast over the airwaves. The popularity of records further changed how people listened to fiddle tunes and old-time music.[28] A wax cylinder recording is short. Although a fiddler could play through a tune once or twice when making a record, the usual context for hearing a hoedown tune required a longer performance timespace. A fiddle tune is difficult to remember if it is heard only once or twice. The shorter timespace of a recording altered the way that people remembered the tunes by increasing the number of songs played while decreasing their length of play. Although marketers worked to capitalize on the commercial appeal of fiddle tunes when they first sold "hillbilly music," the old-time fiddle tune was being selectively displaced by the classic jazz tunes of the 1930s as well as by newer forms of early country music. The radio shows, fiddlers' conventions, and hog-calling contests were all attempts to promote the music. Drawing from the everyday culture of rural life, the producers of these events were brokering a new product. Their marketing appealed to the nostalgia about rural life that animated the parlor song.

Richard used the radio and his appearances at fiddle contests to advertise the talents of the Melody Makers. He also found audiences for his hoedown tunes at house parties and nightclubs throughout the city. By the 1950s, however, dancing the square dance in Jacksonville's homes had been largely displaced by listening and dancing to country and western music in the city's honky-tonk bars. This shift further explains why the neighborhood square dance had fallen apart. Musical tastes changed with the great influence of radio and recordings. The fiddle tune's appeal was usurped by the commercial appeal of more popular musical forms. These media changes also were related to historical changes that influenced a shift away from old-time and into newer forms of music. Young men left the state to fight in World War II, thereby restricting the number of available dance partners and suspending many of the dances. When the soldiers returned home, many had developed other musical tastes and stopped going to the square dances. Roads were improving. They opened up a city's nightclubs to rural residents who left private Florida frolics to cavort in a public bar. Conversely, city folk had greater access to the roads leading to dances in the country. As strangers showed up at country dances, suspicions about the dancers' motives grew. Couple the sense of distrust with the easy availability of bootleg liquor, and it is not surprising that fights erupted. The square dance had broken apart because the scale of social life had changed significantly by the 1950s.[29]

A faded piece of paper, lying in the bottom of Richard Seaman's fiddle case, shows his response to these changes. One night over fifty years ago, the South Land Trail Riders played the following tunes. Their set list reads:

Up Jumped Trouble
Aunt Dina's Quilting Party
When You and I Were Young Maggie
Sweet Bunch of Daisies
Darling Nelly Gray
Red Wing
Good Ole Summer Time
Silver Bell
I'm Going Where the Roses Never Fade
Alabama Jubilee
Shear 'Em
Good Old Summertime

I Don't Love Nobody
No Name Waltz
At a Georgia Camp Meeting

Richard explains that he compiled this set list for a country music show that he had put together for his band. He knew that a show that featured only the hoedown tunes from his core repertory would not hold his audience's interest. The audience had developed its own repertory that had selectively displaced most of the fiddle tunes played at house parties. The new repertory consisted primarily of waltzes, parlor tunes, gospel selections, and western swing. His role as a fiddler had changed from being a participant in a communal dance to becoming a musician in a country band.

In contrast to playing hoedowns at house parties, Richard no longer was featured as the only musician who carried the melody. Instead, he learned to support the other musicians by playing the melody softly in the background as the featured vocalist sang and the piano player or guitarist took a lead. Although the South Land Trail Riders were a country band playing an eclectic array of music—rather than a bluegrass band—they worked together in a style related to bluegrass music. They had to play together as a team, but the cooperative nature of their melody-making also involved spotlighting individual talent. When it came time for Richard to step up to the microphone, he was supported by his fellow musicians and his musical prowess hit home. This creative dialect is negotiated by the unified cooperation within the band as contrasted to the creative competition between its members. It is a major feature of music; Neil Rosenberg writes of how this tension fires up bluegrass bands.[30] It also drives musicians playing western swing and other forms of country music. Richard explains that he modeled his band after Grand Old Opry performers and other commercial recording artists. He cites Ernest Tubb as a major influence, and he also appreciates the music of Bob Wills and the Texas Playboys. In this set list, he includes tunes that they popularized, and this live performance was highly influenced by recorded music.

Between 1920 and 1950, Richard lived through a huge shift in ways that audiences conceptualized music. He found that the record—an attempt to capture the live performance of a country fiddler as he tries to replicate the house party or barn dance—simply did not work over the airwaves.[31] Instead, the record became a performance space for music that fit new aesthetic standards. The professional musicians were creating music for their records and radio shows, thereby establishing new performance standards. Richard was now working to re-create in a live performance what he heard on records. Knowing that they were performing for an attentive audience, members of the South Land Trail

Riders not only played together but competed with each other to create a polished act. Audience members at their country music shows no longer participated in the musical event by dancing. Instead, they sat still, listened, and gave the band a hearty round of applause.

Over time, Richard's fiddling became less a participatory contribution to a community's social event or a resourceful means for scraping together grocery money. During the late 1940s and early 1950s, Richard continued to play at nightclubs for couples who performed the waltz and other new dances. He also found opportunities to play at occasional square dances. But the audience for his band expected country musicians to put together a show. Jacksonville's audiences were fomenting the concept that a country musician is to be a virtuoso performer who will dazzle them on stage. Couple this expectation with the financial machinery of the recording industry, and the result is the birth of the recording star.[32]

Richard went on to meet a number of country music stars. A young singer and songwriter from Mississippi named Jimmie Rodgers occasionally traveled through Jacksonville and spent nights in the railroad bunkhouse. Richard was introduced to Rodgers by their mutual friend Clyde Kirkland, and Richard remembers playing with him. He explains, "I picked up a few of his licks when I could. He was kind of famous."[33] During the 1930s, Richard also met Vassar Clements, a native of central Florida who became known as "The Kissimmee Kid." He remembers that Clements was just learning to play and that the only tune he knew at the time was "Rubber Dolly" and that "he played it over and over again," adding, "you could see he was going to be good." Clements became one of the top session fiddlers in Nashville, and he frequently appeared in Florida folk and country music venues.

Richard also played with the co-composer of the "Orange Blossom Special," Ervin Rouse. He invited him and his band to his home after they performed a show at Jacksonville's Capitol Theater in the late 1930s. As Richard continued to play, he has appeared throughout the years on shows that featured stars such as Charlie Daniels, Doug Kershaw, John Anderson, and Gamble Rogers. Richard has enjoyed his brushes with the famous, but he assembled the South Land Trail Riders mainly because he enjoyed playing for people. He may have once hoped to be a star, but he now plays because he likes the music rather than to "make a million dollars off it."

The South Land Trail Riders' set list shows that Richard changed his repertory to balance the demands of his audiences with satisfying his own musical tastes. To build up his band's following, he knew that they would have to vary their tunes. In the performance recorded by the set list, he set the stage for his show by opening with "Up Jumped Trouble," an old-time hoedown tune. The core of his set list then consisted of commercial country tunes, but he did find opportunities to insert old-time fiddle tunes into the performance. This tension between playing contemporary country tunes while reviving the older tunes in his band's performances is a central dynamic in Richard's musicianship. The audience wanted to hear the South Land Trail Riders play the new songs on the radio, but listeners also appreciated the chance to hear old favorites. In listening to hoedowns, they found allusions to rural life that provided a healthy dose of memories to ameliorate the disease of nostalgia.[34] In hearing the popular country tunes, they learned to pick up on the new sounds that were coming out of Memphis and Nashville. It is an aesthetic value that Richard himself appreciates as he enjoys learning new tunes while remembering the old ones. As S. P. Bayard observes, this dynamic quality has always been a part of fiddling.[35] Fiddlers have been mixing older tunes with the latest sound in their repertory for hundreds of years—long before postmodernists discovered the persistence of the past in contemporary cultural expression.[36]

A repertory is a dynamic resource, consisting of a repertory of repertories. Richard classifies his tunes as hoedowns, waltzes, parlor songs, country tunes, gospel, and blues. He thinks of only the hoedowns and waltzes as "old-time fiddle tunes," but he enjoys playing other styles. As do the Florida Folk Heritage Award winners George Custer and Chubby Wise, Richard views the country classic "Faded Love" as one of the prettiest tunes ever written for the fiddle, and he enjoys playing twin fiddle with other musicians on this tune. He also likes to play parlor songs, such as "The Old Spinning Wheel" and "When You and I Were Young, Maggie," and he frequently closes his shows with the gospel tune "How Great Thou Art." In talking with him, however, one finds that he takes great pride in the old-time tunes that he learned in Kissimmee Park and from Tom Acosta and Jack Pitts in Jacksonville. Richard's eyes brighten when he recounts how he first heard these tunes and how he struggled to learn them. In contemporary performances, he always emphasizes the old-time tunes, and his stage patter includes accounts of how he would play them at house parties, on street corners, and in barbershops. In private jam sessions, he keeps returning to these tunes in his core repertory.

Originally, the tunes in his core repertory were the major components of his primary experience in learning to play the fiddle. Today, the core repertory is a major resource that he uses to express his voice as a fiddler. He appreciates seeing other fiddlers learn his tunes, especially when the attentive musician discovers that the tunes have survived from the nineteenth century through his unmediated link to one of Florida's aural traditions. His core repertory is a source of pride.

Cultural critics might seek to deconstruct the idea of a core repertory by calling into question the idea that there is a center to Richard's fiddling tradition. Noting the dynamic quality of his repertory and the variety of genres, one could argue that the assumption of a center is more a subjective—if not hegemonic—cultural construct of the folklorist rather than an objective aspect of Richard's fiddling.[37] Richard Seaman's cultural categories suggest a different meaning in privileging the older tunes in his core repertory of hoedowns. The collection of tunes is an essential aspect of musical expression and central to his status as an old-time fiddler. The tunes provide a workable center that both honors the past and provides standards for artistic values used in new creations. The center establishes commonplaces of history and culture that create the potential to be a contributing citizen in a community, state, and nation. This core provides an authentic representation of the tunes that are vital to Florida's fiddle tradition.[38]

Boundaries between cultural expressions are permeable. Genres leak and centers change.[39] Richard Seaman, however, makes sharp distinctions between the genres in his repertory. When he breaks outside of his core repertory of hoedowns and waltzes, he is no longer playing old-time fiddle tunes. When he returns to tunes in his core repertory, he establishes the commonplaces that connect him with other fiddlers and with his audience. As he moves through his repertory to play parlor tunes, early country music, hymns, and blues, his center shifts as he explores other repertories and expands his own repertory. Fellow musicians and his audience do find that the newer genres and selections also create musical commonplaces, but Richard always returns to the early tunes that he first learned at home.

Originally Richard played his fiddle as a participant who had a gift that he freely offered to neighbors in his home community. As he added new tunes, he found that the fiddle helped him and his family through hard times just as it added to the enjoyment of good times. With the addition of tunes to the repertory of the South Land Trail Riders, Richard began to see himself more as a musician playing to a crowd rather than as a fiddler playing along with a crowd. These changes all show Richard creatively presenting himself as a musician in response to changes in Florida's social history. As the social structure changed so drastically that the fiddle largely fell out of favor by the middle of the 1950s, Richard stopped playing. Jacksonville's audiences no longer seemed to understand or appreciate the musical gift that he wished to offer.

But there is a final stage in Richard's musical life history. He picked up the fiddle once again at the age of eighty-two. His fiddle provided him an entry point for finding a new audience, and Richard Seaman began to reconceptualize his role as a musician and storyteller. He came to recognize that he is also a historian.

8

Folklife in Education

~

Come with me, dance with me,
Give me your hand,
Hum to me softly an old tune,
Tell me a story of when you were young.
                    —Greg Dale and Erik Sessions*

A fter examining the thousand-year-old etymology of the word *folklore*, a
researcher might regard the phrase "folklife in education" as an oxymoron.
Jeffrey Mazo writes that the Anglo-Saxon term *folclar* was in circulation by the
year 890.[1] Meaning "knowledge held in common," the term that gave us *folklore*
is in contrast with the term *boclar,* which referred to "knowledge kept in books"
or "doctrine." Mazo points out that the contrast runs parallel to the difference
between *folcland* and *bocland,* which marks a distinction between "land subject
to the provisions of common law versus land subject to the provisions of royal
charter." As nineteenth-century Scandinavian thinkers transformed the term
into *folkliv*[2] and twentieth-century English speakers created the American term
folklife, the contrast between academic and nonacademic forms of cultural expression is a salient concern in a "folklife in education" project.[3]

These projects contribute to compensatory education that integrates and
affirms the value of knowledge found outside the canon of academic instruction. American folklorists originally established "folk arts in the schools" programs during the late 1970s.[4] They continue to administer these projects across
the nation today. They are modeled after artist-in-residence programs developed by state and local arts agencies and inspired by numerous projects that use
folklife as a resource for enhancing instruction in language arts, history, music,
and art in primary and secondary schools. I met Richard Seaman because I was

coordinating a folklife in education program in Jacksonville. His interest in participating in the program is one reason why he picked up his fiddle once again at the age of eighty-three and began to play in the summer of 1988.

The following description is typical of the many school performances that I coordinated with Richard. The format, structure, and specific techniques demonstrate how Richard and I designed a classroom presentation from the interview sessions that I had held with him during the project's initial fieldwork. I became interested in folklife in education because I felt that this type of public programming is an excellent approach to public folklife programming. It combined two of my main interests: the study of folklore and the teaching of children. Teaching children about the traditional culture of their communities initially appealed to me because musicians such as Richard Seaman can liven up the material found in textbooks and make lessons relevant to local history and culture. As I continued to work with folklife in education projects, I came to recognize more values to folklife in education programming. The sessions with students, teachers, folk musicians, and traditional artists not only provide opportunities to enhance the social studies and language arts curriculum of schools, but they also offer excellent ways to teach music and art appreciation. I also came to recognize how these programs affirm local knowledge and artistic expression, thereby connecting classroom instruction with community life. My predecessors and supervisors in Folklife in Education at the Florida Folklife Program had explained that these projects can foster cross-cultural and intergenerational understanding, two goals that I value and believe can be taught through folklife studies. In the course of the project, I came to realize that understanding the value of Folklife in Education is an emergent process. People learn different lessons from these projects, and I came to appreciate the sense of epiphanies that emerge in performances.

The following session provides a context for understanding Richard's involvement with playing for students, and it documents some of our early ideas about playing together. The session also consists of numerous teachable moments that are perhaps best understood through ethnographic description rather than theory and analysis.

It is a warm February afternoon. Richard and I are in a library at a school located far into Jacksonville's northside, across the St. Johns River. The media center is crowded with three classes crammed into the facilities where I have been teaching a hundred students during the past two weeks. Richard is the third artist I have brought to the school. Over the past week, one hundred students have learned about Puerto Rican bobbin lace, or *bolillo*, and they also learned some of the trade secrets of a local auctioneer.[5] They received the other artists well. I had prepared them specifically for Richard's visit by giving them a short history of old-time fiddling and bluegrass music and by telling them that they were going to meet a fiddler and storyteller from Florida. Finding major difficulties in arranging for a guitarist to back up Richard, I had broken with the professional protocol of many folklorists and blurred the line between performer and presenter. Rather than juggling other guitarists' busy schedules with my school presentations, I backed up Richard by playing his red sunburst Ovation guitar. As the session begins, half of the students are sitting in uncomfortable library chairs, half on the floor.

As we wait for all of the students to find their seats, I introduce Mr. Seaman to a few of the students. A fourth-grade student is surprised that he is wearing a cowboy hat, bolo tie, and boots as he does not think that cowboys live in Florida. I quickly respond to him by telling him that there are indeed cowboys in Florida. When I introduce Mr. Seaman, he nods, touches the brim of his black felt hat, and says hello.

The students and teachers are ready, and I begin our performance by saying good afternoon to the students. They respond with a *good afternoon,* and we have their attention. I look over to Richard and comment loud enough for everyone to hear that this group is smaller than the last but that what they lack in numbers they will make up for in enthusiasm. Introducing Mr. Seaman to the entire group, I tell the children that we have another guest and explain that Mr. Seaman lives in Jacksonville but that he was born and raised in Kissimmee. I see some blank looks from my students and add that Kissimmee is near Orlando. I finally gain some flashes of recognition when I mention that Orlando is where Mickey Mouse lives.

To put Richard Seaman's fiddling and stories in context, I explain that there used to be square dances in Kissimmee that were held in people's homes. Noting that dances still are held in Florida, I tell the students that these dances are where Mr. Seaman first learned to play the fiddle. To prepare students for the entire session, I explain that Mr. Seaman is going to play some of the tunes that he knows and that they will have the chance to interview him about his music.[6] I conclude the introduction by adding that he also has been known to tell some stories and that they can expect to hear some tales by the end of the afternoon.

Framing the presentation by explaining how fiddling in America has roots in the traditional music of Europe, Richard begins playing "Irish Washerwoman," and some of the students clap along to the jig's beat as soon as Mr. Seaman leads off on his fiddle. He plays through the tune a few times, and I accompany him on guitar. I listen for his familiar tag and end the tune with the appropriate G-chord.

The students politely clap at the tune's conclusion. I announce that the name of the tune is "Irish Washerwoman" and then explain that we are going to play some old-time fiddle tunes. Turning to Richard, I suggest "Soldier's Joy," and he lifts his fiddle to his chin and slides an upbow to kick off a tune that is a common part of the repertory of Celtic and American fiddlers. Richard plays the tune at a fast clip and tags the ending with a musical phrase that I had never heard him play. I compliment him for playing a clever ending, and he thanks the crowd.

The schoolchildren are beginning to listen more attentively. I note that I had played "Soldier's Joy" for them on my pennywhistle a few days ago, and some of the children remember the tune.

We move the performance along after I explain that Americans created their own fiddle tunes in this country and that the tunes came to be used for square dancing. Richard suggests we play "Flop-Eared Mule," and I introduce the tune and tell the students to listen for the sound of a mule going "hee-haw" in the song. He bows out the familiar double-stop that kicks off this hoedown tune. Holding his black fiddle under his chin, Richard occasionally lifts his eyes to the audience to acknowledge the students' interest in his music. At the end of the tune, I ask the students if they heard the mule, and most of them raise their hands.

The students have been clapping along, somewhat in time to the up-tempo beat of old-time tunes. I ask the students what they think of a name for a tune like "Flop-Eared Mule" and explain that some of the old-time tunes have great titles like "Back Up and Push." Richard suggests we play "Mississippi Sawyer," and he bows out the shuffle that opens this hoedown. As he tags this tune to end it, I notice how the students' applause is much more enthusiastic and appreciative. Mr. Seaman thanks them for their interest, and I explain that the name of that tune was "Mississippi Sawyer."

Richard turns to look at his set list as I mention to him that the students like the hoedowns, and I tell the students that we could have a dance if we had someone to call the squares. He replies that we should play "Cindy," and he pulls the downbow that opens this tune. After a few bars, I find the key and the chords that allow me to back his fiddling.

As he finishes this tune, Mr. Seaman begins telling the students about the tunes that he has played. He shares with them that he played these tunes at square dances. Acknowledging that the students probably are not acquainted with the types of dances at which he played, Mr. Seaman tells them that the fiddler used to sit in a corner of a building to play for others. A lively dance tune with a nice tempo like "Cindy," he asserts, would start a square dance off right quick and get the people to dancing.

I ask him to explain how fiddle beaters work, and he tells the children that someone would whittle out two long sticks that looked like long match sticks. He says that the fiddle beater would just tap them against the strings while the fiddler played, and he clarifies that the person beating straws would gently tap the sticks against the strings to give the tune some more bounce. I then ask for a volunteer. Picking the first hand that I see, I call on a boy and ask him to come up with the front of the class.[7] Mr. Seaman takes a seat and softly begins playing "Cindy." I show the fourth-grader how to hold the fiddle beaters and where to tap on the strings. He bounces the beaters on the strings between Mr. Seaman's bow and his left hand and finds the rhythm. After Mr. Seaman plays the tune through a couple times, he congratulates the volunteer for keeping good time.

We slow the tempo down as I explain that fiddlers also play other types of music. Reviewing the idea of the three-quarter time-signature that we had discussed last week, I have the students count out the three-beat cycle of a waltz and ask them to listen for this pattern in the next tune we play.[8] I explain that unlike the square dance, the waltz is not a group dance but rather a dance in which two people dance together as a couple. After my introduction, Richard begins the first notes of "The Waltz You Save for Me." As I am playing, I watch the students and notice that the slow tune has held their interest and that some of the children are swaying along in three-quarter time. After he finishes the tune, he suggests that we play another waltz.

We finish the first half of the presentation with the "Westphalia Waltz." I withdraw my presence as a presenter and shift the emphasis to Mr. Seaman's art by asking the students to interview him. Having never worked as a classroom teacher, Mr. Seaman prefers to have me play a role that is an awkward mixture of teacher, back-up guitarist, and emcee. He is more comfortable answering their questions, but my skills in what teachers euphemistically term "classroom management" are needed owing to his soft voice and quiet way of answering their questions.

An intrepid student initiates the interviewing and puts up his hand to ask, "What's the largest audience that you have played for?"

Mr. Seaman replies that there used to be a lot of people who would come to the dances but that he does not play for big audiences anymore. I mention that Mr. Seaman used to have his own band and that he used to play for some big crowds for country music shows and that this was a way he helped to earn his living.

Another student asks, "How did you learn?"

Mr. Seaman explains that he grew up in central Florida near Kissimmee. He explains that when he was their age, he did not have television, radio, computers, stereos, movies, or any of the modern conveniences that the students have in their homes. Noting that if people in his community wanted any entertainment they would have to make it themselves, he describes going to square dances where he would listen to the fiddlers. He concludes his answer by explaining that he learned from them and then figured out the tunes on his own as best he could. He tells them that after practicing, he would return to the dances and try to play the tune along with the other fiddlers.

A fourth-grade girl raises her hand. When Mr. Seaman calls on her, she asks, "I know that you play the fiddle because it's a tradition, but if you didn't learn it just as a tradition, would you still play the fiddle? And why?"

Richard looks at me and blinks his eyes at the question's depth and breadth. He laughs and says that she should be a reporter after asking a question like that. He responds that he enjoys playing the tunes and that he likes the sound of the fiddle.

A girl asks, "What's the bow made from?" Bending down to show her the bow, Mr. Seaman tells her that it is made from horsehair and wood. He shows her how the bow works by drawing it across the strings of his fiddle, and she touches the wooden part of the bow.

I comment that there is an interesting story that explains why his fiddle is painted black and ask him to share it with the children. He tells them that in 1926 when the hurricane hit Miami, it blew the roof off his dad's house in Kissimmee. The rain soaked into the fiddle, causing the instrument to fall apart. After he put it back together, he decided to paint it with black enamel to cover up the scratches.

Another girl asks, "How long ago did you start?" He replies that he started playing at dances when he was about sixteen and that this was a long time ago. He adds that he is not going to tell them how old he is as he smiles and shakes his head.

Another student asks, "Why did you play the fiddle?" He says that he just liked it.

A boy asks him, "What color was your fiddle before you painted it?" He says that the color was the same as the rest of the instruments. It was a mahogany color, but the instrument is made of maple and spruce.

Another student asks if he plays for concerts. Mr. Seaman replies that he does not and that he just plays at home if someone comes around. He points over to me and smiles.

I ask him if the dances were fun to play for, and he replies that they were actually a lot of work because they would about play you to death. He adds that they had to play all night long.

A fourth-grader asks, "How old is your fiddle?" He answers him by explaining that he does not know exactly how old it was. Disclosing his age, he says that he is eighty-four years old and that the fiddle was in his house before he was born.

"How long did it take to learn?" asks another student. It is a hard question for Mr. Seaman to answer. He jokes that he has been trying to learn the instrument since he started playing. He says that it takes a long time and a lot of practice to learn the fiddle and that he picked up his own method of playing.

A girl asks, "What's your favorite?" He replies that he likes "Rose of San Antone" and a lot of the waltzes.

A boy asks, "Do you play the 'Orange Blossom Special'?" He replies that he does not play it but that he knows the tune. He adds that bluegrass fiddlers play that particular tune, and I clarify that he plays "old-time" and not bluegrass.

A student asks him if he likes to play the fiddle, and Mr. Seaman says "yes." I follow up with "What do you like about playing?"

Mr. Seaman smiles and says that it is just a pastime. He laughs and says that when he gets in the doghouse, then he can take his fiddle out there with him.

The teachers and students pick up on his laughter, and I ask him to describe a square dance.

He tells the students that the houses were like today's and that the neighbors would come over. He says that if there was any furniture, they would clear it out of the living room and that someone would roll back the rug for the dance. Someone would then play the fiddle, and they'd dance all night long. He concludes the description by explaining that they were held every couple weeks and that neighbors also danced at picnics. Richard notes that neighbors either walked there or rode over with a horse and buggy because there were no cars in his part of the state.

"How many songs do you know?" asks a student. He answers that he knows quite a few but that he can't number them. A smile lights up his face as he jokes that he does not know that many good ones.

A girl asks, "Do you play with musical notes?" He tells her that he does not read music, and I explain that he picked up the tunes by ear. The students learn that this way of learning is an important part of the fiddling tradition as I remind them how tunes are passed along from musician to musician.

A student asks, "Do you play other instruments?" He says that he doesn't, but I add that he plays guitar.

Another student asks if he has taught any other people in his family to play. Richard pauses a moment and answers that he has not taught anyone else to play the fiddle but that he used to play in a band with his family.

As I hear how he answers the children's questions succinctly and vividly, I also watch the children listening to his first-hand descriptions of the dances and farm life in rural Kissimmee Park. The children are fascinated, and they are listening well, despite a few boys who are seated and fidgeting next to their teachers. After ten minutes of questions, a few more students start to squirm, and I glare at them with the *teacher's eye* as another classroom teacher leans over to tell them to sit still. Mr. Seaman finishes the interview by explaining how he went to school up to the eighth grade. He tells the children that the teachers were strict and not afraid to use the razor strop to cure the illness of laziness.

We are quickly using up our forty-five minutes. I tell the students that we would like to play another song. I remind the students that we had studied blues music in Florida along with old-time fiddle tunes. I explain that blues were first developed in black people's communities and that they are also played on the fiddle. As I pick up Richard's guitar, a boy asks me, "Is that your guitar?" I explain that it is Mr. Seaman's and that I was going to bring mine but that I could not find my guitar strap that morning. Together, Richard and I play the "Carroll County Blues."

The children like the tune, and a student asks, "Do you like telling stories?"

The students have been waiting to hear his tall tales. After he tells them that he does like to tell stories, I affirm that he is a good storyteller. Playing with the idea of stretching the truth, I tell the kids that every story he tells is true. Richard looks at me and laughs.

Hedging my bet, I tell the children that maybe they are just true because it is true that he tells stories and add that sometimes these stories are called *tall tales* and even *lies*. As Richard is reviewing his list of tales, I reiterate that all of these stories are true.

A couple of the teachers laugh, and one teacher's eyes begin to sparkle. Richard develops the joking frame of reference and begins to tell his tales. "That reminds me of the time that I was in the third grade. I never will forget that the time that I graduated from the third grade. That was a great day of my life. I was so excited, I almost forgot to shave that morning."

As Mr. Seaman finishes rubbing the whiskers on his chin, he places his fiddle and bow down on a nearby table and he tells one of his favorite stories.

> I went down the state one time not too long ago. My sister had a farm down there—a peanut farm. And the back of her farm was growed up. There wasn't much back there. And there was an old abandoned well. It had been dug years ago for water, and they didn't use it anymore. So they covered it up. Somehow or another, her prize milk cow went down there and fell in that well.
>
> So I went down there and went looking around. I told them I didn't think it was no problem getting that cow out of the well. It was

the best milk cow in the county. So we got a ladder, and I crawled down there. And I started milking that cow.

Mr. Seaman motions his hands as if he were milking a cow. He then nods over to me and continues his story.

And I went down there, and I milked till I got tired. And I milked some more. And, you know, we kept on, and we floated that cow right out of that hole. There was nothing to it.[9]

The students are sitting a bit too quietly now, and Richard points over to me, and says, "He was there. He saw it." I reply, "We grew up together!"

One of the teachers laughs the loudest, and I catch her eye as most of the children just continue to listen attentively. Richard tells these tales in a style so convincingly droll that the teacher commented to me later that afternoon when we met at the Jacksonville Landing that she thought the students believed his stories. I told her that it takes some time for the students to understand the humor in the stories but that most of the students usually begin to understand the jokes.[10] She explained that she was really pleased that Richard could come into the school for a special performance and that she liked his stories and tunes.

In the school's library, Richard continues and tells the children another story about his sister's farm:

My sister's farm was in Osceola County. That was awful rich ground, and she used to grow corn. But the ground was so rich that the corn grew so tall that we thought we'd have to get a stepladder to pick it. But it kept on growing. And finally, it got so tall, that the moon had to detour by way of Georgia every night to get over it!

And I had a little farm down there, and I raised popcorn. With all I had to do, I got pretty good at it. I'd take the popcorn to town in a horse and wagon and sell it. Anyway, it got so hot down there. I didn't know whether I was going to get to town or not with that popcorn. The sun would be so hot, it would blow up my popcorn.

But anyhow, about halfway to town, the sun kept getting hotter, hotter, hotter. And them old mules pulling that wagon was just plugging along. And that's when the sun got so hot, that whole wagonload of popcorn just blowed up right in the middle of the road. I lost everything I had, too.

To top it all off, those two mules turned around, looked at it, and they thought it was snow. And both of them froze to death. Tough times. Yeah, it was tough times.

One day, a neighbor boy come over to our house, and he said, "Mr. Seaman, my daddy wants to borrow your cross-cut saw."

"You-know those old-timey saws they used to have?" Richard clarifies his story for the children, who are now beginning to laugh when he completes his stories.

Dad said, "All right, you can have it. It'll be some time this afternoon." He said, "What do you want it for?"
He said, "We want to cut a pumpkin."
Dad said, "Well, it'll be sometime this afternoon before you can get it. We're just halfway through a sweet potato."
Potatoes would grow big down there.

More children laugh as they are figuring out how to listen to his tall tales. Richard continues his storytelling by apparently shifting the frame of the performance: "But, other than that, there wasn't much happening down there. Just daily life. My sister growed a watermelon down there one day. The ground was so rich that she couldn't do much with watermelons because the vines grow so fast. The ground was so rich. Them vines grow so fast that it just wore them watermelons out, dragging them across the ground. Never could save a one."
Richard shakes his head and pauses while more children laugh. He then embeds another tale into his story.

We did save one, one time, I remember. They sent me down there with a horse and wagon to get it. It was a little one. It was too big for me to get in the wagon, so I had to get half a dozen neighbors to come up there and help me get it in the wagon and carry it to the house. And on the way, that watermelon fell off the wagon and drowned the mule—right quick!
We used to take them up there and put a couple sawhorses up there. And we'd lay them right across the sawhorses. And we'd screw a faucet in there and have watermelon juice for two weeks.[11]

Richard chuckles, and comments, "It's the truth, or I wouldn't have told it." He looks over to me and says, "I think that he can verify it. He was down there with me, and he wouldn't story either!" He pauses and adds, "Not unless he got a chance!" I laugh and say, "I don't know about that!"

Richard explains the one condition in which he might tell a story to twist the truth. He says, "I wouldn't either—until my wife catches me."

He pulls me into his act, so I ask him if he ever had lying contests where people would try to top his tales.

Richard answers that he has never been in a lying contest but that no one ever tried to stop him from telling stories. He jokes and says that he has been criticized for telling stories.

We are running out of time. Richard picks up his fiddle, and I pick up his guitar and place the strap around my neck. He continues with a few more stories.

> We had an old clock, a pendulum clock that would sit up on the mantelpiece. You've all seen the old pendulum clocks with the pendulum swinging back and forth. We had one there, and we didn't know how old it was. We tried to find out how old it was. We never could. But I know it was real old because the shadow from that pendulum wore the back of that clock out.[12]

Richard's tale reminds me about one story that he tells about fish that feed on shadows. I ask him, "You also had some bass that hit shadows, right?"

He laughs, "Yeah," and then adds "I never was one much to tell a story, you know." I respond, "That's the biggest lie you've told today!" as Richard laughs and tells one last story to the children:

> There was a little, old pond, down back of the house there. A round pond. About three-quarter of an acre, I guess. Clear water. Bullfrogs used to sit around there and sing all night. All those frogs at night would sit by that, and I never saw so many frogs sitting around that pond in my life.
>
> That winter, there come a freeze. That freeze come through there so fast that when it passed over that pond—just as it passed over that pond—the water froze. That's what it did: it was so severe.
>
> Well, them frogs sitting around that pond was sitting out there behaving themselves. When the freeze come, they jumped in the water to keep from freezing to death, you see. But it happened just like that. That freeze come over, and those frogs jumped in the water to keep from freezing to death.

But that pond froze, just like that!
And I went out there the next morning and looked.
And there was a pond of ice with frog legs sticking up, all around.

With this story, the students are finally figuring out the humor. They laugh and set Mr. Seaman up for the punchline. "Well, I hated to see that. So I went in the house, and I got my lawnmower. And I went out there, and I mowed me up a good mess of frog legs."

The children laugh. A girl yells out, "Oh, gross." A boy calls out, "Nuh-huh, that's not true!" He is promptly hushed by the young teacher. She gives me a look that says, "Sorry about my kids, but we've been studying 'fact versus opinion' this year." Richard hears him and says, "Yeah, they was still kicking, some of them. But we had them!" The girl says, "Oh, gross" once again.

The buses are going to load soon, and we are just about out of time. I ask for a volunteer for a demonstration.[13] Selecting a fourth-grader, I explain that he is going to try to play Mr. Seaman's fiddle. Richard hands him his instrument and shows him how to hold it. Stage-shy at first, the fourth-grader says that he does not know how to play the instrument, but he gives it a try. He scratches the bow up and down the strings as I find a rhythm on the guitar. After he works his way through the tune, I ask for another volunteer and select another fourth-grader to take her first fiddle lesson. Mr. Seaman shows her how to hold the fiddle and bow, and she saws out some less screechy tones before handing the instrument back to him.

I explain that there is time for one more tune. I tell the students that the fiddle is also used in gospel music, and Mr. Seaman and I bring the performance to a close by playing the hymn "How Great Thou Art." I notice some of the teachers are singing along and that many of the students recognize the melody. After the applause fades, I announce that we are out of time.

Mr. Seaman thanks the children by saying, "My pleasure, I really enjoyed it." I acknowledge the appreciation and tell him, "I'd say this was a pretty good audience, wouldn't you?" "Yeah, they were real good. I only got hit by the first egg!" I reply, "And I got hit by the second!"

The buses are arriving, and parents are lining up their cars in the school's driveway. Before we pack up, a teacher asks, "What do we say to Mr. Seaman?" A chorus of "Thank you" resounds, and Richard smiles, waves his hand, and says "You're welcome—I enjoyed it. You're a good audience, the best we had all day."

We had finished a similar session earlier that afternoon and three sessions in the morning, and it has been a good day. Loading the instruments into the back seat of my car, we head back to the Avondale neighborhood near the intersection of I-10 and I-95, turning off the interstate at Lackawanna Elementary School where the South Land Trail Riders played a country music show half a century ago.

On the way back to Richard and Annie's house, I ask him what he would have thought about having this type of program in his school in Kissimmee Park. He answers that he would have enjoyed it as a schoolboy and that he thinks that children just naturally respond to music, especially tunes that have a strong beat. I ask him if he ever thought that he would be playing his fiddle tunes and telling stories in schools, and he laughs and says that he never expected to be a teacher. I thank him for helping me out for the day, and we talk about the possibility that some of the students might learn to play some of the tunes. We note that a student that morning had brought his violin and that he could play the first few bars of the "Orange Blossom Special" without looking at the musical manuscript that he brought into his schoolroom.

We arrive back at his house and unload the instruments. After I helped Richard carry them into his house, we return back to the driveway and I chat with him. He shows me where he is planting collard greens in his backyard garden, and he comments on the hotwire connected directly to the 110-volt outlet in his house that works to keep dogs and rabbits away from his plantings. The scattered tracks and deep gouges in the soil show where a dog had hit the wire earlier that week.

We say our goodbyes, and I head back to the Jacksonville Landing where I am to have a sandwich with the teacher from the school.

Next week, when I return to the administrative office building for the Duval County Public Schools, the director of social studies for the Duval County school system informs me that the school board will no longer fund the Duval County Folklife in Education Program using EOCA Chapter II funds. He explains that a committee and the deputy superintendent for instruction plan to use the funding that covers my short-term contractual services, honoraria for the folk musicians and folk artists, travel expenses, and office supplies for a brand new budget item. The deputy superintendent agrees with a budget committee's recommendation, and he has earmarked the funds for new computers in the schools.

I ask him if I should look for another job.

The director of social studies for the Duval County Public School System nods his head and says, "Yes."[14]

9

A Florida Fiddler

~

No thoughtful student of folklore can possibly become a chauvinist.
—Sigurd Bernhard Hustvedt*

In the late 1980s, Richard Seaman picked up his fiddle from the mantelpiece
and began playing once again. While working at Paschal and Shaw's Hardware, he had met Jack Piccalo, a bluegrass banjo player and salesman in the
hardware business. They found that they shared mutual interests in music, and
Richard explains that Jack encouraged him to play his fiddle once again. Richard
found that he could remember a few of the hoedowns, and Daisy helped him
to relearn some of the tunes that he had forgotten. Jack would come to visit
the Seamans, and he played guitar with Richard after Daisy passed on in 1986.
Richard and Daisy Seaman were married for fifty-six years.

I met Jack at a bluegrass jam session in Jacksonville in July 1988. In early
August, he introduced me to Richard. We spent an evening recording tunes at
Richard's home. I was to return many times to play with Richard and record
more tunes and stories. As Jack and I were driving back from our first visit with
Richard, he asked me if there was any possibility that I could help to open up
a spot for Richard to perform on stage at the Florida Folk Festival as well as in
the schools. I agreed with Jack that Richard's storehouse of tunes and stories is
a treasure worth sharing with audiences and that I would offer my assistance.
Recommending Richard to the Florida Department of State's Florida Folklife
Council, I was given the opportunity to help him find new performance venues.
Over the years, Richard has played for thousands of children in Duval County's

public school system. He has also appeared on stage at the Florida Folk Festival, at local arts festivals, and in numerous community events. I invited Richard to record old-time tunes and waltzes in a recording studio, where he contributed to a sampler tape of folk music from Florida's First Coast, an audio resource used in the county's schools.[1] Richard has been invited to play at events throughout the state, and in his nineties he competed in the "rustic division" of Florida's official "Old-time Fiddler's Contest." Richard and his fiddling have been represented in newspaper feature stories and front page photographs in the *Florida Times-Union* and broadcast on WJKS's "First Coast News" as well as in articles published in *Southern Folklore* and *Midnight Flier.*[2] A small story on Richard, featuring his photograph on the cover, was published in *Florida Fiddler,* the newsletter of the Florida State Fiddlers Association.[3] Interview footage and his playing are also portrayed in a radio series broadcast nationwide on National Public Radio.[4] In these presentations, some may see him as an icon who represents Florida fiddling.

Richard's artistry provides resources for understanding the place of story and music within one life. But can his story be regarded as truly representative of fiddling in the Sunshine State? Critiques about facilely using one traditional artist to represent a region, ethnic group, or nation's folk culture have their validity.[5] Richard's songs and stories are known only by a small group of Floridians, and there are millions of other stories that also symbolize important aspects of the state's history and culture. It is inaccurate to view his artistry as unique and indigenous to Florida, and it is disingenuous to suggest that authentic Florida fiddlers play the tunes in his repertory and that true Florida storytellers tell only his tall tales. There are insufficient compilations of Florida's folk music, and there is little field research on the state's earliest fiddling traditions, to generalize fully about fiddling in Florida. But affirming Richard's status as a Florida fiddler is important to understanding his artistry. He continues to play the tunes that he played in the early part of the twentieth century, and Richard does articulate vivid firsthand experiences about an important regional folk tradition. Furthermore, historically, many of his tunes have been integral to the core repertories of other fiddlers in the state, and Florida's contemporary fiddlers admire his ability to convey an understanding of the instrument's place in the state's history. His tall tales are not unique to the state, but they are part of central Florida's storytelling tradition. Richard's ability to localize them to Kissimmee reveals that he takes a special interest in using them cleverly to express an understanding of daily life in his community. The shifts in his repertory and his mastery of new genres of fiddling strongly support the assertion that his experience of Florida history has undergone a huge shift. The communal orientation of rural life that was symbolized and re-created in the Florida frolic may still be present in some rural areas, but urbanization has stifled this type of community spirit in Kissimmee and Jacksonville. This shift is an important theme in Richard's personal experience narratives and in his reflections on history, and it is a vital part of his old-time fiddle tunes and tall tales in his present performances. In all of these ways, his stories and tunes remain important resources for understanding how an individual examines the past. It is challenging to move beyond the microlevel of one man's life history into a broader view of what his artistry suggests about life in Florida. One useful way to begin to generalize is to examine the symbolic resonance of his fiddling and storytelling in relation to common perceptions about Florida's folklife.

To understand these images, it is first useful to consider that public performances, written publications, and folklore scholarship take Richard Seaman's unique life experience and place his artistry in the public sphere. As the history of country music suggests, this shift from private to public spheres reaffirms, or even establishes, the dominant images of musicians who perform within specific genres and regions. As roots music has been commercialized and promoted by music industries, the image of "the fiddler" has emerged as an interesting character.[6] Whereas Richard sees the fiddler primarily as a playful contributor to social life, the dominant mass media images of the fiddler are different. Along with seeing the fiddler as a potential country music star, those unfamiliar with old-time music may imagine fiddlers as rustic rubes or as unsophisticated good old boys playing on the front porch. These images are rooted in historical antecedents, and fiddlers have toyed with the stereotypes in crafting public personas as "hillbilly" musicians and old-timers. When the less flattering associations of fiddling are coupled with the image of rural Florida, there are major problems in finding ways to present an accurate and sympathetic understanding of a Florida fiddler.

In presenting his music and stories to audiences in public folklore programs, Richard came to recognize that his individual experiences as a fiddler are relevant to wider patterns in Florida's history and culture. On the festival stage and in the classroom, he was faced with the problem of turning accounts of individual experience into representations of Florida folklife. When he plays his tunes, relates the context for house parties, and answers students' questions, Richard is providing firsthand descriptions of fiddling in Kissimmee Park. He makes no claim to speak for all fiddlers, and it would be a stretch to regard his artistry as an all-encompassing icon of Florida. These caveats aside, there is value in considering how his tunes and stories are resonant with symbolic images about the state's folklife.

Florida's image is multifaceted. Margot Ammidown argues that the state's many tourist attractions provide useful ways to view the presentation and self-representation of images that can be described as "mythic."[7] She asserts that from the earliest days of exploration to the present-day construction of contemporary attractions, Florida has been promoted in three characteristic ways. From its beginnings, promoters have touted a visit to the state as a pilgrimage to a shrine, even presenting the peninsula as a source of magic.[8] Many of these images truly are mythic. They first inspired quixotic journeys to discover the Fountain of Youth, just as they continue to inspire millions of forays into central Florida's Magic Kingdom. Ammidown explains that a second dominant image casts Florida as a garden paradise. The interest in visiting beautifully manicured gardens and pristine parks is resonant with a desire to rediscover Eden.[9] A final image is less idyllic. Florida is sometimes represented as the underworld, with its many attractions that promote alligator wrestling, the world of reptiles, and slightly sinister expeditions into the spheres of pirates, outlaws, and chambers of horrors. These dominant themes fuel the state's leading industry and are present in tourist attractions throughout Florida. They attract visitors, but the themes also emerge in Richard's stories about Florida. His tall tales turn Kissimmee Park into an enchanting land of fantasy. The bucolic images of Florida folklife and his smooth, laconic style of storytelling draw listeners further into a magical place where making a living is hard but life is good. His description of rural Florida falls short of Edenic, but his affection for unspoiled wilderness, open range for grazing cattle, and carefully tended fields, orange groves, and gardens evokes images of a paradise that has been lost largely to urban sprawl, highly commercialized development, and no trespassing signs. The harshness of life on the Kissimmee Prairie can be cast in Edenic terms, but life on the scrublands is also harsh. Richard's stories include accounts of snakes, alligators, and vicious underworld beasts lurking in the wilderness. His stories also include accounts of the violence and lawlessness that comprise the human underworld.

These three themes emerge in Richard's presentations of fiddling, but there is a dominant image of Florida that is more resonant with his fiddling tradition. It is that of the Florida Cracker. Typically, "cracker" can refer to a specific group of people in Florida or to specific aspects of Florida's regional culture. Dana Ste. Clair documents that the term was first applied to a specific population in Florida in 1767.[10] He explains that the gentry class adopted the term as an ethnic slur against Scots-Irish frontiersmen and that this use of the term was especially common in southern coastal regions. His thorough discussion of the negative associations with cracker culture cites the pernicious stereotypes that portray Florida's white pioneers as shiftless and ignorant vagrants or outlaws. Early writers continued to portray crackers as eking out an existence at a level slightly above savagery, and they frequently associated them with an isolated rural culture that thrived on cunningness, clannishness, and violence. Although cracker stereotypes have softened, the image of a Florida Cracker still evokes impressions of unsophisticated and bigoted country bumpkins who are prone to hard drinking, violence, and bigotry. The other use of the term "cracker," however, is less derogatory. In Florida, cracker culture increasingly identifies a specific regional culture in the state. It can refer to the old-time Anglo and Celtic/Irish traditions that are integral to the state's early heritage and contemporary identity. This pioneer culture includes traditional activities such as hunting, trapping, storytelling, and fiddling. Although Richard does not consider himself a Florida Cracker, largely because his family settled in Florida following the Civil War, he recognizes that his folk traditions are associated with cracker culture.

The disparate, even conflicting, images of Florida's cracker culture can create major problems in coordinating public programs on Florida's folklife. A focus on the tourist's image of Florida perpetuates the idea that the state is a lost Eden that commercial development has redeemed into a modern "Paradise Regained." The images of Florida as a shrine to the lost magic of the New World, a garden paradise, and a site for escapist entertainment into the underworld all construct the state as a tourist's fantasyland, thereby obscuring rather than reflecting the realities of daily life. Public programs about folklore can thus devolve from an honest attempt to represent the state's history and culture into an exotic celebration of nostalgia. In this respect, presentations of public folklore have been challenged for contributing to a celebratory view of culture at the expense of cultural critique.[11] In contrast to the celebratory image of cracker culture that can emerge in public presentations, public programmers also face a related problem. Folklore can be perceived as a display of quaint and exotic others when traditional artists are presented in the public sphere. In Florida, this can be evident when the image of the Florida fiddler is associated with pernicious regional stereotypes that vilify native Floridians as "crackers." A final problem is that the image of the Florida fiddler can be misinterpreted as an endorsement of nativist ideology.[12] The problem can be especially salient in a state experiencing a constantly booming population. The crowds at folklife festivals, music shows, sporting activities, and other display events can twist a healthy appreciation of their state's history and culture into a sense of ownership that devolves into xenophobia and jingoism.

Richard Seaman's stories and his descriptions of his own life experiences suggest how these varied images about the state are rooted in various historical and cultural contexts that are part of Florida's folklife. When watching him in performance, one can see that he challenges simplistic ideas about representing history and culture, for although he uses Florida history as a basis for tall tales, his commentary provides a thoughtful and sympathetic portrait of rural life. His music, stories, and reflections also offer a richer way to understand these images within the state's contemporary culture. Richard does know stories that he will rarely tell in classrooms and at folklife festivals. His discretion is wise as these stories can be better presented in other media, and children in elementary school would need a great deal of historical understanding and maturity to understand them. While he does not regard his musical venues as appropriate forums for speaking about the "catalogue of crime"[13] that is inscribed in Florida's written history, he wants his knowledge of unjust and oppressive systems to be included in the historical record. He balances the tension between celebrating and critiquing Florida's history by selectively presenting difficult issues in Florida's history and by telling his stories in appropriate times and places. These stories include difficult topics, and the celebratory image of Florida's history that he presents in public performances is balanced by other narratives that deal with controversial topics. To understand how these stories and his music critique dominant images of Florida's folk culture, it is essential to consider some of the stories that he rarely tells in public. An examination of these stories also reveals how his perspectives on Florida's history challenge the idea that fiddling is an emblem for creating a highly romanticized view of Florida's history and fomenting regional chauvinism through the study of folklore.

Richard Seaman knows about the brutality in Florida's history. Precontact Indian nations waged warfare and engaged in ritualistic torture before they, in turn, were slaughtered or driven from Florida by Europeans and Euro-Americans.[14] Florida's First Coast was the site of the total disappearance of the Timucua, who died from disease, forced enslavement, and battles with colonizers from the sixteenth to the eighteenth centuries. The first recorded naval battle between European nations in America was fought off the coast of Jacksonville when French admiral Jean Ribault was fired on by Spanish admiral Pedro Menéndez de Avilés in 1565.[15] That autumn, the Huguenot Ribault, his soldiers, and colonists lost to the Catholic Menéndez, and Ribault and over three hundred men, women, and children were killed by arquebuses and spears in battle, hanged from trees, or hacked to death with swords behind the Atlantic Ocean's sand dunes.[16] Today, this area, Matanzas Bay, a few miles south of St. Augustine, still bears the Spanish word for *slaughter*.[17]

Florida's sand has been bloodied by vicious warfare, ranging from skirmishes to full-scale battles between soldiers of the U.S. Army and those of Britain, France, and Spain. Three Seminole Indian wars were fought in the first half of the nineteenth century.[18] In battles in central Florida's prairies and south Florida's swamps, the Seminole nation was decimated and the Miccosukee nation almost annihilated.[19] The horror of large-scale enslavement of Africans and African Americans was a comparatively late American institution in the state as—for a brief time period—those who escaped could flee southward into freedom before Florida was part of the early United States.[20] It became a full-fledged slave state when it was admitted to the union in 1845. During the Civil War, several battles were fought in Florida. The state's sea forts housed Confederate prisoners as well as other prisoners of war throughout the state's history, including Osceola and Geronimo.[21] By the early part of the twentieth century, Florida industrialists and governmental officials had transmogrified slavery into systems of convict leasing through work camps. Zora Neale Hurston and other writers accurately identified prison labor and peonage systems in turpentine camps as contemporary forms of slavery during the 1920s.[22] The state has been the scene of the vicious Rosewood massacre, lynchings, and race riots.

Florida's violent history is well documented in history books. Grim reminders are preserved in both the popular and scholarly literature and in archival holdings, and the history of violence is presented to the public in documentary and feature films.[23] The brutal reality of Florida history is also part of the state's school curricula.[24] Tragedies in Florida history are also interpreted in its state parks and in museums. As do many Floridians, Richard knows of the violence and oppression of life in Florida. Unlike many Floridians, he has been an eyewitness to major historical changes during the past century, and he has personally experienced huge shifts in the state's social history. He also understands how the brutality in Florida's history is related to racist ideology and institutionalized systems of oppression, for his life spans a significant portion of the Jim Crow era. Although the system of segregation largely kept him away from black people throughout much of his life, Richard's first human contact at birth was with the black hands of a midwife who delivered him. The midwife was to help his mother care for him during his first few months of life, and Richard explains that she helped to deliver many of the infants in Kissimmee. Richard lost contact with her, but he keeps an old photograph that shows her standing on a planked wooden walkway. There are no written notes on the back of the snapshot, and Richard remembers her name only as "Miss Anderson." This black woman was old when the photograph was taken around 1906, and Richard knows little about her life. There is a strong probability that she had survived slavery.

Much of Richard's personal history tells of a life spent in a world apart from black communities. He explains that Kissimmee Park was white and that black people came into the community mainly as seasonal workers to harvest the citrus crops, earning fifteen cents for filling a box of grapefruit and twenty cents for picking a box of oranges. He did not venture into black communities, although he explains that he had heard of a small town called Eatonville that was located across Lake Tohopekaliga a short drive north of Orlando.[25] The various places where Richard worked were predominantly segregated, but he was friends with a few coworkers who told him stories about living as black men in the state.

Recounting stories that merge his knowledge of firsthand experiences with these recounted narratives, Richard begins with a pointed commentary about history.

A lot of things went on down there that I guess nobody will ever know. The negroes down around through there weren't very well liked by anybody.

Clewiston was a sugar mill in those days, and there was no roads down there to amount to anything.

When I was a little boy, there was a constable. If he caught a negro in town and he didn't have no money, he'd put him in jail. If he had money, he'd say "give it here and get."

See? Run him out.

And then he'd put them in jail. He'd get a jail full of negroes.

And then these foremen from Clewiston would come up here about once a month in a truck. And he'd offer that black man, "I'll go your bail, if you'll work it out."

"Yes sir." He was going to get out of jail.

Take him down to Clewiston, and he never got out. That was the last time they'd see him. They didn't get out of there. And they'd give the old constable so much a negro for putting him in jail for them. And they worked that a long time.

That happened.

I talked to an old negro that was down there. He got out. He made it out. I don't remember his last name, but everybody called him "Henry." He got a job at the shop. Some of the tales he told, you wouldn't believe. They worked the hell out of them, and if they didn't work, why, they would whip them. They didn't pay them or anything. And they couldn't get out.

They were guarded by dogs. And that prairie—no man could hardly make that prairie. And he told about them. He said he saw one place—one negro rebelled. They made the negro dig a hole, put him in it, covered him all up in it but his head, and sic the dogs on him.

Well, the others, they went to work. He told that. I ain't seen that, but he told that. So the negroes, they worked. He told me that. Now, I don't know, but he told me that.

He was working at the Seaboard as a helper and he escaped. He escaped. The other ones didn't. They couldn't get away. That swamp down there. My God, that swamp! You either had to swim Lake Okeechobee or—

Listening to Richard's voice trail off, I sit at his table, stunned and unnerved. There is a long silence, and I struggle for something to say: "That was just like slavery." He corrects me:

> That *was* slavery-time.
> And the constable, if he caught a negro come in on a train or something like that—or if he caught him in town—if he had any money, he'd get it. If he didn't have any money, he'd put him in jail.
> I've seen them in the jail there. It was down along the lake, where we come in from the north part of the lake into Kissimmee. There's that electric light plant where they make their own electricity. And they had a jail there. That was a city jail. Now the county jail—the county jail was in the courthouse. And this city jail was—as we come in according to Kissimmee, we had to come in by boat then and walk right by the window like that.
> And we had to walk right by the street. There'd be a bunch of negroes. They'd have their hands sticking out of the bars. "Cigarette, sir, cigarette, sir. Please sir, a cigarette." Wanting you to give them cigarettes. Begging for cigarettes.
> I've seen that.[26]

Richard tells more of this facet of black—and white—history on the next day when I return to see him. He compares conditions in present-day Florida with life during the time of Jim Crow laws.

> In them days, the black man didn't have any voice. He was told what to do, and he couldn't talk back. That's the way it was in the turpentine camps. They'd work them and work them and work them. They had to get stuff at the commissary. That was rough too. The turpentine camps was around Lofton. Lofton is sort of west of Kissimmee out in that section. Lofton mills.
> I used to could see—
> Where we lived on the south end of the lake, we could see the smoke on the horizon, far across the lake. That was the Lofton Turpen-

tine Camp. And they had a mill there. And they had a bunch of negroes that worked there, and they didn't pay them much.[27]

I tell Richard about documents that I found in the Florida Department of State's archives. One is a joint affidavit filed to the National Labor Relations Board on March 11, 1943. The deposition is from Thomas Evans and Taylor Sneed of Orlando. It affirms what Richard has been explaining about the arrests of black people on trumped-up vagrancy charges.[28] I also mention information gleaned from field notes written by Zora Neale Hurston during her time in Cross City during August 1939. Her notes assert that workers owed money to the commissary in the turpentine camps in the area, and she writes that the Ku Klux Klan had paraded that weekend. Another report describes how Hurston took the WPA photographer Bob Cooke into the turpentine distillers' camp, where he documented working conditions that were later published in the popular press. Florida's history books record that the area was known for its brutal working conditions, peonage systems, and violence at the camps.[29]

Richard offers another story about an area close to where he was living during the time that Zora Neale Hurston researched folklore in African-American communities:

> Around where Disney World is today, that was what was known as "Reedy Creek." Reedy Creek. It wasn't nothing but a little cypress swamp and water. And the ground was so poor that a rabbit would have to carry his lunch to go across to the next acre down. It was that poor.
>
> Disney bought that for a little of nothing. Nobody knew what he wanted it for and what was going on. He bought that and them old turpentine camps and lumber camps below Kissimmee.
>
> I got this from an old negro man that used to live there, and he was working at the railroad. And he told me what it was down there when he was a boy. And I lived down there too—and I lived east of where he was. I lived east of that lake, Lake Tohopekaliga. Kissimmee is right on top of it, and Orlando was north of that.
>
> West of that section in Florida was where all the turpentine camps and sawmills were. And they were all operated by blacks. And in those days, if a negro got killed, the section foreman, he didn't know nothing about it. There was just trouble in the camps down there. See it was in the "nigger quarters." They did never bother to investigate it. It was blacks. And a lot of them are buried out down that way. Murdered and buried.[30]

Richard's legends and personal experiences show how the state's troubled race relations are important themes in the state's folklore. Fiddling is often associated with Anglo culture, and it is too easily regarded as a white tradition. There are numerous tunes like "Nigger in the Woodpile" that embody racist ideology. His frank accounts show that there is a historical context for associating Florida's folklife with racism, and he honestly acknowledges this troubling aspect of the state's history. He affirms, however, that contemporary race relations are not as severe as what he witnessed as a young man. He notes that there are changes in fiddlers' repertories that reflect changes in racial attitudes. As we talk, he explains that, for example, the fiddle tune "Run Nigger Run" is now called "Trouble Amongst the Yearlings," and he comments that racist stage patter is no longer as acceptable in the present as it was when he was younger. He also observes that his neighborhood is becoming more integrated. He regards the dismantling of segregation laws as one of the major changes in his lifetime. He reflects: "Times have changed. The black people have been discriminated upon in many ways. I don't hold things against them because of their race or color or anything like that. They've got as much right to be here as I have. They're born and raised the same way I was. A long time ago, the black man, he was discriminated upon to where he couldn't come to your front door. He had to go to the back door. He had to take his hat off. All like this, you see?"

Richard concludes by looking at me and saying that the racism he has been speaking of is immoral. He thinks that Florida has made progress in working through racial problems, but he is unsure whether the problems will ever be resolved. In the silence that follows his stories and reflections, I search for something to say. I think about values that are important in his own life. I tell him that I think segregation kept him away from people who could have been his friends, and he nods and agrees.

Later that day, I ask him about regional prejudices, "What was a Yankee in your community when you were growing up?" Richard smiles and responds, with a "Hmm" before giving another eyewitness account of history.

> He wasn't too well thought of.
>
> People didn't travel too much then—like they do now. Once in a while you'd see a stranger come through. Traveling preachers would come through on a horse and buggy, and they'd go from house to house. They knew they'd get dinner when dinner come. They knew that night that somebody would put his horse up in that stall and he'd get something to eat. So he'd go there and talk to them a little bit. And they'd give a little change, you-know.
>
> So that was about the only strangers we'd see. But if a stranger

would come through, and he looked like he had a temper or something, all of us boys would say, "He looks like a damn Yankee to me." Yankees wasn't too well thought of.

Nowadays with the automobile and people's traveling now, they don't think about it.[31]

Mentioning field notes from WPA writers, I tell Richard of a definition for the appellation "Yankee" that I had read: "In the 1930s, people in your area of the country said a Yankee is anybody from north of Georgia."[32] Richard answers, "Oh yeah. They sure did."

I ask, "Did people call themselves 'Crackers' back then?" He answers with a common etymology of the term "Florida Cracker."

Yeah. Yeah, the "Florida Cracker." I think that originated from the cowboys, cracking their whips there. They'd make more noise with them whips on a cattle drive than the Spanish-American War did altogether. Everybody had him a whip, and they was "pow, pow, pow, pow." And the dogs were barking. And the whips were popping. And they'd have a round-up down there.

That would be once a year, every fall. They'd have a fall round-up. They'd get the cattle up and brand the calves. If they didn't, the calf would grow up without a brand and anybody could have him. And they'd sell their beef and all.

Oh, it was a mess. I didn't like it.[33]

When spoken by nonwhite people, the regional nickname for white residents of Florida and Georgia is sometimes a two-word epithet: "white cracker." In these usages, it is a racial slur. When spoken by native-born white Floridians, "cracker" is a sobriquet that carries some appeal, if said with pride and affection. The state has experienced its dizzying population growth only since the widespread adoption of central air-conditioning systems, and there are few Floridians who can claim the status of "native" and the accompanying cachet associated with a newly emerging sense of "Florida Cracker Chic."[34] When spoken by Yankees and Southerners, the nickname "cracker" can be an offensive regional slur akin to the term "redneck." Guidebooks for Florida tourists properly warn visitors to be cautious about using the nickname and to say it with a smile.[35]

Northern visitors have not always provided sympathetic representations of Florida cracker culture throughout the state's history. At times, the representation reveals a virulent contempt for the types of communities that nurtured

Richard. A travel writer, George M. Barbour, describes cracker customs in his hundred-year-old travel guide, *Florida for Tourists, Invalids, and Settlers*.[36] He explains what he saw during a trip through Brookville, Florida, in the nineteenth century.

> The entire trip that day was through an unsettled region, the only human beings living anywhere along the road being four or five families of Florida natives, the genuine, unadulterated "cracker"—the clay-eating, gaunt, pale, tallowy, leather-skinned sort—stupid, stolid, staring eyes, dead and lusterless; unkempt hair, generally tow-colored; and such a shiftless, slouching manner! Simply white savages—or living white mummies would, perhaps, better indicate their dead-alive looks and actions.
>
> Who, or what these "crackers" are, from whom descended, of what nationality, or what becomes of them, is one among the many unsolved mysteries of the state. Stupid and shiftless, yet shy and vindictive, they are a block in the pathway of civilization, settlement, and enterprise wherever they exist. Fortunately, however, they are very few and rapidly decreasing in numbers, for they cannot exist near civilized settlements.[37]

If Richard's friends had seen Mr. Barbour passing through Kissimmee, they probably would have taken one look at him and muttered, "There's a damn Yankee."

They would have been right. Barbour had come down to see the South from Chicago, and he was traveling the state with General Ulysses Grant's touring party in order to write a newspaper story on the state. Touring America's Southland in a stagecoach, he writes of what he saw:

> As the stage was slowly climbing a rise in the road, we were surprised to see four women, seated on a fallen tree close by the roadside; all were of precisely the same size, with the same features, eyes, and hair, and a vacant, stupid stare; each wore a light colored, faded calico dress, of plainest, scantiest possible make, quite clean (a surprising fact), and large, plain cotton sun-bonnets; each wore a cheap, bright-hued, cotton handkerchief around her neck; and they were all barefooted, carrying their low, thick-soled shoes in their hands. The dress and kerchief appeared to be their only garments—no underwear whatever.[38]

After Barbour explains how his driver initiated contact with the natives, he explains where the women were headed:

> They were going to a dance at a "crackers," some fifteen miles farther on, and they had already walked about five miles. Think of woman—lovely, tender woman!—walking barefoot twenty miles to dance all night in a close cracker cabin, with whisky-perfumed cracker males, to the scraping of a wheezy violin in the hands of an old darkey; the scene lighted with pine knots; the feast of hog, hominy, beef, sweet potatoes, and likely a few villainous compounds of flour, cheapest brown sugar, or syrup, and called *cake* or "risin'-bread." And, perhaps, that cracker ball will be kept up two or three days and nights, until all the stock of eatables and whisky is used up.[39]

Regional prejudices die hard in America. Whether Barbour actually attended a Florida frolic seems to be a moot point. Nevertheless, he does describe a house party held in rural Florida:

> The "cracker" when resolved to give a dance, shoots some game and carves a hog, finds a market and sells his game for a little cash, lays in a stock of whiskey, a little flour, cheap sugar, syrup, tobacco, hominy, or grits, more whiskey, coffee, or cheap tea, goes home, sets the "wimmin-folks" to baking, while he resolves himself into an invitation committee, and sets out on his lean, lank, cracker pony, and invites all the crackers for miles around to "cum round." And they come. A fight generally ends the dance, and the best man wins the girl, for these dances are usually prolific of "jinin" matches. It should be said, however, *per contra,* that there is very little sexual immorality at these half-civilized gatherings, for the mothers—as in this case—are also on hand, and keep a sharp eye on proceedings; while the men—the fathers—will shoot.[40]

The Florida frolic remained an important aspect of cracker culture following Barbour's expedition into the state. In his *Vicissitudes and Casathrophics,* Orange County native Carl Dann provides a more sympathetic description of the dance.[41] Geographically and temporally, his representation of the dance is situated close to Richard Seaman's Kissimmee Park. Conceptually, Dann tells virtually the same story, supporting and complementing Mr. Seaman's description. Dann's representation verifies how Richard envisions the dance and its place within cracker culture:

I have attended many "Cracker breakdowns" that lasted three days and nights. You would dance until you tired, then sleep a while, then up and dance some more. The music for a real country square dance is one fiddle and a second man who would beat the fiddle straws.

A real "Cracker" square dancer has a little jig all his own that he does on the corner before he swings his partner, or at any time when he has a chance. At a real "Cracker Shindig" a man keeps dancing. You would see jigging, clog dancing and the Highland Fling and other steps that you never saw before. You would see no loving on the side. You would not see a girl take a drink or smoke; you would, perhaps, see a number of old ladies smoking pipes, but never the daughter.

The girls, in those days, wore petticoats and corset covers. If you would mention the word brassiere, a "Cracker" would think you were speaking of some French fruit. The girls wore lots of ribbon in their sashes, around their necks and on their hair. Snap fasteners had not been heard of, so they used a lot of pins. When the caller would holler "Do-se-Do," "Birdie in the Cage," "Four Hands Around," "Balance All," and "Swing Your Partner," occasionally you would get stuck with these pins.

In the old days you could attend a dance at a big country house and find a big room with the floor covered with pallets for the babies. I have seen as many as forty little children sleeping on the floor in one large room, while their parents danced. Young and old would dance together.[42]

Stetson Kennedy takes these descriptions and provides a more expansive representation of cracker culture in *Palmetto Country,* his social history of the state. His writing includes a wealth of folktales, descriptions of occupational folklife, and ample mention of old-time fiddling, jook joints, and other vibrant aspects of Florida's folk culture.[43] He provides a vivid historical context for understanding how Richard's stories and tunes are linked to large-scale Anglo migration into Florida from Georgia and states in the Upland South, beginning after Florida became a U.S. territory in 1821. This cracker migration was further sparked during the Reconstruction years that followed the Civil War.[44] One southerner who was part of this immigration wave was Richard Seaman's grandmother, Elizabeth Sharpe. Her family was forced to find new land in Florida because their family farm near Savannah had been burned out when General William Tecumseh Sherman marched his army from Atlanta to the sea.

Richard regards his music as an important part of southern culture, and it is not surprising that the tune "Dixie" shows up in his repertory. Although not written as an old-time fiddle tune, it underwent a process called "metaphrasis" through which it shifted genres.[45] The anthem was a stirring military march for the Confederate troops, whose ranks included ancestors on Richard's mother's side of the family. Upon the surrender of Robert E. Lee's army, President Lincoln had his military band strike up "Dixie" as an anthem to initiate healing between Rebel and Union troops; the ranks of the latter included ancestors on Richard's father's side of the family. Since the surrender, southern fiddlers have transformed the tune into a hoedown. This type of tune commemorates people and places in America's Southland, and Richard regards the connection between his fiddling and southern history as an intriguing part of his cultural heritage. He notes that other Florida fiddlers also view old-time fiddling as a southern tradition and that when he was growing up they had to call one particular tune, "John Brown's Body," or local crackers would "slap the hell out of you."

Although fiddling and fiddle tunes are part of a history that includes racism, xenophobia, regional prejudices, and other sordid themes, it is unfortunate that the fiddle is too easily associated with the negative aspects of southern history and culture. Today, some continue to regard fiddling in Florida as an anachronism, carrying little more than embarrassing reminders of the worst of cracker culture. In Florida and neighboring southern states, fiddling has sometimes fallen out of fashion partly because of the traces of separatism and nativism allegedly evoked by the tradition.[46] Jingoists such as Henry Ford did promote old-time fiddling and square dancing to foment xenophobic nationalism and fuel racist ideology.[47] The performance situations did exclude groups of people. The system of segregation kept black people from attending these events, and the contests and dances were promoted to dampen the fires kindled by hot jazz. But I would suspect that many fiddlers who performed in the 1920s and '30s in contests and dances sponsored by the Ford Motor Company shared motivations similar to Richard's interest in playing. They were not particularly concerned with representing fiddle tunes as nationalist anthems. Rather they simply enjoyed playing for others, and they took advantage of the opportunity to use contests to compete for needed prize money.[48] Furthermore, there were numerous fiddlers who, like Richard, also enjoyed listening to, dancing to, and playing ragtime, jazz, and blues music during the 1920s and '30s.

In today's Florida, times have changed. Whereas many early venues for Richard's fiddle playing were open only to white people, contemporary event coordinators work hard to develop diverse audiences. Richard Seaman and many Florida fiddlers are open to playing with others, and they are interested in a range of musical styles from a variety of cultural traditions. I found it especially interesting that Richard and other fiddlers are intrigued by black Americans' contributions to the state's fiddling tradition. He agrees that their contributions to fiddling and to country music should be included in the written historical record. The tunes in Richard's repertory provide clues for recognizing that old-time fiddling cannot be accurately represented as an "Anglo" tradition. The presence of blues and ragtime in Florida fiddlers' repertories demonstrates that fiddling is also a part of African-American history and culture. When Richard plays the "Carroll County Blues," he is demonstrating that African Americans have contributed to America's fiddling tradition. Tracking down the origins of many fiddle tunes is a difficult task, and numerous states claim a "Carroll County" that is honored by the tune. The folklorist and fiddler Howard Marshall writes that a Mississippi string band recorded the tune in the 1920s and that it was a popular two-step in southern states.[49] Richard learned the tune from an eight-track tape produced by Chubby Wise, who played it with Bill Monroe's Blue Grass Boys. Whatever the tune's origin, its twelve-bar blues chord progression, syncopated rhythms, jazzy feel, and bent notes are all vibrant characteristics of African-American musical traditions. This tune and other bluesy selections in the repertoire are verifiable records that document how Chubby Wise, Howdy Forrester, Bill Monroe, and other innovators blended blues, jazz, and ragtime into the old-time and early country forms of music to create bluegrass fiddling fifty years ago. Despite the conservative quality of old-time music, the general open-mindedness to jazz, blues, and other genres suggests that fiddlers and their audiences were not necessarily attached to the promoters' nativist ideologies.

Not only did blues music have a strong influence on fiddling in Florida, but early in Florida's history, numerous black fiddlers also played old-time tunes for square dances. Wiley Housewright documents that by the early 1800s, fiddling was highly valued in both black and white communities.[50] He explains that fiddling and square dancing were vital aspects of African-American culture and provides eyewitness descriptions of well-known black fiddlers. A WPA interview with Ella Lassiter, a one-hundred-year-old American who survived slavery, shows not only that square dancing was a form of recreation in black communities but that the fiddle was also favored by black musicians during antebellum times. In an interview on June 18, 1940, in Sebring, she describes to Barbara Darsey how the slaves in Florida would "swing up and down the room while the fiddle played."[51] Zora Neale Hurston also vividly describes how the hoedown was a popular form of socializing in black communities during the 1920s and '30s. She establishes an important scene in *Mules and Men* by writing of a dance in Polk County in a community that was located a few miles south of Kissim-mee.[52] The historical record shows that there were black fiddlers who played at Florida dances, just as George Barbour asserted over one hundred years ago. This strong presence of black fiddlers and their contributions to Florida fiddling is part of a wider pattern of American history.[53] Fiddling's history reveals that the tunes are part of a common cultural heritage derived from multiethnic sources. Florida's history thus belies the validity of promoting fiddling to bolster a racist or nativist ideology. Old-time fiddling is not solely a white tradition.

Racism remains a hidden wound that also often festers in the open in America. The fiddle has been used to symbolize regressive politics, regional prejudice, and jingoism. Housewright affirms that despite the acclaim for black fiddlers, white slave-owners also used the fiddle as a mechanism for social con-trol.[54] Although fiddlers' repertories shows that there is a historical basis for as-sociating old-time music with racist, provincialist, and nativist ideology, the history of fiddle tunes also supports a far more diverse history than is often recognized. Today, it is possible to find exclusionary and chauvinistic ideological implications in fiddling, but these ideologies are not the dominant interests among musicians like Richard Seaman. His current repertory and his contem-porary perspectives show that ideological resonances from the past have been replaced by different views. His performances show that the fiddle tune has a great potential to connect people—rather than to divide them—across lines of ethnicity, regional affiliation, class, and gender. He appreciates opportunities to play his fiddle for the scores of children in Duval County's schools, and black and white children alike show their appreciation for him by their applause and through the thank-you letters that Richard has saved from his time playing in the schools. Mr. Seaman performs at folklife festivals and educational programs to share his knowledge of Florida with others—not to exclude them from un-derstanding the state's history.

What does his fiddling represent? Old-time fiddling is not readily under-stood by most people. It is too easy to overlook a fiddler's artistry and humanity by seeing the fiddler only through the veil of regional prejudices, ageism, and a myopic lens created through believing in the grand master narrative of progress. A concern with the messages that are communicated is an importance aspect of thinking of cultural representation as a problem. Critiques that examine how some voices are excluded add to our understanding of the complexity of cul-tural representation. A discussion of ways in which cultural representation con-tributes to erasing people from the historical resource and creating inaccurate representations of history and culture should remain a vital concern to those engaged in cultural study. There are problems, however, in thinking of the symbolic resonance of a tradition such as fiddling as an all-encompassing symbol of culture.

Complete and accurate representations of culture are impossible. All historical descriptions and all cultural studies will remain incomplete pictures of people's lives.[55] History and culture constantly change, and people will continue to negotiate their descriptions and interpretations of what is being represented. There is no all-seeing eye that gazes at all things and then projects the complete event back to all people. Everyone has a different history, and we all have different sets of cultural assumptions that influence how we interpret history and cultural expression.

Consequently, ambiguities and crises over representation are inherent in ethnographic and historical study. These problems make presentations of history, culture, and folklore challenging to understand. But rather than a crisis of representation, there is a greater problem.[56] It is a crisis of reading. The larger challenge is developing skills for reading presentations of history and culture. Readers need to recognize that Richard's story is but one story of one Florida fiddler. His history is only one of many that millions of Floridians are constructing. It is a rich and fascinating story, and Richard's keen observations are as sensitive as they are eloquent. He wants to record a history that is an accurate reflection of his life experiences, and he trusts that I will provide an accurate and fair presentation of the tunes and stories that he so generously shares. It is possible to critique his cultural presentations to expose the historical contexts and ideological constructs that perpetuate the current political, economic, and social order. It is more accurate and rewarding to read Richard's stories and tunes to understand why my old friend likes to play his fiddle.

10

The Voice of a Fiddler

~

I keep talking wild theory, but it keeps somehow coming out stuff everybody knows, folklore. This Quality, this feeling for the work is something known in every shop.

—Robert M. Pirsig, *Zen and the Art of Motorcycle Maintenance*, 256

The voice of the emcee is clear on the videotape of the 1992 Florida Folk Festival that Richard has recorded and sent to me.[1] She is off-camera, but the video frame shows the amphitheater's stage setup. Shading a brick floor, this wooden pavilion is the main stage at the Stephen Foster Folk Culture Center State Park. Since its inception in 1953, the festival has been held on the banks of the Suwannee River, and it is coordinated each year during Memorial Day weekend in the small north-central town of White Springs. As Richard steps up to the microphone, which is being adjusted by a member of the sound crew, the emcee's expression becomes upbeat as she shifts from announcing that there is a lost child at the festival to introducing Richard Seaman's band.

She exclaims, "You're in for a treat now. This tall fellow in the black hat here is Richard Seaman, and I understand he's been known to tell a story or two from time to time. This could be one of those times." She laughs and continues, "And he's accompanied by Jack Piccalo—he plays fine guitar—and also by Frank Farley on bass at this moment."

Carrying his Martin D-28 guitar, Jack steps into the video frame. He walks out with Frank, who positions his string bass to the left of Richard, who is talking with the soundman who is adjusting their microphones and setting up the plug-in for Frank's upright bass.

The announcer continues her introduction to key the performance. "Now

I understand that Richard learned his stuff in Kissimmee. He used to play home square dances, and he was taught by a lot of fiddle players when he was a younger fellow about how to do what he does. So there's really a history and romance that goes back a hundred years with Richard."

She pauses, waiting to see if the sound crew is ready, and then makes a reference to Richard's band. "Most of these folks are from Jacksonville, and we'll see if he's got few stories to tell us too.

"You about ready, Jack?" Jack nods to her, and she continues. "Okay, Frank, Jack, and Richard. How about a nice, warm welcome for them to our stage."

The sun shines brightly on the audience seated on folding chairs under the live oaks draped with Spanish moss. Looking down the hillside to the stage, the viewer's eye goes right to Richard as he steps up to the microphone.

"Well, it's mighty nice to be back here. We wasn't here last year. I guess it was because we was too lazy to get out here. I don't know. I never will make excuses, but that's the best I could think of. In other words, we just forgot to put our name in the pot, so we didn't get no peas. But we're here today.

"We're going to try to play a few old-time fiddle tunes that was popular way back in the first of the century. Maybe some of you've heard them and some of them you haven't. But the old fiddle tunes was played many years ago in our part of the country, where we would go to a square dance and get out there and dance all night long. And some of us didn't know but one or two tunes to play, but that's what they had to dance by. If they'd get tired of one tune, we'd play the other one."

There is laughter from the crowd, and a woman who is seated next to her partner looks to him and smiles. She turns her head back to watch as Richard continues his introduction.

"When I first started learning to play the fiddle, I didn't know much about it. It was one that was in the house where I was born and raised. So when I first started playing, my mother said, 'Look here son, I can't stand that.' She said, 'I can't stand that. That's too much.'

"So she wouldn't let me play in the house. She made me go out there and practice, sitting on a stump out in the field. And I went out there to play and to try to play. She finally told me the better that I played, the closer I could get to the house. It was five years before I ever played a tune in the house."

The audience laughs at Richard's story, and he delivers a final commentary to finish his stage patter: "Even that was risky!"

Richard then introduces his first tune of the twenty-minute set. "One of the old tunes we used to play many years ago for a square dance was called 'Mississippi Sawyer.' And we'd like to try to play that for you today. It goes something like this."

He raises his fiddle up to his chin and bows out the familiar shuffle that opens the tune. Jack and Frank join in to back him up on the familiar hoedown from his core repertory. After they finish the tune, Richard introduces his next tune.

"That was one of those tunes to dance by. Here at the old country dances, we'd have to go to somebody's house, if they'd let us. And about two-thirds of the way through the evening, someone would have a few drinks, and the dance would get right lively. You was lucky if you didn't kick the plaster off the wall."

Richard pauses and laughs, "Another little tune we played was called 'Soldier's Joy.'" The Richard Seaman Band plays through this lively hoedown, and the crowd generously claps for them after he tags the tune and brings it to a close.

His patter acknowledges their interest, "When you applaud for us, it's like making love to an old maid: you can't overdo it."

Jack and Frank smile as Richard continues, "I'd like to introduce these boys that are helping me out so well here. This gentleman on the right, he's a fine guitar player and a master on the five-string banjo. I'd like you to make welcome Mr. Jack Piccalo."

After the clapping fades, Richard turns to his left and says, "Lookit here girls, lookit here. He's handsome, and he's single! Yes sir. He's looking around, though. He's got his eye out. He's looking around. He's looking around for a rich widow. If there's any rich widows out there, the line forms on the left. Mr. Frank Farley." Laughing along with the audience, Richard explains, "He paid me a quarter to say that!"

He then introduces the next tune, "Here's another old one, called "The Flop-Eared Mule.' We had a few of them around home to work with. Some of them are ornery as the Devil, especially the white ones. This song is called 'The Flop-Eared Mule.'"

After they play the tune, Richard continues to talk about his old homeplace. "I was raised on a farm down below Kissimmee. Many years ago, it was quite unlike it is today. We had to do everything we did by hand. We didn't have farm tools like front-end loaders or tractors and so forth, and most of it was done by hand."

This introduction introduces his first set of tall tales. He tells about the rich soil on his sister's farm by telling about the need to plant corn on the run and about the tall corn that makes the moon detour by way of Georgia just to get through. The crowd gets the joke and anticipates more stories and tunes.

Jack glances at the set list taped to the floor of the stage and whispers to Richard, "Let's play 'Westphalia Waltz.'"

The waltz is well known at the Florida Folk Festival. Richard varies the tune with each repetition, and the tune evokes a sense of nostalgia with each variation.

As the applause settles, Richard shifts right into more tall tales. He tells three of them, first explaining how the rich soil made the watermelon vines grow so fast that they wore out the fruit by dragging them along the ground. He then tells how a huge watermelon broke when it fell from a wagon, thereby drowning his mule. Richard concludes this set of stories by noting that they could place a tap on a big watermelon and open up the spigot for fresh watermelon juice.

"This is a little tune called 'Up Jumped the Devil,'" Richard says to introduce his spirited version of the old hoedown. After they finish this tune, he thanks the audience for their applause and announces the next tune on the set list.

"There's a waltz that I like to play called 'The Waltz You Saved for Me.'" He plays through the waltz, changing his ornamentation with each variation. The vibrato, double-stops, drones, and shuffles embellish the elegant melody line of this piece. When he finishes the small run that ends this tune, he returns back to his tall tales and tells the story of his sister's milk cow that he rescued from the well.

Jack turns to Richard and whispers, "How about 'Maple Sugar?'" They play through the square dance tune, and the audience gives them a final round of applause.

"Thank you very much. It's been a pleasure to play for you," Richard says to close the set.

As this performance shows, Richard has created his own sense of self-presentation and interpretation of folklore through his involvement with public programs. This type of performance is different from playing for house parties or country music shows. Rather than using stage patter mainly to entertain, Richard uses his stories to key his tunes beautifully and to provide a context for his music to an audience unfamiliar with what he has experienced in life. His patter not only indexes a shift from story into song, but his narratives also establish a frame for the audience to gain a better understanding of his fiddle tunes and his life experiences. Taking his cues from the insistent questions and tropes posed by folklorists and curious schoolchildren, Richard transforms the arcane interpretive commentary of the social scientist into captivating narratives. His stories and commentary provide engaging resources for him to present the salient aspects of the tunes' context in a way that is resonant with his audience's expectations.

The content of his stories, his stage patter, his tall tales all portray details of everyday life experiences, and the music carries with it the emotional associations evoked in thinking about one hundred years of Florida folklife.

What are the consequences of this blurring of the boundary between the folk musician and the folklorist through events such as the Florida Folk Festival? The event changed the context for Richard's artistry. Whereas his early performances were grounded in the everyday fabric of his community's social life, his contemporary performances are now highly mediated by the intervention of arts administrators, park rangers, educators, and folklorists. My role as a folklorist started out by documenting, presenting, and interpreting his fiddling as a folk tradition, but Richard's involvement with public folklore events changed this role. Watching him perform, I realized that he could gracefully present his own stories and tunes to an audience and that my best place was to sit in the audience and observe how he crafts his own artistry from his own vast storehouse of tunes, stories, and memories. In watching his performances, I came to realize how we shared similar goals and techniques for presenting folklife in public. We both value the opportunities for public events to foster an appreciation for his tunes and an understanding of his storytelling. We both recognize how exposing the public to his old-time fiddle tradition can preserve the music. Not only are the tunes preserved in the immediate performance venues, but we also found that other musicians come to Richard to learn his tunes. We both agree that his stories and tunes are vibrant resources for learning about Florida's history.

Others express concern that showcasing his tunes as "Florida Folklife" can foster ideologies of regional chauvinism, romantic nationalism, nativism, and jingoism.[2] Richard Seaman is a native Floridian, but he is not a nativist. His tunes and stories are authentic aspects of Florida's folk culture, but he knows that they are not unique to the state. They are rooted in the cultural expressions of Irish, Scots-Irish, Anglo, African-American, and American folklore, and Richard localizes these texts to reflect his experiences as a Floridian. His folklife is rooted in a past that yields stories reflecting an array of images and experiences from his history. For some, his folk expressions may symbolize romantic images that mask ideologies of provincialism and nativism.[3] Interpretations and theories offered by outsiders provide lines of inquiry for examining why Richard finds value in his folklife, and some members of the audience may take from his performances a sense of regional chauvinism and facilely exoticize Richard as the embodiment of a "real-live native Floridian." When they view him this way, they may regard his fiddle tunes and stories as symbols of a pure and prelapsarian Florida.

But it is too easy to read his artistry through these outside lenses. Thomas

McLaughlin provides a corrective viewpoint by arguing that researchers need to balance academic discourse with the willingness to listen to the vernacular.[4] By listening to Richard's stories, watching him perform, and hearing him reflect on his own motivations for continuing to play the fiddle, his audience discovers that he privileges other values through his artistic creativity. A close look at his performances in festivals and school classrooms shows that he does not regard his folklore as symbols for retreating into reactionary views of Florida's past. He does not use his tunes to foster ideologies of separatism. Rather, he plays his tunes and tells his stories to share his experiences with others. Because he invites his listeners to imagine a history that includes a wide range of people with an array of experiences, his willingness to offer his own life experiences is a refreshing break from other perspectives about Florida's complex cultural landscape. Through his stories, stage patter, and direct discourse, Richard shows how his stories and fiddle tunes are essential resources for finding equilibrium and sanctuary in the face of dramatic change. Finding balance, order, and harmony for himself through artistic expression, he generously offers his gifts of story and song to others.

The need to find balance and sanctuary is especially salient when placed in the context of his life in Florida. A close look at Florida reveals a sense of disjointedness that drifts off into surrealism. A reading of the state's history and cultural landscape supports Susan Orlean's characterization of Florida as a land of incongruity and paradox.[5] The state's economy is largely supported by tourism, but it is easy to find nativist sentiments in the Sunshine State. A pickup truck carrying a surfboard is decorated with a Confederate flag in its rear window and a bumper sticker that reads "Welcome to our beach—now go home!" The majority of the state's population consists of people who have moved from outside its borders, yet residents who have recently moved to the state frequently develop a sense of propriety about Florida that can border on xenophobia. Florida is the southernmost state in the Old South, but outsiders often do not think of the state as "southern." The northern part of the state is culturally the most southern, and much of south Florida feels like it is its own Caribbean nation. Miles of beaches attract vacationers, yet many denizens of Jacksonville rarely cross the intracoastal waterway to spend the day at the beach. Florida is a frontier state, and its open-range grazing was closed by fences only a half-century ago. It is also one of the Earth's major spaceports, and the Kennedy Space Center is surrounded by a wildlife preserve right at the edge of Richard Seaman's home community. The state is urbanized. The entire Atlantic coastline is essentially a megalopolis from Jacksonville to Key West, but a few miles west of south Florida's coastline lie the state's most desolate swamplands and its harshest prairies, where approximately five hundred cowboys still work livestock in the state.

The common images of Florida as a modern fantasyland, however, obscure its pioneer heritage. Despite the huge metropolitan areas throughout the state, much of the land remains undeveloped, seeded with pine trees or cultivated as farmland.

Florida's frontiers remain even though the state's long history has been drastically changed in a short period of time. These types of rapid changes violate a sense of equilibrium in the state's history that contributes to a sense of disorientation about contemporary life. The disparate mixing of old and new challenges environmentalists and historic preservationists. Not only are the state's ancient and fragile ecosystems stressed by development, but the state's historic structures are also under siege by the physical elements of wind, rain, sun, and rot as well as by the human element of rapid population growth.[6] Managing old and undeveloped lands while supporting economic growth remains a major challenge throughout the state, and these tensions can affect all Floridians.

On a personal level, the tension between old and new directly affects Richard Seaman. He has seen his home community changed drastically by central Florida's rapid growth, and much of the wilderness where he hunted and fished as a boy has been either paved over or subsumed by Orlando's urban sprawl. Visual blight and audio pollution threaten the quality of life in contemporary Florida.[7] If he viewed his tunes and stories as fodder for nativism, it would be understandable.[8] Despite experiencing a certain nostalgia for his lost homeplace, Richard feels more of a loss of human connection in the striking disparities between what is young and old in Florida. The state's elderly population is large, and it includes citizens of old Florida families and retired snowbirds who have chosen to remain in the state. But he has lost his immediate family and most of his long-time friends, and he feels that much of his modern urban life is isolated when compared to the close community connections that he made earlier. He recognizes that he has lived through a century of major changes, and he could use his stories and tunes to escape into a fantasy world of maudlin nostalgia that only admits fellow natives. He has a fresher and healthier view of what he has experienced, however, as his stories and tunes emerge as resources that ameliorate tensions created when balancing the need for continuity while adapting to the drastic changes that he has experienced.[9]

Too often, researchers leave interpretation and theorizing to the scholars. Scholars also frequently privilege the insights and agendas of academic theoreticians at the expense of understanding the value of insights and reflective comments by folk artists, musicians, and other carriers of folk tradition.[10] But those who work with folk performers discover that theorizing is not solely the work of scholars. In their work with folklife festivals, Joe Wilson and Lee Udall discovered that the musicians who perform in public folklore programs often develop rich and interesting conceptions about their participation in these events.[11] Richard Seaman's own ideas, reflections, and interpretation of his folklore should be the basis for understanding his art, and he has also developed a clear sense of what he wishes to accomplish when sharing his talents with the public through school presentations and festivals. His articulate statements about his role in performing tunes and folktales from Florida's history are an important resource for understanding why he continues to present his music and stories to audiences well into his nineties. These values reveal how he regards folklore as an essential resource for living within history as he finds meaning and inspiration in his life in the present.

His interpretive commentary about public folklore and his own theoretical perspectives emerged in an interview that he gave to a local television reporter, Glen Fisher, who produced a news feature story on Mr. Seaman's participation in Folklife in Education programs.[12] Fisher's story includes footage of classroom performances, but he also completed an interview with Richard following one of his presentations. When Fisher asked him what he wanted to accomplish in playing for children, he replied that students need to understand what it was like to live without electricity, cars, and modern conveniences so that they could understand his fiddle tunes. He explained that members of his community were starved for entertainment and that they had to make do on their own if they wanted any recreation. He explained that playing for children helps him "bridge a gap between youngsters and oldsters." He sums up major aesthetic values in his storytelling by explaining that he tries to "paint a picture on the children's minds of what it used to be like in 1910 and '12, way back yonder."

Intrigued by Mr. Seaman's theory of public presentation, I follow up Fisher's interview with questions of my own. I ask him what he would like students to remember from his performances, and he explains that his stories and tunes provide links between his own past and the lives of contemporary schoolchildren: "It's an old tradition. It's something of the past being brought back. The way of life in this country, many years ago, is being renewed, brought back to the public where they can see it. I think that's one of the main things."

He recognizes that his fiddle tunes and stories are valuable artistic expressions for creating intergenerational understanding, but he also assumes a responsibility for telling the stories in a vivid, understandable style. He works to create strong visual imagery through his tall tales and accounts of daily life, and he clearly articulates this storytelling aesthetic, explaining why it is appropriate for classroom presentations. Carefully selecting and presenting concrete images to explain new concepts to children, he provides a solid rationale for his storytelling's aesthetic values: "If a child is paying attention to what it's all about, he can't help but wonder, you know? It comes to the mind of a lot of them. If you can tell a child something clear enough that he has a picture of it, then he's got it."

Richard's concise descriptions of his own vernacular theories suggest deep implications in his subtle statements. Placing value on creating vivid images that he selects from his rich storehouse of knowledge, Richard's storytelling aesthetic addresses a central concern in rhetorical theory. The eighteenth-century rhetorician George Campbell used the term "vivacity" as a central aspect of his rhetorical theory, and much of his writing in *The Philosophy of Rhetoric* analyzes ways in which speakers create lively images through their choice of words, their organization of narrative and discourse, and their abilities to balance perspicuity with elaboration.[13] Richard Seaman uses this aesthetic value to link mechanical technique with the artistic spirit as his stories' vivid images link his own consciousness to the thinking of schoolchildren. The rich details familiarize students with a history that is difficult for them to imagine, but the stories can connect the contemporary present with the historical past. Just as the act of storytelling unifies teller and listener, physical imagery and artistic creativity blur the boundaries between young and old in the artistry of performance. The content of Richard's stories engages children in listening to a story as a creative activity, and he invites his listeners to recognize the value of the concrete image as a spark for creativity.[14] The performance of his stories and tunes creates a sense of even calmness, and his artistry restores a sense of balance and harmony as he provides listeners with a chance to assess huge changes that have occurred within a relatively short span of Florida's history.

Richard can create vivid images because he has lived the social life of his stories' context. Because many of his stories are fanciful and explore the dynamics of truth telling, he works hard to turn quotidian reality into stylized artistic expression.[15] With its complex history of rapid change, Florida provides him with great fodder for playfully stretching the truth, and this play reveals the seriousness with which he honors the importance of speaking the truth. In his tall tales, he emphasizes separating the truth from lies, thereby demonstrating the need to cultivate honesty as a personal resource for daily life. In all of his narratives, he reveals his belief that truth involves a correspondence between the subjective ideas in his mind and the objective reality of experience. His skill at spinning a vivid tale demonstrates how he relies on truthful experience and accurate images to connect with his listeners' imagination. The tales' truths create continuity in ideas as each story flows from a plausible scenario into the hyperbole of fantasy. Throughout all of his storytelling, the truth emerges as a pragmatic resource for working out the exigencies of daily life. He thus affirms that telling the truth is a value essential for social cohesion as his stories teach children to discriminate the truth from a lie. In all of these respects, his story-telling allows Richard to disclose his sense of himself to others.

To understand his artistry fully, it is helpful to imagine the storytelling persona that he has created as a mechanic whose job is to fix things. A highly skilled mechanic himself, Richard Seaman's task in telling stories and playing tunes is one of maintaining and repairing systems. This quality of his artistry begs the question "What is broken?" One answer emerges through considering why he tells stories to establish relationships and reconnect with others. He says that he is often asked if communities were closer in the past. He perceives contemporary communities as fractured, and he sees people as isolated. The system of neighborly survival exists only in vestiges, and neighbors rarely visit with each other. In an untapped conversation, he recounts how a new neighbor once moved in across the street. When Richard saw him working under the hood of his truck and went over to say hello, the new neighbor saw him but did not even respond. Richard explains that he turned around and went back home, feeling "like a damn fool." Even though family and friends still stop by for visits, he has seen the rich social networks of his earlier life broken apart, and much of his socializing now centers around playing and visiting with his friends in Jacksonville's bluegrass music community. With the decline in community cohesiveness, his stories and music reemerge as a center for building and sustaining relationships with others. Part of the pride he places in remembering the past and being able to relate witty tales in the present is derived from ways in which music and story can re-create some of the neighborly bonds that have been broken with the passage of time.

Richard is ambivalent about the major historical changes that he has seen in life. He sees progress as bringing along new opportunities, and he enjoys the new technology and comforts of modern life. His interest in history is not so much a nostalgic appeal for returning to the good old days, which he does not necessarily see as "all that good." Rather, he tells his stories to communicate what he has seen in his life. He communicates his perceptions of what he has experienced through his stories, enfolding his ideas about the value of sharing a spirit of neighborliness within his music. Recognizing why these values are important to him provides a way to understand how he presents himself in performance.

In his public presentations, his stories and fiddling are linked. He wants his listeners to understand the tunes' contexts, knowing that this understanding can bring about a greater appreciation for the tunes. Just as he wishes to have his stories and memories preserved and passed on to future generations, he also wishes to see the tunes preserved. He appreciates the opportunity to let audiences hear a style of fiddling that may be new to them, and he views his participation in festivals and school presentations as doing his part toward preserving the old-time music. When he began playing again in the late 1980s, his style of fiddling was an endangered tradition, and there were virtually no public venues for hearing old-time fiddlers in what is geographically Florida's largest city. Although a recent revival of roots music has opened up new performance spaces, old-time fiddling remains a rarely heard form of cultural expression in Duval County and throughout much of Florida. Searching through Jacksonville's music superstores, it is difficult to find recordings of old-time fiddling anywhere in the greater metropolitan area of over one million people. As the state's oldest active fiddler, Richard is aware of his tunes' value as rare and vibrant links to the early years of the twentieth century, and he knows that their history runs deep into the nineteenth. Modest about his own abilities, he views his performances as doing his part to preserve the old-time music by keeping old favorites alive.

The physical link between Richard's old age and his vital artistic spirit opens up a major facet of his artistry. His answer to a question that I waited to ask—because it seemed like a cliché—further explains why he believes that his old-time tunes and stories continue to have value. I asked him if he had a secret to living such a long and full life. He began by acknowledging his spiritual center. This center makes possible the free play of creativity and imagination that supports his storytelling and musicianship. The center grounds his artistry in a profound sense of the spiritual presence that emerges through artistic expression. His answer transforms a quotidian statement of vernacular theory into poetry:

> Well, I think, I would say—trust in the Good Lord, and don't believe in sickness. Instead of believing that you're sick, believe that you're well. The body is governed by your mind, and your body responds to whatever you want it to do. If you want to go somewhere, it will take you there. And if you let it tell you "you're tired," you're tired. Don't believe it. Don't believe a lie. If you feel a pain, deny it. Don't say "I got it." Just deny it to yourself, "I don't have it." Don't give in to it. That's the way I do it. Don't let your body govern you. God gave you the mind to govern it. If you believe that you're well and healthy, you'll be so. If you believe that you're sick, you'll be sick. Fight against it.
>
> Annie and I, we've been here a long time. And she don't give in. She don't give in, and I don't either. Sometimes, she can't hardly go, but she'll get up, and she'll get there.
>
> We've had to fight a battle in a lot of ways.

I've lost all my people. It leaves a mark on you. When you're a happy family and then all of a sudden, there's nobody but you, it leaves you feeling sort of lost. But you can't let it be. If you let yourself sit around and mope, that's the way you'll be.

If something don't go right, then get your mind on something else and pretty soon you've forgot it. And you've got your mind on what you're doing, and pretty soon, you'll be all right.

You've seen a little boy hollering, "I don't feel good, wah, wah wah, I don't feel good!" Something come around and interest him—he's forgot that and he's going on and having a big time. He's forgot it. A child is more susceptible to that than a grown-up.

Richard laughs, and Annie agrees with what he has told me. Intrigued by what he is saying, I remember the time that he played for an arts festival a week after he had been released from the hospital following surgery for cancer. He continues:

So, don't feel sorry for yourself. A lot of times, I feel out of sorts. Well, I get busy with something. I pick up the fiddle or get some tapes I like to hear and get my mind off myself. That's what I attribute it to because—if you admit it, you got it, if you deny it, you won't have it.

If somebody handed you a hot potato, you wouldn't stand there hollering and raising hell because it's hot, you'd throw it down. If you throw it down, you ain't got it no more. If you accept, you got it. Don't accept it. It's hard to do. Don't accept it. Don't accept anything you don't want. Because if you accept it, you got it.

His music heals. The self, he asserts, is made up of mind, body, and soul, and music will lift the spirit, provided one uses the will to create. Just as his stories link concrete images with the imagination, his fiddling links the mechanical techniques of playing an instrument with the creative spark summoning him to pick up his fiddle and choose to play. His tunes offer a chance for others to share his artistic spirit. The rich associations of his life experiences interanimate the affective appeal of musical expression, and his stories and tunes invite others to share his own life experiences. His performances establish new connections in a fragmented social sphere.

In his study of old men crafting meaning through woodcarving, the folklorist Simon Bronner writes how crafters create similar meanings through artistic acts. The carvers whom Bronner interviewed retreated to their workshops to engage in the creative act of carving wood. Through their artistry, they found release from the feelings of loneliness and isolation that often accompany aging.[16] Master woodcarvers George Blume, Floyd Bennington, Wandley Burch, and Earnest Bennett all revealed how focusing on the order they created by cutting chains from blocks of wood soothed their everyday cares and concerns. Their artistry provided a respite from stress, anxiousness, and the desire to grasp at unfulfilled emotions as their handwork helped them lose their sense of time and released them from an awareness of the self. Their artistry healed through the physical activity of focusing the mind while working with the hands. The carvers worked alone, yet they stopped individual projects to emerge from their workshops, thereby sharing their woodwork with family and friends and finding fulfillment in giving their carvings to others.

Unlike the carvers who worked alone, Richard rarely plays by himself. He prefers to play music with others, and he enjoys opportunities to share his tunes and stories with willing listeners. His will to create emerges through musical expression, and his tunes in turn invigorate his creative will. Just as his tunes create that something that inspires dancers to step through the lively patterns of a dance, his tunes also create a sense of artistry that he shares with fellow musicians and listeners. He prefers the smooth yet lively quality of his tunes to the "banging and crashing" of rock music, and along with playing the old hoe-downs, he especially enjoys playing waltzes and parlor tunes with his friends. Like the carvers, he notes that artistry creates a sense of self-release, and he finds this peace of mind essential to playing well.[17]

This sense of releasing the mind of distractions to cultivate mindfulness was written down twenty-five centuries ago in the *Bhagavad-Gita* as Sri Krishna's "Yoga of Renunciation."[18] The idea was later taught by the Buddha as the principle of detachment.[19] It is a familiar idea to Richard, and he speaks of discovering facets of this way of being when he was a child. One day he told his mother that he was bored with nothing to do, and she told him to play outside. He sat in the yard and watched ants crawling over a leaf and then realized that "all is one" and his boredom turned into fascination. Throughout his life, Richard continues to discover that he can seek and find ways to engage in life while at the same time learn to free himself from worldly cares and concerns. He trusts the Divine reality of healing, and he uses his faith to cast aside anger and fear, finding ways to release what he wishes to discard. Through this precept, his spirituality grounds his creativity just as it demands honest reflection in his stories. Preferring to play his fiddle with friends, he dwells less on the mystery of how art can heal and more on the desire to share and affirm the artistic spirit. Authentic storytelling and careful musicianship communicate this reality to others.[20]

As Richard reflects on his longevity, the tape recorder runs out of tape. As the tape machine's capstan pulls the last few inches of tape over the recording head and onto the take-up reel, the cassette tape preserves Richard's voice as he reflects on his life. Collecting a peace of mind that allows for quiet contemplation, he affirms that he has had a good life. Eyes dancing, he smiles as he tells me that the first thing he does when he wakes up in the morning is to say thanks to God. Not even sure what the day will bring, he just exclaims his gratitude for awakening to find a new day. The recorder winds to a stop with a dull click, and he tells me that he enjoys speaking of the events that we have recorded. He says that at night, lying in bed before falling asleep, he often plays through the tunes in his mind and that he thinks of the stories he holds in his memory. He remembers his childhood in Kissimmee Park, his work with the railroad, his fiddling with his family bands, and his performances in schools and at the festivals. And he thinks of Annie as she sleeps next to him.

11

The Icing on the Cake

~

When from a satchel,
A fiddle, he drew.
He played her a message,
That made the hills ring.
          —From "The Nightingale's Song"*

O n the first day that I interviewed Richard, he asked me to come early in the afternoon. We talked for an hour while the tape recorder was running, and we spent some time visiting after I packed away all of the recording equipment. He explained that he needed to make sure that he had time open later in the afternoon because he was going to meet a friend. Richard told me that he had been spending time with her following his wife Daisy's death, and they usually had dinner together every evening.

Three years later, I am interviewing Richard once again, and he tells how he first met Annie.

When I first come to Jacksonville and went to work for the Seaboard, I went to work in 'twenty-six, and I didn't get married till 'thirty. But in 1929, I met Annie.

She was a young girl—quite a bit younger than I was at the time. Still is. But anyhow, we used to go around. We were nothing serious— you know what I mean. We'd go to parties. Whenever it was convenient, we'd take a ride somewhere, or things like that. I didn't consider marriage or anything like that. Finally we just sort of drifted around, and I met my wife. We got married. I lost all contact with her and didn't see her all those years. I was married fifty-six years.[1]

Annie tells almost the same story as Richard. But she notes that she did see him after they had courted each other when she was in her late teens. She remembers catching glimpses of Richard during the 1930s: "He was staying at a boardinghouse, and my brother-in-law had a barber shop. And so when we'd go down to take his lunch to him—and things I'd go down there for—I used to see Richard. And just see him. We got together, but before then, I got married, see? Richard and I weren't seeing each other, and I got married to T. K. Bivins."[2]

Their story is emerging as Annie picks up the narrative after their initial courtship. I ask her to return to the earlier time when she was courted by Richard. "Before you married Mr. Bevins, you went out with Richard a little bit?"

Annie recollects that she went on only a few dates with Richard before they each met their different spouses, concluding that they were never serious and that he must have been just playing the field. For decades, Richard and Annie lived only a few miles away from each other, yet they never saw each other for over half a century. Annie continues her story: "I didn't even see him, but when his wife passed away, I recognized the name. And that's how we started back together. I didn't know who he married or anything about him. I didn't know anything about his family. So that started it."

Richard picks up their story: "She saw my wife's obituary in the paper and called me up to offer condolences. I didn't know what her name was. She'd married, and I didn't know who she'd married. And so we started going together and sort of started up where we left off way back in time. I went to see her a couple times. We just went together for about a year after we met. And we went different places, saw different things, just traveled around—pass the time away and do different things—eat out. Whatever we'd want to do, just to pass the time away. And I guess she liked it. When I asked her to marry me, she said, 'Huh?! Yeah, I guess so.'"

Annie comments on receiving a marriage proposal while she was in her mid-seventies, explaining that Richard's offer was unexpected: "I didn't think he was ever going to propose. We were at the house, and he asked me would I marry him. And I kind of hesitated, and I told him 'Yes.' So that started being serious about it. It's just been great. Great."

Annie reiterates that she hesitated to accept the proposal for a while, so I ask her if Richard had swept her off her feet. Her eyes brighten and her laugh sweetens the soft southern accent that carries her strong voice: "Yes, he did! No, I had it made. But living alone—it's different."

Richard provides his rationale for offering a marriage proposal when he was in his mid-eighties: "Well, the thing of it was, she needed somebody, and I needed somebody."

Annie adds that she was not looking to remarry after the loss of her husband, explaining that she did not go out on any dates following her thirty-year marriage to T. K. Bivins. Affirming what she says, Richard adds: "We didn't intend to get married. I didn't. But after we got to going together, I guess it just sort of grew on us. It just sort of happened. And so we decided that we'd finish up our time on earth here and try and help one another. She needed help, and I did too."

Annie provides more details about remarrying late in life: "We was both nervous when we started the courtship. We had about a year before we got married. We got married the seventeenth of December in 1988."

Richard and Annie remain happily married. Annie made a decision to leave her home to live with Richard. They have set up housekeeping at Richard's home in the Avondale section of Jacksonville. They spend most of their time together, traveling throughout the state where they enjoy listening to bluegrass and old-time music. Annie is usually in the audience, seated in a lawn chair when Richard steps out on stage to play his fiddle and tell his tales.

Richard and Annie Seaman complete their love story. "We've made a go of it. We've never had an argument. We've got our freedom. She does what she wants to do, and I do what I want to. I help her, and she helps me. And we couldn't want nothing better."

I comment, "And you've got a good life now with Richard."

"Oh Lord, that put the icing on the cake. It sure did. We get along good. No problems. No problems. Richard, he's just had so many disappointments that I wouldn't hurt his feeling for nothing in the world. He's just a fine, fine person. I've never seen anybody just like him. I sure haven't. He's great. I've never known anybody like him. He sure is a wonderful person. He's just God-sent as far as I know. Being with Richard, I was blessed."

We both were.

Postscript

~

It was my privilege to know Richard Seaman for over fifteen years. The story of Richard and Annie's courtship is an important part of their life histories, and it provides the context for the "Annie Seaman Waltz." This tune has been picked up by fiddlers throughout Florida, and musicians who knew Richard often tell the story when introducing the waltz. I feel that his musical life history is concluded with this story, but the historical record needs completion.

I returned to Florida in March 2000 when I accepted a position as a folk arts coordinator with the Florida Folklife Program. I continued to interview Richard and document his stories and tunes while in Florida, but I also spent numerous afternoons visiting Richard and Annie when I could make the trip across the state from Tallahassee to Jacksonville. One morning I had a call from Richard. When I asked how he was doing, he told me he was "all busted up." He had taken a fall at home and was in a nursing home recocovering from surgery. I visited him that weekend, and he was in good spirits, feeling more embarrassed than in pain about his accident. A few weeks later, his doctors released him and he returned to his active life.

Shortly after he came home, Richard called me once again. This time it was Annie who had fallen. After surgery she convalesced in a nursing home, but she didn't pull through the recovery period. Annie Johns Bivins Seaman died on March 7, 2001.

When I was working in Florida during this time, one of my responsibilities was to coordinate the Florida Folk Heritage Award Program offered by the Florida Department of State. This program, initiated in 1985, honors traditional artists and musicians who have made lifelong contributions to the state's folklife. Florida's program is modeled after National Heritage Fellowships awarded by the National Endowment for the Arts to honor the contributions of folk artists to our nation's cultural heritage. Past winners in Florida include fiddlers Chubby Wise and George Custer, with whom Richard played during the First Coast Folklife Exploration. After a conversation with Jack Piccalo, I found that he had reactivated Richard's nomination, and I sent a large packet of support materials for the Florida Folklife Council to review during their quarterly meeting. On Memorial Day weekend in 2001, the State of Florida honored Richard Seaman with one of the state's heritage awards in recognition of his contributions as a fiddler and storyteller. Richard gave his acceptance speech on the stage of the Florida Folk Festival anad graciously thanked his friends and supporters for this recognition. Jack Piccalo sat on the stage as his guest of honor.

I had the chance to visit Richard and play tunes with him after this time, and Richard continued to play with his band at the annual Florida Folk Festival the next year. Whenever travel took me to Jacksonville, I would be sure to stop to see him in the white frame house on Bridal Street. Because of cuts to the state's budget for folklife and historic preservation, I moved from Florida in August 2002. After this time, Richard accepted his family's offer to move in with them in Palm Coast. His usual good health had failed, and he recognized that he needed to accept their help. Richard died on October 18, 2002, a couple of months before his ninety-eighth birthday.

Tunes

Annie Seaman Waltz

Dance All Night with a Bottle in My Hand

Stoney Point

Ragtime Annie

Sally Gooden

Shear 'Em

Whistling Rufus

Unnamed tune learned from Willie Jones

Notes

~

Introduction: Fiddler's Stories

1. Simon Bronner, *Old-Time Music Makers of New York State,* xiv.
2. "Performance theory" describes an eclectic array of approaches, methods, and theories used in the study of folklore. Within the vast literature, the following sources provide an essential basis for examining how an analysis of folklore within its performative contexts yields an understanding of a system of knowledge and ability termed "competence." Dan Ben-Amos and Kenneth Goldstein's edited volume *Folklore: Performance and Communication,* Richard Bauman's *Verbal Art as Performance,* and Dell Hymes's *"In Vain I Tried to Tell You": Essays in Native American Ethnopoetics* include foundational articles that brought the study of performance into folklore. Henry Glassie centers his ethnographic methods on performance studies in numerous works, including *Passing the Time in Ballymenone: Culture and History of an Ulster Community.* Edward D. Ives used a performance-centered orientation in his study of a ballad singer's life in *Joe Scott: The Woodsman-Songmaker* as well as in subsequent scholarship. Kenneth Burke's theory of dramatism underlies various approaches to performance; his *Dramatism and Development* provides a unified view of his theory. Performance theorists adapted, and critiqued, Noam Chomsky's articulation of distinctions between competence and performance in his early theories of transformational-generative grammar, especially as presented in *Aspects of the Theory of Syntax.* Recent overviews and applications of

contemporary performance-centered approaches are discussed in Deborah A. Kapchan's article "Performance" and in a special issue on performance theory edited by Harris M. Berger and Giovanna P. Del Negro in the *Journal of American Folklore* ("Toward New Perspectives on *Verbal Art* as Performance").

3. The critique of logocentrism offered by Jacque Derrida in *Of Grammatology*, 9–29, provides a basic text for his program of poststructuralist deconstructionism. In replacing the phonemes of the spoken word with the grammatological "grapheme" and foregrounding the importance of traces, Derrida provides an approach to critiquing empirical foundations in literary criticism. Performance theory can be read through deconstructionism, but I find there to be great value in what Derrida critiques as "logocentrism." Namely, most performance-centered approaches are built from an empirically grounded science of the concrete. There are intricate systems within Richard's fiddling and storytelling, and a logocentric perspective is closer to his theory of artistic creativity.

4. James Deetz, *In Small Things Forgotten: The Archaeology of Early American Life*, 131.

5. Kenneth Burke's distinction between the "psychology of information" and the "psychology of form" is presented in a number of his writings. The essential essay is "Psychology and Form," in *Counter-Statement*, 29–44. In distinguishing between the content of what is said versus the range of aesthetic qualities and emotional associations that accompany this information, Burke provides important perspectives for expanding ideas about analysis and interpretation.

6. David E. Whisnant, *All That Is Native and Fine: The Politics of Culture in an American Region*, 13–15.

7. Nancy Michael, Preface to *A Teacher's Guide to the Duval County Folklife in Education Program* by Gregory Hansen, v.

8. Thomas McLaughlin, *Street Smarts and Critical Theory: Listening to the Vernacular*.

Chapter 1. Arts Mania

1. Although The Landing was not established to create venues for folklife programming, the staff has supported various folk culture programs. In "Cultural Conservation and Economic Recovery Planning: The Pennsylvania Heritage Parks Program," Shalom Staub provides a model and case study for examining folklife programming in relation to economic development within urban environments.

2. Joe Wilson and Lee Udall provide a good discussion of various genres of folklife festival presentations in *Folk Festivals: A Handbook for Organization and Management*, 77–87. Their discussion on matching musicians with appropriate stage settings is essential reading for those thinking about full performance stages versus workshop presentations at festivals. Richard Kurin's *Reflections of a Culture Broker: A View from the Smithsonian* provides additional case studies and discussion of the major concerns in staging folk culture presentations in appropriate venues.

3. I have presented these renditions in this chapter to provide a verbatim transcript of a festival performance and to show ways in which Richard varies his storytelling within performances. For tale types and motifs, see the discussion in Chapter 4, "Your Words Was Your Bond," where I provide historical context and commentary on these tales and other stories in his repertoire.

4. This text is a variant of Aarne-Thompson Tale Type 1414: *The Returning Husband Hoodwinked*. The story is rooted in Irish, English, Anglo-American, and African-American oral traditions.

5. When Richard refers to "Kissimmee Prairie," he is discussing the ranchland and orchards between Kissimmee and the Everglades. At times, he refers to this area simply as "Kissimmee," but he also distinguishes the rural area from the actual town of Kissimmee.

6. Interest in how a musician and storyteller uses folklore to craft an effective performance is central to performance-centered approaches to folklore. While the theory has limited value for assessing how all members of the audience evaluated Richard's performance, the approach is useful in examining the knowledge, skill, and abilities that Richard Seaman and Jack Piccolo have displayed in various presentations. Americó Paredes and Richard Bauman's edited volume *Toward New Perspectives in Folklore* includes a new introduction to this work of key theoretical essays. The volume's central idea of examining folklore within various performance contexts provides a useful way to compensate for a purely grammatological reading as suggested by Jacques Derrida in *Of Grammatology*.

7. Folklorists tend to avoid a preservationist approach in their research. Steve Siporin defends the concept of "eleventh-hour ethnography" by arguing that important artistic and cultural resources are lost and derided in a quest for documenting "modern" forms of cultural expression. "On Scapegoating Public Folklore," 89.

Chapter 2. And the Merry Love the Fiddle

*Yeats' poem is commemorated through Sligo's prestigious "Fiddler of Dooney" competition and festival.

1. From an interview with Richard and Annie Seaman that I conducted on May 19, 1998, at their home in Jacksonville, Florida.

2. Between 1880 and the mid-1920s, Florida's population experienced its first major period of growth. In 1880, the population was estimated to be 270,000. A major migration during Reconstruction brought many southern farmers as well as northern entrepreneurs and workers into the state. By the mid 1920s, Florida's population reached 1 million. Richard's home community of Kissimmee Park was a sparsely populated rural area that was carved out as a subdivision following Hamilton Disston's major land purchase in central Florida. Charles Tebeau's *New History of Florida* provides an excellent history of booms and busts in Florida history.

3. The majority of Richard's stories in this chapter are from interviews that I conducted with him on May 18 and 19, 1998, at his home in Jacksonville, and there

are short excerpts from an interview on September 28, 1991. Rather than editing all of this interview material into one massive life history, I have compiled them into a series of stories and descriptions to reflect the unity of his narratives. I have included transitional comments drawn from notes and informal conversations with Richard to unify his descriptions. My commentary also marks points where individual stories begin and end.

4. Sandra Dolby Stahl's *Literary Folkloristics and the Personal Narrative*, 12–14, provides an important description of this genre. Richard Seaman is most comfortable talking about his life history through personal experience narratives and descriptions of his home community. He also provides biographical information through stage patter and tall tales.

5. Scholars of American fiddling provide special attention to the square dances held primarily in homes. These are sometimes known as "house parties," and numerous stories about house parties that are similar to Richard's can be found in Philip Martin's study of Wisconsin fiddling, *Farmhouse Fiddlers: Music and Dance Traditions in the Rural Midwest*.

6. Along with the stories in Martin's book, Drew Beisswenger offers a thorough presentation of "roll back the rug" stories in *Fiddling Way Out Yonder: The Life and Music of Melvin Wine*.

7. A thorough discussion of square dancing and callers can be found in Paul L. Tyler's "'Sets on the Floor': Social Dance as an Emblem of Community in Rural Indiana." The square dance figures that Richard describes are all common patterns.

8. This patter call is from a cartoon that Richard drew.

9. Improved transportation and changes in social life were major factors in the demise of house parties by the 1950s. Joyce H. Cauthen provides a good discussion of these changes in *With Fiddle and Well-Rosined Bow: A History of Old-Time Fiddling in Alabama*, 37–40.

10. Numerous fiddlers tell stories of fights at dances that are similar to Richard's account. A good discussion of violence at square dances can be found in Gerald Milnes's *Play of a Fiddle: Traditional Music, Dance, and Folklore in West Virginia*, 118–23.

11. Although the guitar is commonly used to accompany contemporary fiddlers, Richard's account of solo fiddling appears to be typical. In *Southern Music/ American Music*, 10, Bill Malone and David Stricklin assert that widespread adoption of guitar accompaniment began with innovations in guitar manufacturing and the introduction of steel strings in 1900. Banjos and mandolins were sometimes used earlier to accompany fiddlers, but it was common for fiddlers to play solo or with someone beating straws.

12. Jill Linzee, *A Reference Guide to Florida Folklore from the Federal WPA Deposited in the Florida Folklife Archives*.

13. Wiley L. Housewright, *A History of Music and Dance in Florida, 1565–1865*, 295–97.

14. The associations of the fiddle with the Devil are rich in folklore. See Charles

Wolfe's *The Devil's Box: Masters of Southern Fiddling*, xv–xvii, and Milnes's *Play of a Fiddle*, 69–73.

15. Yehudi Menuhin's *The Violin*, 100–116, includes discussion of various diabolical associations attached both to fiddling and to classical violin playing.

16. This communal system of reciprocity is evident in numerous rural communities. Marjorie Kinnan Rawlings describes the same values in a nearby community in *Cross Creek*, 67.

17. Henry Glassie, *Passing the Time in Ballymenone*, 291.

18. This theme of valuing both personal freedom and communal cooperation is present in the literature on rural Florida during the time period that Richard is describing. J. T. Glisson's writing on Cross Creek, Florida, in *The Creek*, 173, explores these values in his discussion of a similar farming and fishing community in central Florida.

19. Kathy Neustadt, *Clambake: A History and Celebration of an American Tradition*, 158.

20. Burt Feintuch, "Square Dancing and Clogging," in *Encyclopedia of Southern Culture*, 1034.

21. The history and development of various dance figures and their relation to social structure are described in Tyler's " 'Sets on the Floor.' " Forming "the big circle" means that all of the participating dancers create one massive circle in one room. This formation was often used to complete an evening of square dancing, especially in Richard's home community. This tradition was apparently common in dances in America's southern states.

22. The value of reciprocity and helping the neighbors with no expectation of payment shows up in Glassie's study of Ballymenone. It also is evident in Rawlings's writing on central Florida in *Cross Creek*, 117.

23. Many older residents have provided me with similar descriptions about leaving their homes open to neighbors. Rawlings, *Cross Creek*, 123, and Glisson, *The Creek*, 96, support Richard's memory that doors were rarely locked in their rural communities.

Chapter 3. Workshop

1. Betty Belanus provides a realistic description of the preparation and coordination of similar folklife festivals in her novel *Seasonal*.

2. Chubby Wise frequently used local bluegrass bands when playing in his later years. Salt Run accompanied Chubby for various events and backed Wise later that evening for a concert on the festival's main stage.

3. Instrument makers and repairers are considered elite crafters, and their use of water-soluble glue is essential for preserving instruments. Part of the humor revolves around the potential for Richard to ruin a badly damaged instrument by his willingness to take the matter into his own hands.

4. Numerous musicians swap stories about learning to play instruments.

Similar stories told by blues players can be found in Barry Lee Pearson's *"Sounds So Good to Me:" The Bluesman's Story*.

5. Chubby Wise played an important role in popularizing "The Orange Blossom Special," but it is most likely that Ervin Rouse wrote the tune. For a different account of the tune's origin and a discussion of Rouse and Wise's musical careers, see Randy Noles's *Orange Blossom Boys: The Untold Story of Ervin T. Rouse, Chubby Wise and the World's Most Famous Fiddle Tune*.

6. Chubby Wise is featured in a full-page color photograph in Bruce Watson's article "This Here's All for Foot Tappin' and Grin Winnin'."

7. For a discussion of this tune, see Charles Wolfe's "'Over the Waves': Notes toward a History" in his volume *The Devil's Box*, 183–85. The waltz is common to many fiddlers' repertories, and Richard occasionally plays it.

8. Chubby Wise is recorded on a number of records, tapes, and compact disks. A recording that preserves his playing at the time of this workshop is "Chubby Wise in Nashville" (Orlando: Pinecastle Records, 1994).

9. Bill Malone's *Country Music USA*, 158–75, includes a thorough discussion of the development of western swing. See also Malone and Stricklin's *Southern Music/American Music*, 82–89.

10. Some fiddlers use the term "busking" to refer to playing for small change or meals. Kenner C. Kartchner's *Frontier Fiddler: The Life on a Northern Arizona Pioneer* provides excellent descriptions of busking in a fiddler's life history.

11. *The Texas Fiddle Collection* (Los Angeles: CMH Music, 1988) is an excellent recording of old-time, western swing, and jazz tunes by Johnny Gimble.

12. Jill Linzee's *A Reference Guide to Florida Folklore* includes "Shear 'Em," but the tune was misidentified by WPA fieldworkers as "Sharon." It is likely that some fiddlers called the tune "Sharon" and that Chubby's story reflects either a local fiddler's nickname or a folk etymology. Chubby did pronounce the title as "Sharon," and the transcript is my phonetic representation.

13. It is likely that the derisive exclamation "fiddle sticks" is derived from a reference to fiddle beaters. A plausible rationale for this association is that someone playing fiddle sticks is posing as a sham fiddler. A violin bow is also sometimes referred to as a "fiddle stick," so a precise etymology is difficult to ascertain.

14. It is common for bluegrass musicians to include hymns in their shows, and in his later years, Chubby Wise typically played a gospel song to close out each show.

15. Kathy Neustadt provides relevant discussion of ways that an intensified sense of identity emerges in festivals in her book *Clambake*, 154–58. George Custer's comments affirm individual participation within an increased sense of communal creation.

16. George Custer, Richard Seaman, and Chubby Wise never performed together following this presentation, and this was the only workshop that Chubby Wise ever participated in at a folklife festival. Chubby continued to play actively until his death on January 6, 1996, at the age of eighty.

17. Joyce Cauthen includes a good discussion of trick fiddling and photographs of Charlie Atkins playing "Pop Goes the Weasel" in various trick positions in *With Fiddle and Well-Rosined Bow*, 174–75.

18. Cauthen's description (37–39) of fiddling's waning popularity and its revival in Alabama supports Wise and Custer's description.

19. Chubby Wise's story complements Neil Rosenberg's description of Bill Monroe's incorporation of fiddling into bluegrass in *Bluegrass: A History*, 55–64.

20. Although fiddlers strive to conserve a particular old-time sound in their playing, Richard's comments demonstrate that his aesthetic values include an emphasis on honing an individual style within the tradition. An emphasis on innovation is perhaps stronger among bluegrass and western swing fiddlers, but its roots are in an aesthetic system shared by many old-time fiddlers.

Chapter 4. An Anthology of Tall Tales

1. Lewis Seaman is described as the charter captain in Joseph T. Rothrock and Jane Rothrock's *Chesapeake Odysseys: An 1883 Cruise Revisited*. Richard does not recall when Lewis arrived in Florida, but he believes that this voyage encouraged the move from Pennsylvania. Lawrence E. Will's *Okeechobee Boats and Skippers* provides illustrations and historical information on the types of vessels that plied Florida's inland waters during Lewis Seaman's time as a waterman.

2. J. T. Glisson outlines this same value in rural Florida's folk culture in *The Creek*, 188. "Your word is your bond" is a traditional proverb that I first heard in Florida.

3. Linzee, *A Reference Guide to Florida Folklore*. A number of Richard's tunes and stories were documented in central Florida by WPA fieldworkers during the 1930s. Audio recordings and fieldnotes are archived at the Division of Historical Resource's archives in Tallahassee, and Linzee's guide is a valuable aid for locating materials. The Library of Congress's American Folklife Center has produced "Florida Folklife from the WPA Collections, 1937–1942." This Web site includes selected audio recordings and can be accessed at http://memory.loc.gov/ammem/flwpahtml/flwpahome.html.

4. Stetson Kennedy, *Palmetto Country*, 221–24. Kennedy collected this legend while directing the WPA's Federal Writers Project in Florida. His social history of Florida folklore contains ample material on Florida folklife. Two other excellent sources for myths, legends, tall tales, and other narratives collected in Florida are J. Russell Reaver's *Florida Folktales* and Kristin G. Congdon's *Uncle Monday and Other Florida Tales*. All three volumes include versions of tales in Richard's repertory.

5. Tape-recorded interview with Richard Seaman, Jacksonville, December 17, 1999. All other interview material in this chapter is from this session.

6. Henry Glassie, *Passing the Time in Ballymenone*, 39. Glassie argues that

ethnopoetic renditions emphasize differences between the oral qualities of spoken prose and the written word. This style of visual representation is surprisingly controversial. Brian Swann's edited volume *Coming to Light: Contemporary Translations of the Native Literatures of North America* is an excellent volume for reading additional examples of texts rendered in ethnopoetics, and the book's introduction, headnotes, and bibliography provide a range of arguments about the controversy.

7. This perspective on Richard's tall tales is derived from discussions that I held with him and observations of his performances. These generalizations are also supported by Richard Bauman's fine summary of research on tall tales presented in *Story, Performance, and Event: Contextual Studies of Oral Narrative*. This volume includes the article "'Any Man Who Keeps More'n One Hound'l Lie to You': A Contextual Study of Expressive Lying," 1–32, an especially useful article for understanding the tall tale genre in relation to Richard's storytelling.

8. Richard recorded this tape sometime between 1990 and 1994. He often documented his own fiddle tunes, public performances, and stories with his audio tape recorder or his video camera. I found his idea of a folk musician serving as his own folklorist incredibly useful, and each narrative in this chapter is from this recording.

9. The idea that there are prototypic patterns for understanding a story's syntax is presented in Vladímir Propp's foundational study, *Morphology of the Folktale*. Propp regarded the pattern of Russian fairy tales to be an idealized construct of the researcher, and he outlined thirty-one specific elements within a narrative's plot. This approach is useful for looking at the basic structure of Richard's tall tales at the abstract level. "Sister's Milk Cow" includes basic features that are present in numerous variations in most of his other stories.

10. William Ferris, "The Dogtrot: A Mythic Image in Southern Culture," 75.

11. An important part of documenting the history and distribution of folklore involves identifying tale types and motifs using indexes developed by Stith Thompson and Ernest Baughman. In this chapter, all references to these types and motifs are in the following sources: Ernest W. Baughman, *Type and Motif Index of the Folktales of England and North America*; Stith Thompson, *Motif-Index of Folk Literature*; and Stith Thompson, *The Types of the Folktale*. Thompson's landmark study *The Folktale* contains a fine description of tall tales (214–17) and includes a concise type and motif index.

12. Vance Randolph, *We Always Lie to Strangers: Tall Tales from the Ozarks*, 184; Roberta Strauss Feuerlicht, ed., *The Legends of Paul Bunyan*, 107–9.

13. Richard Dorson, *Negro Folktales in Michigan*, 179. It is likely that the majority of the stories that Dorson collected from African-Americans in the 1950s were originally part of southern folklore. Their presence in Michigan is due to the great migration of black Americans from the South.

14. Douglas R. Hofstadter has an excellent discussion of recursion in *Gödel, Escher, Bach: An Eternal Golden Braid*, 127–33. Recursion is a process that also allows for the creation of new systems and subsystems from an open-ended set of compo-

nents and formal processes. It is a common property of mathematics, computer programming, linguistics, music theory, and storytelling.

15. Kennedy, *Palmetto Country*, 25.

16. Glen Simons and Laura Ogden provide a fine discussion of folklife in the Everglades, especially in relation to environmental change and life history in their book *Gladesmen: Gator Hunters, Moonshiners, and Skiffers*.

17. Richard Dorson, *Buying the Wind: Regional Folklore in the United States*, 350.

18. Zora Neale Hurston, *Mules and Men*, 109–10.

19. Sandra Dolby Stahl argues that reader-response criticism can be applied to folklore genres. She uses the approach mainly to look at personal experience narratives, and I have loosely adapted her ideas as a major resource for some my own commentary. Dolby discusses this model in *Literary Folkloristics and the Personal Narrative* (Bloomington: Indiana University Press, 1989), 6–11.

20. Bauman, "'Any Man Who Keeps More'n One Hound'll Lie to You'," 22.

21. In contrast to Propp's syntagmatic structuralism, Claude Lévi-Strauss's voluminous writing on paradigmatic structuralism provides useful ways to understand symbolic mediators that bridge gaps between concepts in binary opposition. Lévi-Strauss's *The Story of Lynx* brings his earlier formulations of structuralism into contemporary scholarship and addresses some of the critiques of structuralism present in poststructuralist discourse.

22. It is too simple to make a sharp distinction between "feminine interiors" and "masculine exteriors," but an ironing board carries strong symbolic associations of feminized domestic spaces, just as a fur stretcher evokes masculine associations with outdoor sports. In her book *Homeplace: The Social Use and Meaning of the Folk Dwelling in Southwestern North Carolina*, Michael Ann Williams applies the concept of gendered space as an integral component of vernacular architecture.

23. Kenneth Burke's *Counter-Statement* remains an essential resource for examining artistic uses of form. Merging Burke's formalism with perspectives from structuralism and performance theory provides a useful resource for discovering how the infrastructure of Richard Seaman's tall tales is united with his aesthetic sensibilities.

24. Randolph, *We Always Lie to Strangers*, 102.

25. Keith H. Basso, "Stalking with Stories," and N. Scott Momaday, *The Way to Rainy Mountain*.

26. Lowell Thomas, *Tall Stories: The Rise and Triumph of the Great American Whopper*, 36–41.

27. Robert Thomson, "*Non Nimium Credendum Antiquitati:* But Don't Throw the Baby out with the Bathwater," 40–42. A similar version of Richard Seaman's text can be found in Randolph, *We Always Lie to Strangers*, 226. This tall tale has also been set to music. Dorsey Dixon wrote "Fisherman's Luck," and the Dixon Brothers recorded this old-time version of the song in 1937. It is available on a compact disc reissued in 2001 as *The Dixon Brothers*, vol. 2, *1937* on Document Records. Their melody is close to the melody of the "Washbash Cannonball." Slats Klug and

Stephen Miller's audio recording *Liar's Bench: Musical Portraits of Brown County* also includes a variant of the story in song that they entitled "The Snake that Liked His Brew," performed by Steve Miller. This rendition is more of a tone poem than a country tune, but it is closer to Richard Seaman's version of the tale.

28. A good discussion of local taxonomies as they pertain to relationships between humans and animals can be found in Elizabeth Atwood Lawrence, *Rodeo: An Anthropologist Looks at the Wild and the Tame*. Lawrence's reading of the metaphorical quality of rodeo as a symbol of taming the Wild West provides a useful way to think about Richard's stories about fish, game, livestock, and pets. Marjorie Kinnan Rawlings provides an interesting discussion of Florida's wildlife taxonomies in rural Florida and discusses how local residents make major distinctions between "varmints" and "beasts" in *Cross Creek*, 156–57.

29. Marjorie Kinnan Rawlings, *The Yearling*.

30. J. T. Glisson's *The Creek*, 156–61, includes an incident in which the author's pet sow causes major damages in the Cross Creek community. Glisson lived next door to Rawlings, and he served as a model for Jody. Many of the values that relate a community's social order to the conceptualization of the natural order are present in his writing.

31. Lawrence, *Rodeo*, 223.

32. Dorson, *Negro Folktales*, 46.

33. Kristin Congdon's excellent anthology *Uncle Monday and Other Florida Tales* includes numerous animal tales from Seminole and African-American storytelling traditions. Congdon also includes a few animal tales that are derived from European sources, but these texts would be considered household tales rather than tall tales.

34. Dorson, *Negro Folktales*, 46, and Hurston, *Mules and Men*, 108–9.

35. Clifford Geertz, *Works and Lives: The Anthropologist as Author*, 14. Robert Cantwell's *Ethnomimesis: Folklife and the Representation of Culture* provides an interesting discussion of stereotyping in public presentations of folk culture. Although Cantwell critiques pernicious stereotypes that can emerge in display events, his argument about the futility of attempts to abolish stereotyping is a strong one. Linking stereotyping with myth-making, he provides a useful way to understand how a stereotypical symbol can serve as an entry point for negotiating cross-cultural interaction. His discussion of stereotyping as an important component of the infrastructure of display events can be found in his chapter "The Ink Spots: Folklife and Stereotypes," 150–84.

36. Milan Kundera, *Immortality*, 332.

37. This characteristic antipathy to snakes is common in writing on Florida's folk culture; see Glisson, *The Creek*, 44–48.

38. Another of Milan Kundera's novels, *The Joke*, is a masterful treatment of the schisms between mind and body and a serious inquiry into the role of humor in totalitarian states.

Chapter 5. Uncle Josie's Farm

*In the spring of 1985, I recorded a fiddler named Marvin Tingle in Milton, Kentucky. His fiddle-playing son, Philip, provided this quote after the recorder was turned off.

1. Michael Gannon, *Florida: A Short History,* 85.

2. Stetson Kennedy, *Palmetto Country,* 213–38.

3. Improved rail service contributed to Florida's boom in population and economic development during the 1920s. The Seaboard Air Line opened regular rail service from Jacksonville to Miami, and other companies established lines throughout the eastern seaboard and into the Midwest. Employment with the railroads was attractive because of its security and relatively solid wages. Gannon, *Florida: A Short History,* 53–61, 77.

4. Various urban communities also maintained the tradition of hosting frolics, although square dancing at house parties in the South is usually associated with rural farmhouses as in Malone and Stricklin's *Southern Music/American Music,* 11–12.

5. Gerald Milnes provides similar stories about busking in *Play of a Fiddle,* 126.

6. Richard Blaustein writes that the first known fiddling contest in the United States was held as part of a St. Andrew's Day celebration in Hanover County, Virginia, in 1736; see *The Thistle and the Brier: Historical Links and Cultural Parallels Between Scotland and Appalachia,* 73. For a discussion of fiddle contests and fiddlers' conventions during this time period, see Joyce H. Cauthen's *With Fiddle and Well-Rosined Bow,* 163–200. Richard agrees with Cauthen's view that contests flourished in the 1920s and '30s as a way to preserve older styles of fiddling. His perspective that fiddling was popular in Jacksonville is well supported, for this particular contest drew a sizeable audience of 1,000 people in a city of 190,000 (*Florida Times-Union,* May 16, 1930).

7. *Florida Times-Union,* May 16, 1930. An announcement for the contest was published on May 15 and May 8.

8. Richard is not precise in dating his time on the radio, but it was in the early 1930s. WJAX (900/AM) was a 1,000-watt station that the City of Jacksonville owned at this time. Its station and tower were located in the downtown area in the Klutho and Confederate Park complex. The station hosted old-time and gospel musicians from the area. The call letters are now owned by Jones College, and WJAX (1220/AM) is the sister station of WKTZ (90.9/FM). Jones College Radio markets its programming as "Beautiful Music and Easy Listening."

9. Richard's view that radio programmers opportunistically capitalized on old-time fiddling in the late 1920s and early 1930s is well supported in Joyce Cauthen's *With Fiddle and Well-Rosined Bow,* 24–33. She documents an early radio broadcast of old-time fiddling on WAPI in Birmingham by the Johnson String Band in March 1926. Cauthen notes that informal broadcasts of fiddle tunes continued into the

mid-1930s. These types of informal live performances contributed to the popularity of radio programs with a rural theme by the 1930s, as described in Peter Stanfield in *Horse Opera: The Strange History of the 1930s Singing Cowboy*, 66–70. "Uncle Josie's Farm" never reached the popularity of the Grand Ole Opry and the National Barn Dance, but it was typical of smaller radio programs of the era.

10. Bill C. Malone's *Singing Cowboys and Musical Mountaineers: Southern Culture and the Roots of Country Music*, 93–97, discusses how early radio programs and recordings established enduring images of "hillbillies," rural southerners, and cowboys. The images were established by the time Richard began playing on the radio, and he views the show as providing opportunities to advertise his band and make jokes about tensions between country and city life. The show ended when WJAX had access to other performers and more marketable recordings.

11. Ferdinand Tönnies, *Community and Society*, 59.

12. Tönnies intended this dichotomy to be an idealized description of abstract systems of order rather than a caricature of country folk versus city people. Much of his writing asserts that little communities are formed within urban areas, and he argues that there are multiple configurations of social life within any population. The argument that old-time fiddling and dancing is related to *Gemeinschaft* social structure has ample support in the literature. Philip Martin writes, for example, how Wisconsin fiddlers use the term "neighboring" to describe Richard's system of "neighborly survival" in his study *Farmhouse Fiddlers*, 49. His argument is supported by Henry Glassie's discussion of fiddling and storytelling in Ballymenone in *Passing the Time in Ballymenone*, 96–102. Simon Bronner develops the argument in his study of chain carving, *The Carver's Art: Crafting Meaning from Wood*.

13. Glen Simons and Laura Ogden provide an extended discussion of bootlegging and moonshining activities in south Florida in their book *Gladesmen: Gator Hunters, Moonshiners, and Skiffers*. They explain that moonshining was especially popular in the Everglades because of the region's remoteness. Rural north Florida of the 1920s and '30s also was sparsely populated, and the nearby swamps and timberlands provided similar cover for illegal activities.

14. There are other stories of moonshining fiddlers who knew how to work the law. Joyce Cauthen provides a similar story in *With Fiddle and Well-Rosined Bow*, 128–29.

15. Although Richard and other fiddlers in Florida associate Florida frolics with moonshining and fighting, various fiddlers in the Midwest remember playing for house parties that were relatively free of alcohol and violence; see Martin, *Farmhouse Fiddlers*, 58. Richard's descriptions of country dances suggest that fistfights and immoderate drinking became common only after improved roads opened rural dances to "rowdies" from town.

16. Tim Cooley describes how fiddlers who play by ear often pick up tunes from the printed page by this process in "When a Tune Becomes a Folk Tune: Fiddling in Southern Illinois." This process of learning tunes in print through an aural tradition greatly expanded fiddlers' repertoires and modified the oral tradition of

learning old-time tunes. Richard never learned to read music, and he expanded on this process by learning additional tunes from records and tapes. Consequently, his repertory includes tunes characteristic of Florida's early years of fiddling as well as more widespread songs made popular after the 1930s. Contemporary fiddlers continue to learn tunes directly from other fiddlers, but most acquire new tunes from recorded sources.

17. The South Land Trail Riders did not complete any commercial recordings, but Richard did record some tunes on a small Emerson record player designed for home use. Outside of these recordings, his band's reputation is preserved only in the memory of the region's older residents.

18. Richard does not have an exact date for his last performance, but he thinks it was by the mid-1950s. A number of old-time fiddlers have similar stories of "laying the fiddle up." Drew Beisswenger gives an account of Melvin Wine's refusal to play in *Fiddling Way Out Yonder*, 76–83. Whereas Wine gave up fiddling for at least fifteen years largely because of religious reasons, Richard stopped fiddling for almost thirty years mainly because he simply lost interest in playing. The shifts in public tastes in music by the late 1950s contributed to a loss of venues for old-time music as described in numerous publications and articulated especially well in Malone and Stricklin, *Southern Music/American Music*, 129–54.

Chapter 6. Richard's Fiddle

*The Hoosier Poet, James Whitcomb Riley, was also a fiddler. His poem "My Fiddle" was first published in 1882, and it is the inspiration for this chapter's title and content. Riley's poem and a representative sample of his other poetry can be found in Donald C. Manlove's edited volume *The Best of James Whitcomb Riley*, 78–79.

1. In the chapter titled "Workshop," George Custer makes the point that fiddling is best learned through the oral and aural tradition by direct interaction with other musicians. This important idea is commonly shared among violinists as evident in Yehudi Menuhin's eloquent description of the violin's place in an aural soundscape in *The Violin*, 8.

2. Judith Becker uses Pauline Oliveros's term "deep listening" to describe a intense practice of attentive listening that connects music with emotion and trance states in *Deep Listeners: Music, Emotions, and Trancing*, 2. This type of listening is often present when square dancers move through their sets while hearing a hoedown, and it also can emerge when an attentive listener simply hears a piece of music. The intense and careful cultivation of listening necessarily involves emotional engagement and is essential to learning to appreciate a fiddler's artistry.

3. Menuhin elegantly describes the sensual appeal of the instrument in *The Violin*, 11–40. His argument that playing the instrument involves smoothing out the unnatural and abrasive qualities of the instrument itself is essential for understanding the tactile qualities of handling the instrument.

4. The shape of most violins is derived from Stradivarius's instruments. Numerous violin-makers and manufacturers have used the name "Stradivarius" on labels glued on the inside of their instruments. The resultant confusion about the true origins of a specific instrument is a common theme in many stories about fiddles. Joyce Cauthen, in *With Fiddle and Well-Rosined Bow*, 55–59, includes a discussion of stories about "acquiring the strad."

5. This story is given as a personal experience narrative throughout this book. The 1926 hurricane and a second hurricane in 1928 mark important eras in south Florida's history. These two are unnamed because Florida did not adopt the practice of naming hurricanes until the 1940s.

6. Luthiers often tell their customers that the worst that their instrument will sound is on the day that they buy it. Sound quality generally improves as musicians play an instrument and "put some tone into it" over time.

7. Placing rattlesnake rattles in a fiddle is a prominent feature of "fiddle lore." There are various explanations for the custom's origin and meanings. Along with Richard Seaman's explanations are the claims that the rattles contain a scent that keeps mice from chewing on the wood. None of these assertions appears to be valid, and mice are known to chew on rattlesnake rattles. Associating fiddling with snakes is sometimes related to the idea of the fiddle as "The Devil's Instrument," as filmmakers Les Blank, Cece Conway, and Alice Gerard playfully suggest in their documentary of Tommy Jarrell, *Sprout Wings and Fly*. There are a number of tunes that reference rattlesnakes. The Kentucky fiddler Perry Riley played a tuned called "Rattlesnake," which Jeff Todd Titon relates to the more common tune "Frankie" in *Old-Time Kentucky Fiddle Tunes*, 78.

8. Joyce Cauthen describes this common pattern of learning to play as "the lure of the forbidden" in *With Fiddle and Well-Rosined Bow*, 48–50. In *Fiddling Way Out Yonder*, 35–37, Drew Beisswenger writes how Melvin Wine also learned to play by taking down his father's fiddle. As Melvin Wine's ability to play improved, his father encouraged his interest in music just as Lewis Seaman eventually supported Richard's playing.

9. Richard's perspective on learning a tune is complicit with Judith Becker's discussion of deep listening. It involves a blend of listening in a highly analytical sense to acquire an exact knowledge of the music as well as an approach to listening that focuses on emotionally absorbing the sound and feeling of the music. See *Deep Listeners*, 73–74.

10. Folklorists have developed educational models based on indigenous forms of learning. Judith Haut provides theoretical and practical approaches for using teaching methods based on ways of learning in her article "How Can Acting Like a Fieldworker Enrich Pluralistic Education?"

11. Joyce Cauthen includes a photograph, ca. 1890, of John McDougal beating straws while Charlie Sellers fiddles in Alabama in *With Fiddle and Well-Rosined Bow*, 72. Jeff Todd Titon includes a photograph, ca. 1923, of an unidentified woman playing fiddlesticks to accompany the Kentucky fiddler Sam Davidson in *Old-Time Ken-*

tucky Fiddle Tunes, xx. Gerald Milnes also includes a photograph, ca. 1956, of Gilbert Massey beating the strings while Andrew Burnside plays in West Virginia in *Play of a Fiddle,* 13. The common use of fiddle beaters in Florida is most likely derived from migrations of fiddlers from the Deep South, Appalachia, and other regions into the state, and, as Richard's account demonstrates, the practice was part of the tradition prior to the introduction of recorded fiddle tunes. The recording "Florida Folk Festival: The First 25 Years (1953–1977)" includes a field recording of the important Florida fiddler Cush Holston playing with "Old Coon Dog" to the accompaniment of strawbeating.

12. The rhythmic movements of the bow fuse fiddling with dancing. Yehudi Menuhin makes the same connection between playing the violin and dancing in *The Violin,* 104.

13. Julie Youmans's thorough analysis of "bounce" as a component of the generative system of performing fiddle tunes systemically and insightfully links aesthetics to the mechanics of playing. See "Warming the Cold Notes: Style and Boundaries in Old-Time Fiddling."

14. Most fiddlers use this shuffle as a basis for their playing. Most instructional books provide a more complete description of this technique, and Miles Krassen's *Appalachian Fiddle* demonstrates techniques that Richard uses in playing basic shuffles. Numerous instructional DVDs and videotapes also provide careful analysis and clear presentations of fiddle tunes. Alan Jabbour's "Learning Old-Time Fiddle Appalachian Style with Alan Jabbour" provides an excellent discussion and demonstration of fiddling techniques used in ten tunes.

15. Menuhin, *The Violin,* 164–71.

16. Charles Wolfe writes how short-bow fiddling is associated with Appalachian fiddling in *The Devil's Box,* 84–85. He notes how fiddlers such as Clayton McMichen originally played using "jiggy-bow" styles but later adapted the long-bow techniques from Marcus Lowell Stokes, a fiddler from Georgia who picked up the style from the Alabama fiddler Joe Lee. Bill Malone writes that long-bow fiddling was associated with Texas fiddling but that it cannot be considered unique to that region (*Country Music USA,* 23–24). He asserts that numerous styles are evident within a particular region because of mutual influences from itinerant fiddlers. The popularity of the mass media by the 1930s further blended regionally distinctive styles. Owing to these factors and limited documentation, it is difficult to ascertain whether long-bow or short-bow was more common in Florida.

17. Chubby Wise played hoedowns prior to learning long-bow styles associated with western swing, but he also remarks that he learned new long-bow fiddle techniques when playing with Bill Monroe. His contributions to the long-bow fiddling style of bluegrass fiddling are featured in Neil Rosenberg's *Bluegrass: A History,* 56–71. Because the long-bow style was seen as a novel way of playing old-time tunes, it is likely that Chubby originally used short-bow fiddling when playing hoedowns.

18. The controversy over whether short-bow historically was predominant in Florida also is a topic of informal conversation among fiddlers in the state. The long-

bow style of old-time fiddling is sometimes referred to as "Georgia long-bow," after the style of Gid Tanner and the Skillet Lickers, but Joyce Cauthen writes that the technique is also rooted in Alabama fiddle styles (*With Fiddle and Well-Rosined Bow*, 121). Reviewing Richard's comments in relation to the influences from early string band recording and bluegrass fiddling, it is most likely that the current popularity of long-bow over short-bow is linked primarily to media influences and bluegrass styles rather than to a high prevalence of long-bow players early in Florida's history. Early recordings of Florida fiddlers dating to the 1930s are archived in the Folklife Collection in the archives of the Florida Department of State. These recordings show the use of both techniques, but there is a heavy presence of short-bow players.

19. Richard's use of "breaking time" is interesting. In a general sense, a fiddler tries not to break time by losing the beat, especially when accompanying dancers. In Richard's view, "breaking time" can also refer to *rubato*, or the artistic toying with minute differences in time between notes. Richard plays with a steady beat, but he will borrow time from one note and add it to another to personalize his tunes.

20. Two open tunings used in Florida are *D G D G* and *E A E A*. Because of a dearth of field recordings, it is difficult to assess how widely these tunes were used, but a number of contemporary fiddlers in the state learned a few hoedowns in these tunings from older fiddlers.

21. As does Richard, many old-time fiddlers play mainly in the sharp keys of *D, G,* and *A.* A few of Richard's tunes are in the key of C, but he also plays in some of the flatted keys. I have also heard him play in 4th position, but he avoids playing up the neck in public.

22. Julie Youmans takes the idea that a limited number of patterns and techniques can be used to create an infinitely large number of creative expressions from Noam Chomsky's linguistic theory and applies to it music by terming this process the "generative" aspect of fiddling ("Warming the Cold Notes," 134). The idea is central to structuralism and is evident in Vladímir Propp's *Morphology of the Folktale*. The idea is also present in Claude Lévi-Strauss's approach to structuralism in various works such as *The Story of Lynx*, 239.

23. Drew Beisswenger completed the transcriptions for each tune in this book.

24. It is common to hear the terms "A-part" and "B-part," but these divisions are sometimes also refered to as the "first part" and "second part." Occasionally, a fiddler will use the terms "top part" and the "bottom," but these often apply only when the B-part begins on a lower note than the A-part.

25. There is a certain arbitrary quality in breaking down fiddle tunes into various phrases. I have identified these phrases in order to show similar musical qualities, but the divisions are also based on ways that Richard plays the tunes. It is also plausible to divide each segment further to find sequences of notes that a fiddler must master in learning to play by ear. In the interest of clarity, I have omitted or included pick-up notes that are not necessarily integral to the melodic phrase.

26. The Parry-Lord hypothesis asserted the basic ideas of oral-formulaic theories of composition forty years ago. Stephen Mitchell and Gregory Nagy provide a

good introduction to the approach and an insightful discussion of ways that the theory has proven useful in a range of disciplines in their introduction to the second edition of Albert B. Lord's *The Singer of Tales.*

27. Youmans, "Warming the Cold Notes," 126.

28. Richard composed this waltz in the late 1980s. It involves musical phrases and themed waltzes that he has played or heard, including "Cherokee Waltz," "Westphalia Waltz," and "The Waltz You Saved for Me."

29. Robert M. Pirsig's fusion of aesthetic quality with essential quality remains an inspiring way to merge aesthetic appreciation and rational understanding as set forth in *Zen and the Art of Motorcycle Maintenance: An Inquiry into Values,* 208.

30. Jack Piccalo's article "Richard Seaman Is a Treasure" was published in the August 1997 edition of the *Midnight Flier,* the monthly newsletter of the North Florida Bluegrass Music Association. It includes Richard's poem "The Voice of a Fiddle."

Chapter 7. Core Repertory

*Philip Martin, *Farmhouse Fiddlers,* 41.

1. Matthew Guntharp, *Learning the Fiddler's Ways,* 7.

2. Roger Abrahams's work with ballad singer Almeda Riddle provides a comprehensive and insightful means for studying repertoire in relation to life history in their book *A Singer and Her Songs.*

3. Fiddlers have compiled numerous books of traditional fiddle tunes that both preserve local repertoires and provide sources for new tunes for fiddlers. An excellent tunebook that includes many tunes in Richard's repertoire is David Brody's *The Fiddler's Fakebook.*

4. Raymond William's discussion of the popular structure of feeling provides a useful phrase for integrating an individual's aesthetics with wider aesthetic values held to varying degrees within a broader community of listeners. He describes this aspect of cultural expression in *Marxism and Literature* (Oxford: Oxford University Press, 1977). The idea is provided a neuroscientific basis in Judith Becker's *Deep Listeners.*

5. Numerous studies include careful examinations of fiddlers' repertories. Larry Shumway edited Kenner C. Kartchner's life history in *Frontier Fiddler.* This exemplary study of a fiddler's life includes ample documentation and discussion of Kartchner's repertory, as do Guntharp's *Learning the Fiddler's Ways* and numerous other studies of individual fiddlers.

6. Alan Dundes, "The Devolutionary Premise in Folklore Theory," 17. Henry Glassie argues that skill in the folk arts often improves with the passage of time in his book *Turkish Traditional Art Today.* A number of fiddlers acknowledge that the overall musicianship is improving as Ernie Hodges expresses in an interview with Charles Wolfe in Wolfe, *The Devil's Box,* 214.

7. Kenneth Burke's groundbreaking discussion of literary and artistic form can be found in *Counter-Statement.* Two of the essays in this volume, "Psychology

and Form" (29–44) and "Lexicon Rhetoricæ" (123–83), provide essential resources for understanding how writers, storytellers, musicians, and other performers vary their artistry in response to their audience's interests and demands.

8. Samuel Preston Bayard, *Hill Country Tunes: Instrumental Folk Music of Southwestern Pennsylvania.*

9. Samuel Preston Bayard, *Dance to the Fiddle, March to the Fife: Instrumental Folk Tunes in Pennsylvania,* 8.

10. Malone and Stricklin, *Southern Music/American Music,* 63.

11. Jill Linzee, *A Reference Guide to Florida Folklore.*

12. Linda L. Danielson, "Oregon Fiddling: The Missouri Connection," 85.

13. Richard's core repertory includes many of the tunes documented by Joyce Cauthen in *With Fiddle and Well-Rosined Bow.* A number of his tunes are also common in Appalachian fiddlers' repertories, and variants of these tunes are preserved in Miles Krassen's *Appalachian Fiddle.* It is also important to consider Simon Bronner's argument that it is too simple to label fiddle tunes "southern tunes" or "Appalachian tunes" when many of them are in the repertoires of fiddlers from other geographical regions, as Bronner verifies in *Old-Time Music Makers of New York State.*

14. Wiley L. Housewright, *A History of Music and Dance in Florida,* 147.

15. Sandra Dolby Stahl, *Literary Folkloristics and the Personal Narrative,* 4.

16. Ibid., 14.

17. Charles Briggs and Richard Bauman, "Genre, Intertextuality, and Social Power," 147.

18. Trudier Harris, "Genre," 522.

19. Historical continuity and canonical authenticity are two of the seven characteristic ways of defining "tradition" as discussed in Dan Ben-Amos's "The Seven Strands of *Tradition:* Varieties and Its Meaning in American Folklore Studies." Henry Glassie develops Ben-Amos's ideas to assert that *tradition* is a resource to derive the future from the past through dynamic and volitional action in the present in his article "Tradition," 409.

20. In describing the place of the waltz in old-time fiddling, Joyce Cauthen writes that waltzes and other round dances were introduced to America's Deep South fiddling tradition from Europe in the middle of the nineteenth century. She notes that numerous rural communities that preferred the hoedown rejected these new dances, often seeing them as too scandalous (*With Fiddle and Well-Rosined Bow,* 157).

21. Joyce Cauthen's discussion of the shift from house parties to public social dances (ibid., 157–63) provides a useful way to examine the different social associations that cluster around various dance styles.

22. Richard's view is that most fiddlers were not seen as stars in their home communities. He sees the performance of music in urban areas as bringing about a change in the fiddler's status. He views waltzes and slower tunes as more difficult to play than the old hoedowns and regards these tunes as important pieces for developing his sense of himself as a musician. He also recognizes that "brag" fiddlers were

also known for their ability to play hoedowns, and throughout time they showcased their artistry in fiddle contests.

23. Timothy Cooley, "When a Tune Becomes a Folk Tune," 47.

24. It is tempting to ignore Tin Pan Alley's influence on old-time fiddling, especially when examining a fiddler's core repertory. Researchers note that many hoedowns are actually rooted in songs from minstrel shows, Tin Pan Alley, and even classical repertories (Malone and Stricklin, *Southern Music/American Music*, 11; Wolfe, *The Devil's Box*, 185). Richard does not consider the sentimental parlor tunes to be hoedowns, but he considers them to be important components of his repertory.

25. These tunes are primarily western swing selections and hymns. Richard learned them from his family, fellow band members, and other sources. Charles Wolfe explains that the popularity of the long-bow style is linked to western swing (*The Devil's Box*, 153). Richard typically plays these tunes with longer bow strokes, and the Texas style of western fiddling is a major stylistic influence. As Wolfe notes, the aesthetic value of drawing from traditional hoedowns to create a new genre is a characteristic of both western swing and bluegrass. While Richard enjoys bluegrass fiddling, he never learned that particular style.

26. Marshall McLuhan presents his popular buzz phrase "the medium is the message" in *Understanding Media: The Extensions of Man*, ix. He overgeneralizes a bit, for it is more useful to recognize that "the medium" is but a part of the message.

27. Charles Wolfe explains that by the late 1920s, many of the recordings and broadcasts of fiddlers were produced specifically for square dancing (*The Devil's Box*, 104). The popularity waned, but record producers also engineered a square dance fad through recordings during the 1950s (ibid., 192). The availability of square dance music through the mass media thus both contributed to the increased availability and popularity of fiddling and to the demise of live fiddling.

28. Erika Brady, *A Spiral Way: How the Phonograph Changed Ethnography*, 6–8.

29. The demise of square dancing in Jacksonville homes and the decline in the popularity of fiddling contributed to Richard's decision to quit fiddling for almost thirty years. Numerous fiddlers' life stories include a similar pattern of "laying the fiddle aside." Drew Beisswenger's discussion of Melvin Wine's twenty-year hiatus from playing the fiddle reveals that Wine quit playing largely because of his dislike, following his religious conversion, of the raucous social life at dances (*Fiddling Way Out Yonder*, 80–83). Other fiddlers explain that they stopped playing for other reasons such as lack of time, family commitments, and interests in other forms of music or recreation.

30. Neil Rosenberg, *Bluegrass: A History*, 20.

31. Wolfe, *The Devil's Box*, 104.

32. Bill Malone and David Stricklin discuss how early recording stars, such as the Carter family and Jimmie Rodgers, were popularized during the 1920s (*Southern Music/American Music*, 64–67). Malone also discusses the shift in old-time fiddling as dance music into a component of "hillbilly music" in his book *Country Music*

USA. His study provides special focus on the economics of the music industry and record producers and promoters' abilities to create recording stars.

33. Jack Piccalo, "Richard Seaman Is a Treasure," 4.
34. Anthony Brandt, "A Short Natural History of Nostalgia," 200.
35. Samuel Preston Bayard, *Dance to the Fiddle*, 9.
36. Henry Glassie, *Material Culture*, 342.
37. Barbara Kirshenblatt-Gimblett, "Mistaken Dichtomy," 36.
38. Roger Abrahams, "Phantoms of Romantic Nationalism in Folkloristics," 18.
39. Briggs and Bauman, "Genre," 149.

Chapter 8. Folklife in Education

*Greg Dale and Erik Sessions wrote "The Highlandville Waltz" in honor of an old-time dance held outside of Decorah, Iowa, at the Highlandville School. The old schoolhouse is used as a community building, and the dances draw an intergenerational crowd who perform old-time dances, waltzes, and Scandinavian folk dances. A fine recording of the tune is on the compact disk "Decorah Waltz" by the band "Foot-Notes."

1. Jeffrey Mazo's important revisionist etymology is in "'Good Saxon Compound'."

2. N.F.S. Grundtvig's call for reforming Danish culture through the study of folklife is a major theme in this nineteenth-century religious leader's writings. His 1847 article "Folk-Life and Christianity" and his 1838 article "The School For Life" are essential readings for linking the preservation of folklife to educational reform. These and other articles are in *Selected Writings: N.F.S. Grundtvig*.

3. Don Yoder, "The Folklife Studies Movement," provides an early link between Scandinavian *folkliv* scholarship and the inception of American folklife studies. The term "folklife" is commonly used among contemporary public folklorists, and it is essentially synonymous with "folklore."

4. An excellent presentation of this history of folklife in education programs can be found in Nancy Nusz's "Folklife in Education."

5. Jacksonville resident Ana Mercedes Rodriguez demonstrated bobbin lace, and Randy Kerr performed and demonstrated auctioneering techniques. I was able to add Richard Seaman's performance to this program because of additional time available, but most two-week sessions involved eight days of my instruction and two days of demonstrations or performances by traditional artists. For a more extended discussion of the goals and format of the Duval County Folklife in Education Program, see Nancy Nusz, ed., "Folklife in Education."

6. A good discussion of ways to use fieldwork techniques for classroom instruction is found in Judith Haut's "How Can Acting Like a Fieldworker Enrich Pluralistic Education?"

7. This description is from a videotape that a teacher gave to me after this program. Because of legal restrictions in working with children in Jacksonville's

public schools, I have not identified the school and the students' names. This particular event occurred in February 1990.

8. One of the advantages of coordinating folklife in education programs relates to ways that abstract ideas can be related to indigenous cultural traditions. Demonstrations by folk artists and performances by folk musicians provide culturally relevant resources for teaching. Two excellent resources that develop these ideas are Elizabeth Radin Simons's *Student Worlds/Student Words: Teaching Writing Through Folklore,* and Bonnie Stone Sunstein and Elizabeth Chiseri-Strater's *Fieldworking: Reading and Writing Research.*

9. I have included different renditions of some of the same tall tales to show how Richard Seaman performs his stories in different settings. It is especially interesting to see how he strings together tall tales and how he varies his style of storytelling for different audiences. Compare the selection of tales he performed at the Arts Mania festival with these renditions. He includes more stories and jokes about marriage when performing to adult audiences, and he sticks mainly to stories about rural life when performing for children. The longer and more ornate tellings show up in the tape that he made, and he simplifies the stories for children. He also uses more hand gestures and a bit more animation in his voice when he tells stories to children.

10. In informal conversation, Richard noted that he enjoyed seeing that some children actually believed his tall tales. Children learn to recognize the fantasy frame through hearing fictional stories, and Missy Elder explained that tall tales are included in various instructional materials that she uses in her classes.

11. These tall tales are variants of Baughman's Tale Type 1960D: *The great vegetable* and Aarne-Thompson motif F816: *Extraordinary vegetable.* This telling illustrates how he links a story with other stories in performances for children. Usually, he tells individual stories between tunes when performing for adults.

12. This performance is the only time that I have heard Richard Seaman tell this tale based on Baughman's motif X1762(c): *Shadow of pendulum of old clock wears hole in back of case. The clock is very old.* The index notes that this story was documented in Pennsylvania in the 1940s. Richard does not remember when he first learned this tale, but he notes that his father also was a storyteller. Because Lewis Seaman was originally from Pennsylvania, it is possible that Richard learned this particular story from his father.

13. To help engage students in these types of presentations, it is helpful to include a hands-on component where students have opportunities to try different activities. Certain activities such as Japanese origami and sweetgrass basket-making lend themselves well to these types of demonstrations, and all students can participate. Students also have participated by singing or dancing to various forms of music. Richard would allow a couple students to try to perform for others, and this type of selective volunteerism provided ways to vary activities sufficiently to keep children's attention and provide them with a sense of the skills required to play the instrument.

14. Securing permanent funding for residency programs is a challenge. The Duval County Folklife in Education Program was funded one additional year from a mixture of EOCA funds and support from Florida's arts council. After this funding cycle was complete, I wrote a grant to coordinate folklife programs at John E. Ford Elementary School in Jacksonville and was able to bring Richard into the classroom for additional performances.

Chapter 9. A Florida Fiddler

*Sigurd Bernhard Hustvedt, *Ballad Books and Ballad Men,* 237.

1. One thousand copies of the tape were produced, and it was distributed at no charge to teachers in the Duval County school system. Master studio recordings are preserved in the Florida Department of State's archives in Tallahassee.

2. Gregory Hansen, "The Relevance of 'Authentic Tradition' in Studying an Oldtime Florida Fiddler"; Jack Piccalo, "Richard Seaman Is a Treasure."

3. Gregory Hansen, "A Portrait of a Florida Fiddler."

4. Bob Stone produced the series "Music from the Sunshine State" in 2002 for the Florida Folklife Program. The hour-long segment entitled "Old-Time and Bluegrass Music" has been broadcast on stations affiliated with National Public Radio throughout Florida and the United States.

5. Kimberly J. Lau, "Serial Logic: Folklore and Difference in the Age of Feel-Good Multiculturalism," 75.

6. Bill C. Malone, *Singing Cowboys and Musical Mountaineers,* 72.

7. Margot Ammidown, "Edens, Underworlds, and Shrines: Florida's Small Tourist Attractions," 243.

8. It is not surprising that the fantasy writer Piers Anthony casts his magical kingdom of Xanth as a magical land that resembles the mundane Florida peninsula. See *The Source of Magic.*

9. This theme of Florida as a lost paradise is common in numerous histories, novels, short stories, and articles about Florida. Anne E. Rowe discusses this dominant image and other themes in *The Idea of Florida in the American Literary Imagination,* 20.

10. Dana Ste. Clair, *Cracker: The Cracker Culture in Florida History,* 41.

11. Barbara Kirshenblatt-Gimblett presents this challenging idea in "Mistaken Dichotomy," 29–42.

12. David E. Whisnant's analysis of nativism and cultural heritage programming focuses on nativism as a regional and nationalist ideology in *All That Is Native and Fine.* His analysis also suggests that nativism can be manifested in individual states in America.

13. This phrase is a lyric from Sting's "History Will Teach Us Nothing" on his recording . . . *Nothing Like the Sun.* A & M Records, Inc. SP-6402, 1987.

14. Jerald T. Milanich, *The Timucua,* 67–92.

15. Charles W. Tebeau, *The New History of Florida,* 34.

16. Herbert E. Bolton, *The Spanish Borderlands: A Chronicle of Old Florida and the Southwest*, 140–47.

17. Stetson Kennedy, *Palmetto Country*, 47.

18. Tina Bucuvalas, Peggy A. Bulger, and Stetson Kennedy, *South Florida Folklife*, 5–8.

19. Patsy West, *The Enduring Seminoles: From Alligator Wrestling to Ecotourism*, 2.

20. Jerrilyn McGregory, *Wiregrass Country*, 15–16.

21. Michael Gannon, *Florida: A Short History*, 28–46.

22. Zora Neale Hurston, *Mules and Men*, 65–75.

23. Kristin Congdon summarizes major themes in Florida's violent history in her introduction to *Uncle Monday and Other Florida Tales*, 3–19.

24. There has been a recent movement to include incidents such as lynching, the Rosewood massacre, and race riots in statewide school curricula, and the Department of State's historic markers program has established commemorative plaques throughout the state to mark scenes of violence.

25. Zora Neale Hurston documented much of the folklore that she presents in *Mules and Men* in the community of Eatonville and in towns located near Kissimmee. Richard's folktales and descriptions of folk music provide additional contexts for adding to her study of African-American folk culture.

26. Jerrilyn McGregory documents similar stories of forced labor, convict leasing, abuses of the tenant farmer system, and lynchings in Florida in *Wiregrass Country*, 70–73.

27. Hurston's accounts of life in turpentine camps and sawmills in *Mules and Men*, 64–81, support Richard's stories. It is significant that Hurston presents slave stories that she had collected as part of the context for the occupational folklife of black men working in the camps.

28. The archival materials are part of the Stetson Kennedy files in the WPA collection in the Florida Department of State's Folklife Collection in the state archives in Tallahassee. The classification and ordering system is a bit loose, but these documents can be perused in the archives located in the R. A. Gray Building in Tallahassee. They include fieldnotes from Stetson Kennedy and numerous fieldworkers including Zora Neale Hurston.

29. Kennedy, *Palmetto Country*, 259; Gannon, *Florida: A Short History*, 86–88.

30. It would be difficult to ascertain this story's historical veracity, but the story is complicit with the oppression of black communities during the twentieth century. The story also evokes poignant symbolic associations about building one of the world's major tourist centers in what was originally a remote swampland. Patricia A. Turner's reading of narratives in black history in her book *I Heard It Through the Grapevine: Rumor in African-American Culture* provides insight into ways that attacks on African Americans are a persistent theme in legends. The metaphor of paving over the violence of central Florida to establish the tourist industry is a rich symbol for understanding this important aspect of the state's history.

31. Dana Ste. Clair writes of the violent reputations of central Florida's cow towns in *Cracker: The Cracker Culture in Florida History,* 16. He notes that the area near Arcadia was especially known for its thirty-year range war between cattlemen and rustlers around the turn of the century. Kissimmee also shared this reputation for violent clashes between local cattle barons and rustlers. The dislike of "Yankees" was part of a wider suspicion of outsiders.

32. Stetson Kennedy copied down this definition of a "Yankee" in his WPA fieldnotes.

33. Al Burt's *The Tropic of Cracker* includes a discussion of the term, as does Dana Ste. Clair's *Cracker: The Cracker Culture in Florida History.* Numerous etymologies have been suggested, and Richard's story is the most common explanation. Ste. Clair's etymology is the most convincing. He argues that the term is related to Anglo and Celtic usages that refer to a "cracker" as a storyteller or even as an uncouth braggart. The term is related to the semantic cluster of "wisecracker," "cracking jokes," and "crack wit," and it was used in this way prior to the introduction of the style of cow whips that are unique to Florida.

34. The term "cracker chic" shows up in Charles Reagan Wilson and William Ferris's *Encyclopedia of Southern Culture,* 1132. The Florida singer and songwriter Gamble Rogers also popularized the phrase "Florida Cracker Chic" in his stage patter and in his comedic monologues.

35. Paul Zach, ed., *Florida: Insight Guide,* 70.

36. George M. Barbour, *Florida for Tourists, Invalids, and Settlers.* (New York: D. Appleton and Company, 1882).

37. Barbour, 54.

38. Barbour, 54, 55.

39. Barbour, 55.

40. Barbour, 56.

41. Carl Dann, *Carl Dann's Vicissitudes and Casathrophics, Vol. One.*

42. Ibid., 71–73.

43. Kennedy, *Palmetto Country,* 183–191.

44. Burt, *Tropic of Cracker,* 12.

45. Charles L. Briggs and Richard Bauman, "Genre, Intertextuality, and Social Power," 141.

46. Informal communication with folklorists and fiddlers in Florida and surrounding states in the Deep South support this view.

47. Bill C. Malone, *Southern Music/American Music,* 64.

48. Richard Blaustein makes this argument in relation to folk culture revivalist movements in *The Thistle and the Brier,* 71. Although fiddling can support jingoism, it is likely that most fiddlers in past centuries were motivated more by pragmatic concerns and personal interests rather than ideology.

49. Howard Marshall and John Williams recorded an excellent version of this tune on "Fiddling Missouri." Marshall's liner notes provide background on the tune. W. T. Narmour and S. W. Shell Smith likely made the first recording of the tune on

March 11, 1929. They both grew up in Carroll County, and they knew local African-American blues musicians. They are also credited with bringing blues musician Mississippi John Hurt to the attention of the recording industry. This selection is featured in a 1988 reissue on the compact disc "Mississippi String Bands, Volume 2: Traditional Fiddle Music of Mississippi." County Records 3515. County Records: Roanoke, Virginia.

50. Wiley L. Housewright, *A History of Music and Dance in Florida, 1565–1865*, 247–51.

51. Archival holdings in the Stetson Kennedy papers at the Florida State Archives, Tallahassee.

52. Hurston, *Mules and Men*, 66.

53. Gerald Milnes provides an extensive discussion of black fiddlers in West Viriginia in *Play of a Fiddle*, 96–107.

54. Housewright, *History of Music and Dance*, 249.

55. The argument that all representations are incomplete is an axiom of contemporary ethnographic study. Charles L. Briggs provides techniques to work with some of the subjective biases inherent in field research and ethnographic study in *Learning How to Ask: A Sociolinguistic Appraisal of the Interview in Social Science Research*.

56. Barbara Kirshenblatt-Gimblett, "Mistaken Dichotomy," 33.

Chapter 10. The Voice of a Fiddler

1. At this time, the festival was produced by the Department of State's Bureau of Florida Folklife Programs in White Springs. The festival's director, David Reddy, and the bureau's staff coordinated over 400 performances for the three-day weekend. The festival continued to be produced by the Department of State until 2003, when it became sponsored by Florida's state park system. Emcees tend to change quite a bit at this festival, and unfortunately I was unable to identify the emcee of this Saturday afternoon performance.

2. Mary Hufford's edited volume *Conserving Culture: A New Discourse on Heritage* includes numerous essays on various aspects of public folklore programming. Roger Abrahams's article "Powerful Promises of Regeneration or Living Well with History" cautions against the overt and inadvertent use of folklore to bolster all of these ideologies. These issues are also thoroughly addressed in Robert Cantwell's *Ethnomimesis*. He argues that the culture industry is implicated in a system of signs, symbols, and social institutions that can reinforce the various ideologies that folklorists may seek to critique.

3. In *All That Is Native and Fine*, David E. Whisnant discusses how the representation of folklore can be both a vibrant resource for cross-cultural understanding as well as a highly contrived project that obscures and depoliticizes a region's social and cultural dynamics. The argument that folk culture can be co-opted for ideologically driven motives is an important consideration, especially when old-time fid-

dling and storytelling are presented in public sector folklife programs. Whisnant's central arguments have provided a base for examining other representations of cultural heritage in other regions. Brooks Blevins's study of the Ozarks demonstrates how dominant regional images are fostered through cultural heritage programming, including public sector folklore, in *Hill Folks: A History of the Arkansas Ozarkers and Their Image*, 227–34, 247–60.

4. Thomas McLaughlin, *Street Smarts and Critical Theory: Listening to the Vernacular*.

5. Susan Orlean, *The Orchid Thief*, 11. Kristin Congdon interprets surreal qualities of Florida life to the state's dramatic environmental features, complex history, and cultural diversity in *Uncle Monday and Other Florida Tales*, 3.

6. The novelist Carl Hiaasen writes a playful yet scathing critique of the commercialism associated with Florida's tourist industry in *Team Rodent: How Disney Devours the World*. His attempts to be banned for life from the Disney theme parks have thus far remained unsuccessful.

7. Stetson Kennedy, *Palmetto Country*, 343.

8. The loss of Florida's environmental, historical, and cultural richness is a major theme in writing about the state. Ernest F. Lyons's *My Florida*, 19–22, includes essays and reflections on the consequences of overdevelopment in the Sunshine State. The theme is also common in numerous stories, songs, and folktales that are currently performed, especially at the annual Florida Folk Festival in White Springs.

9. In his study of Appalachian folk culture, Richard Blaustein argues that dramatic changes in a region's culture can create a sense of psychological and emotional disjunction that the Scots-Irish term "anti-syzygy." Part of the value of folklore is that it provides vibrant resources for merging the past with the present to ameliorate stresses in both personal and social spheres. See *The Thistle and the Brier*, 67.

10. In *Material Culture*, 9, Henry Glassie argues that collegial exchange between scholars and nonacademic intellectuals will provide important insights into serious intellectual questions. He challenges writers to take vernacular theories and perspectives as seriously as we evaluate high theory.

11. Joe Wilson and Lee Udall, *Folk Festivals*, 20–22.

12. Glen Fisher worked as a sportscaster and a reporter for WJKS "First Coast News" in Jacksonville. His feature story on Richard Seaman was broadcast on October 16, 1992.

13. George Campbell, *The Philosophy of Rhetoric*, 285. The work was first published in 1776, and Campbell's discussion of the appeal of imagistic language in speaking remains an important base for both prescriptive and descriptive studies of language.

14. Kristin Congdon discusses listening to stories as a creative act that provides essential resources for education as it stimulates the imagination and preserves culture in *Uncle Monday and Other Florida Tales*, 17.

15. Characteristic patterns of examining truth as a correspondence between subjective mind and physical objects, a resource for interpersonal connection, a so-

cial construction within culture, a pragmatic resource for functioning in society, and a resource for self-disclosure are all evident in Heidegger's essay as well as in Richard Seaman's stories. Martin Heidegger's "On the Essence of Truth" in *Basic Writings*, 114–41, provides an intriguing way to examine various approaches to thinking about truth. Although his interpretation of the Greek term *aletheia* as "unconcealment" is problematic, his discussion of relationships between truth, freedom, and authenticity fit Richard Seaman's ideas about telling stories. Poststructuralist critiques of truth such as those found in the writing of Michel Foucault, *Histoire de la Folie à L'âge Classique*, often explore implications of truth as a subjective social construction. The poststructuralist critique of truth has been critiqued by recent writers including historian Gertrude Himmelfarb in *On Looking into the Abyss: Untimely Thoughts on Culture and Society* and physicists Alan Sokal and Jean Bricmont in *Fashionable Nonsense: Postmodern Intellectuals' Abuse of Science.*

16. Simon Bronner, *The Carver's Art: Crafting Meaning from Wood.*

17. Judith Becker discusses entrainment as a way of listening that creates deep trance-like states of consciousness. Her analysis of entrainment as a shared experience among deep listeners explains what is colloquially known as "fiddle zen." See *Deep Listeners*, 127–30.

18. Swami Prabhavananda and Christopher Isherwood, trans., *The Song of God: Bhagavad-Gita*, 56–62.

19. Walpola Rahula, *What the Buddha Taught*, 99–105

20. Richard Blaustein discusses ways that folk expression can provide a resource for healing fractured psyches and communities in *The Thistle and the Brier*, 63–68.

Chapter 11. The Icing on the Cake

*One of my favorite renditions of this old ballad (Laws P14) was sung by Shorty and Juanita Sheehan on September 16, 1962, for folklorist Art Rosenbaum. An excellent recording appears on "Fine Times at Our House: Indiana Ballads, Fiddle Tunes, and Songs" on Smithsonian/Folkways 03809.

1. Tape-recorded interview with Richard Seaman, on September 28, 1991, in Jacksonville, Florida.

2. The remaining stories and reflections in this chapter are from a tape-recorded interview with Annie Seaman and Richard Seaman, on May 19, 1998, in Jacksonville, Florida.

Works Consulted

~

Abrahams, Roger D. 1993. Phantoms of Romantic Nationalism in Folkloristics. *Journal of American Folklore* 106:3–37.

———. 1994. Powerful Promises of Regeneration or Living Well with History. In *Conserving Culture: A New Discourse on Heritage*, edited by Mary Hufford, 78–93. Publications of the American Folklife Center at the Library of Congress. Urbana: University of Illinois Press.

Alburger, Mary Anne. 1983. *Scottish Fiddlers and Their Music*. London: Victor Gollancz, Ltd.

Ammidown, Margot. 1998. Edens, Underworlds, and Shrines: Florida's Small Tourist Attractions. *Journal of Decorative and Propaganda Arts* 23:238–60.

Anthony, Piers. 1987. *The Source of Magic*. New York: Del Ray Edition.

Attebery, Louie W. 1979. The Fiddle Tune: An American Artifact. In *Readings in American Folklore*, edited by Jan Harold Brunvand, 324–33. New York: W. W. Norton and Company.

Barbour, George M. 1882. *Florida for Tourists, Invalids, and Settlers*. New York: D. Appleton and Company.

Basso, Keith H. 1996. *Wisdom Sits in Places: Landscape and Language Among the Western Apache*. Albuquerque: New Mexico University Press.

Baughman, Ernest W. 1966. *Type and Motif-Index of the Folktales of England and North America*. The Hague: Mouton.

Bauman, Richard. 1984. *Verbal Art as Performance.* Long Grove, Ill.: Waveland Press, Inc.

———. 1986. *Story, Performance, and Event: Contextual Studies of Oral Narrative.* Cambridge Studies in Oral and Literate Culture 10. Cambridge: Press Syndicate of the University of Cambridge. "Any Man Who Keeps More'n One Hound'l Lie to You": A Contextual Study of Expressive Lying, 1–32; "I Go into More Detail Now, to be Sure": Narrative Variation and the Shifting Contexts of Traditional Storytelling, 78–111.

Bauman, Richard, Patricia Sawin, and Inta Carpenter. 1992. *Reflections on the Folklife Festival: An Ethnography of Participant Experience.* Bloomington: Folklore Institute, Indiana University, Special Publications, No. 2.

Bayard, Samuel Preston. 1944. *Hill Country Tunes: Instrumental Folk Music of Southwestern Pennsylvania.* Philadelphia: American Folklore Society.

———. 1982. *Dance to the Fiddle, March to the Fife: Instrumental Folk Tunes in Pennsylvania.* University Park: Pennsylvania State University Press.

Becker, Judith. 2004. *Deep Listeners: Music, Emotion, and Trancing.* Bloomington: Indiana University Press.

Beisswenger, Drew. 2002. *Fiddling Way Out Yonder: The Life and Music of Melvin Wine.* Jackson: University Press of Mississippi.

Belanus, Betty. 2002. *Seasonal.* Rockville, Md.: Round Barn Press.

Ben-Amos, Dan. 1984. The Seven Strands of *Tradition*: Varieties in Its Meaning in American Folklore Studies. *Journal of Folklore Research* 21:97–131.

Ben-Amos, Dan, and Kenneth Goldstein, eds. 1975. *Folklore: Performance and Communication.* The Hague: Mouton.

Berger, Harris, and Giovanna P. Del Negro, eds. 2002. Toward New Perspectives on *Verbal Art as Performance. Journal of American Folklore,* Special Issue, 115 (Winter).

Berry, Wendell. 1974. *The Memory of Old Jack.* New York: Harcourt Brace Jovanovich.

———. 1996. *Another Turn of the Crank.* Washington, D.C.: Counterpoint.

Birnbaum, Robert. 1988. *How Colleges Work: The Cybernetics of Academic Organization and Leadership.* San Francisco: Jossey-Bass Publishers.

Blank, Les, Cece Conway, and Alice Gerard. 1983. *Sprout Wings and Fly.* Video documentary. El Cerrito, Calif.: Flower Films.

Blaustein, Richard. 1975. Traditional Music and Social Change: The Old-Time Fiddlers Association Movement in the United States. Ph.D. dissertation, Indiana University.

———. 1992. Jake and Lena Hughes: Grassroots Promoters of the Old-Time Fiddling Revival in Missouri and the Great Plains Region. *Missouri Folklore Society Journal* 13–14:1–16.

———. 2003. *The Thistle and the Brier: Historical Links and Cultural Parallels Between Scotland and Appalachia.* Jefferson, N.C.: McFarland & Company, Inc.

Blevins, Brooks. 2002. *Hill Folks: A History of Arkansas Ozarkers and Their Image.* Chapel Hill: University of North Carolina Press.

Bluestein, Gene. 1996. *Poplore: Folk and Pop in American Culture.* Amherst: University of Massachusetts Press.

Boas, Franz. 1982. *Race, Language, and Culture.* Chicago: University of Chicago Press.

Bolton, Herbert E. [1921] 1996. *The Spanish Borderlands: A Chronicle of Old Florida and the Southwest.* Albuquerque: University of New Mexico Press.

Brady, Erika. 1999. *A Spiral Way: How the Phonograph Changed Ethnography.* Jackson: University Press of Mississippi.

Brandt, Anthony. 1991. A Short Natural History of Nostalgia. In *A Living History Reader.* Vol. 1, *Museums,* edited by Jay Anderson, 200–205. Nashville: American Association of State and Local History.

Briggs, Charles L. [1986] 1994. *Learning How to Ask: A Sociolinguistic Appraisal of the Interview in Social Science Research.* Reprint edition. New York: Press Syndicate of the University of Cambridge.

Briggs, Charles L., and Richard Bauman. 1992. Genre, Intertextuality, and Social Power. *Journal of Linguistic Anthropology* 2:131–72.

Brody, David, ed. 1983. *The Fiddler's Fakebook.* New York: Oak Publications.

Bronner, Simon. 1985. *The Carver's Art: Crafting Meaning from Wood.* Lexington: University Press of Kentucky.

———. 1987. *Old-Time Music Makers of New York State.* Syracuse: Syracuse University Press.

Brunvand, Jan Harold, ed. 1979. *Readings in American Folklore.* New York: W. W. Norton and Co.

Bucuvalas, Tina, Peggy A. Bulger, and Stetson Kennedy. 1994. *South Florida Folklife.* Folklife in the South Series, edited by William Lynwood Montell. Jackson: University Press of Mississippi.

Burke, Kenneth. [1931] 1968. *Counter-Statement.* Berkeley: University of California Press.

———. 1972. *Dramatism and Development.* Barre, Mass.: Clark University Press.

Burt, Al. 1999. *The Tropic of Cracker.* Gainesville: University Press of Florida.

Camp, Charles, and Timothy Lloyd. 1980. Six Reasons Not to Produce Folklife Festivals. *Kentucky Folklore Record* 26:67–74.

Campbell, George. [1776] 1963. *The Philosophy of Rhetoric,* edited by Lloyd Bitzer. Carbondale: University of Southern Illinois Press.

Cansler, Loman D. 1992. The Fiddle and Religion. *Missouri Folklore Society Journal* 13–14:31–43.

Cantwell, Robert. 1984. *Bluegrass Breakdown: The Making of the Old Southern Sound.* Urbana and Chicago: University of Illinois Press.

———. 1991. Conjuring Culture: Ideology and Magic in the Festival of American Folklife. *Journal of American Folklore* 104:148–63.

———. 1993. *Ethnomimesis: Folklife and the Representation of Culture.* Chapel Hill: University of North Carolina Press.

Carter, Tom. 1991. Looking for Henry Reed: Confessions of a Revivalist. In *Sounds of the South,* edited by Daniel W. Patterson, 73–89. Occasional Papers, No. 1. Chapel Hill: Southern Folklife Collection at the University of North Carolina.

Cauthen, Joyce H. 2001. *With Fiddle and Well-Rosined Bow: A History of Old-Time Fiddling in Alabama.* Tuscaloosa: University of Alabama Press.

Chomsky, Noam. 1965. *Aspects of the Theory of Syntax.* Cambridge: M.I.T. Press.

Christeson, R. P., ed. 1973. *The Old-Time Fiddler's Repertory: 245 Traditional Tunes.* Columbia: University of Missouri Press.

Congdon, Kristin G. 2002. *Uncle Monday and Other Florida Tales.* llustrated by Kitty Kitson Petterson. Jackson: University Press of Mississippi.

Cooley, Timothy J. 1992. When a Tune Becomes a Folk Tune: Fiddling in Southern Illinois. *Missouri Folklore Society Journal* 13–14:45–79.

Dale, Greg. 1990. Highlandville Waltz. From the audio compact disc *Decorah Waltz* by Foot-Notes. Decorah, Iowa: Foot-Notes, FN101.

Daniel, Wayne. 1980. The Georgia Old-Time Fiddlers' Convention: 1920 Edition. *JEMF Quarterly* 16:67–73.

———. 1981. Old Time Fiddlers' Contests on Early Radio. *JEMF Quarterly* 17:159–65.

———. 1990. *Pickin' on Peachtree: A History of Country Music in Atlanta, Georgia.* Urbana and Chicago: University of Illinois Press.

Danielson, Linda L. 1992. Oregon Fiddling: The Missouri Connection. *Missouri Folklore Society Journal* 13–14:81–100.

Dann, Carl. 1929. *Carl Dann's Vicissitudes and Casathropics, Vol. One.* Orlando: Florida Press Club.

Deetz, James. 1977. *In Small Things Forgotten: The Archaeology of Early American Life.* New York: Anchor Books, Doubleday Press.

Derrida, Jacques. 1976. *Of Grammatology.* Translated by Gayatri Chakrovorty Spivak. Baltimore: Johns Hopkins University Press.

Dixon, Dorsey, and Howard Dixon. 1937. *The Dixon Brothers.* Vol. 2, *1937.* (Reissued 2001). Document Records, Catalogue number 8047.

Dorson, Richard M. 1956. *Negro Folktales in Michigan.* Westport, Conn.: Greenwood Press.

———. 1964. *Buying the Wind: Regional Folklore in the United States.* Chicago: University of Chicago Press.

Dundes, Alan. 1975. The Devolutionary Premise in Folklore Theory. In *Analytic Essays in Folklore,* edited by Alan Dundes, 2–27. The Hague: Mouton.

Dunford, Pat, and Art Rosenbaum, eds. 1993. Fine Times at Our House: Indiana Ballads, Fiddle Tunes, and Songs. Audio tape recording. Smithsonian/Folkways 03809.

Ehrenreich, Barbara. 1999. Farewell to a Fad. *The Progressive* 63:17–18.

Feintuch, Burt. 1975. Pop Zeigler, Folk Fiddler: A Study of Folkloric Performance. Ph.D. dissertation, University of Pennsylvania.

———. 1989. Square Dancing and Clogging. In *Encyclopedia of Southern Culture,* edited by Charles Reagan Wilson and William Ferris, 1033–35. Chapel Hill: University of North Carolina Press.

Feldman, Peter. 1975. How to Play Country Fiddle: Vol. One. (Instructional booklet accompanying Sonyatone record ST 101 "How to Play Country Fiddle".) Santa Barbara, Calif.: Sonyatone.

Ferris, William. 1986. The Dogtrot: A Mythic Image in Southern Culture. *The Southern Quarterly: A Journal of the Arts in the South* 25:72–85.

Feuerlicht, Roberta Strauss, ed. 1966. *The Legends of Paul Bunyan.* Illustrated by Kurth Werth. New York: Collier Books.

Folk Festival: The First 25 Years (1953–1977). 1981. Record album produced by the Florida Department of State/Florida Folklife Program. NR 1285.

Foucault, Michel. 1961. *Histoire de la Folie à L'âge Classique.* Paris: Plon.

Gannon, Michael. 1993. *Florida: A Short History.* Columbus Quincentenary Series. Gainesville: University Press of Florida.

Geertz, Clifford. 1988. *Works and Lives: The Anthropologist as Author.* Stanford: Stanford University Press.

Gimble, Johnny. 1988. *The Texas Fiddle Collection.* Los Angeles: CMH Records, Inc. No. CD-9027.

Glassie, Henry. 1982. *Passing the Time in Ballymenone: Culture and History of an Ulster Community.* Philadelphia: University of Pennsylvania Press.

———. [1975] 1983. *All Silver and No Brass: An Irish Christmas Mumming.* Philadelphia: University of Pennsylvania Press.

———. 1993. *Turkish Traditional Art Today.* Bloomington: Indiana University Press.

———. 1995. Tradition. *Journal of American Folklore* 108:395–412.

———. 1999. *Material Culture.* Bloomington: Indiana University Press.

Glisson, J. T. 1993. *The Creek.* Gainesville: University Press of Florida.

Grundtvig, N.F.S. 1976. *Selected Writings: N.F.S. Grundtvig.* Edited by Johannes Knudsen. Translated by Johannes Knudsen, Enok Mortensen, and Ernest D. Nielsen. Philadelphia: Fortress Press.

Guntharp, Matthew. 1980. *Learning the Fiddler's Ways.* University Park: Pennsylvania State University Press.

Handler, Richard. 1988. *Nationalism and the Politics of Culture in Quebec.* Madison: University of Wisconsin Press.

Hansen, Gregory. 1989. *A Teacher's Guide to the Duval County Folklife in Education Program.* Preface by Nancy Michael. White Springs: Florida Department of State/Bureau of Florida Folklife.

———. 1991. A Portrait of a Florida Fiddler. *Florida Fiddler: The Newsletter of the Florida State Fiddlers Association* 10:2–7.

———. 1996. The Relevance of "Authentic Tradition" in Studying an Oldtime Florida Fiddler. *Southern Folklore* 53:67–89.

Harkreader, Sidney. 1987. *Fiddlin' Sid's Memoirs: The Autobiography of Sidney J. Harkreader.* Edited by Walter D. Haden. JEMF Special Series, No. 9. Los Angeles: John Edwards Memorial Foundation.

Harris, Trudier. 1995. Genre. *Journal of American Folklore* 108:509–22.

Haut, Judith. 1994. How Can Acting Like a Fieldworker Enrich Pluralistic Education? In *Putting Folklore to Use*, edited by Michael Owen Jones. Lexington: University Press of Kentucky.

Heidegger, Martin. 1977. *Basic Writings*. Edited by David Farrell Krell. New York: Harper & Row.

Hemenway, Robert E. 1977. *Zora Neale Hurston: A Literary Biography*. Urbana: University of Illinois Press.

Hiaasen, Carl. 1998. *Team Rodent: How Disney Devours the World*. New York: Library of Contemporary Thought.

Hill, Fred. 1980. *Grass Roots: Illustrated History of Bluegrass and Mountain Music*. Rutland, Vt.: Academy Books.

Himmelfarb, Gertrude. 1994. *On Looking into the Abyss: Untimely Thoughts on Culture and Society*. New York: Vintage Books.

Hobsbawm, Eric, and Terence Ranger, eds. 1983. *The Invention of Tradition*. Cambridge: Cambridge University Press.

Hofstadter, Douglas R. 1979. *Gödel, Escher, Bach: An Eternal Golden Braid*. New York: Vintage Books.

Horkheimer, Max, and Theodor W. Adorno. [1947] 1996. *Dialectic of Enlightenment*. Translated by John Cumming. New York: Continuum.

Housewright, Wiley L. 1991. *A History of Music and Dance in Florida, 1565–1865*. Tuscaloosa: University of Alabama Press.

Hufford, Mary, ed. 1994. *Conserving Culture: A New Discourse on Heritage*. Publications of the American Folklife Center at the Library of Congress. Urbana: University of Illinois Press.

———. 1995. Context. *Journal of American Folklore* 108:528–49.

Hurston, Zora Neale. [1935] 1978. *Mules and Men*. Bloomington: Indiana University Press.

Hustvedt, Sigurd Bernhard. 1930. *Ballad Books and Ballad Men*. Cambridge: Harvard University Press.

Hymes, Dell. 1981. *"In Vain I Tried to Tell You": Essays in Native American Ethnopoetics*. Philadelphia: University of Pennsylvania Press.

Ives, Edward D. 1978. *Joe Scott: The Woodsman-Songmaker*. Urbana: University of Illinois Press.

Jabbour, Alan. 2003. Learning Old-Time Fiddle Appalachian Style with Alan Jabbour. Instructional DVD/video. Amherst, Mass.: In the Groove Workshops.

Jay, Martin. 1988. *Fin-de-Siècle Socialism: And Other Essays*. London: Routledge.

Jones, Michael Owen, ed. 1994. *Putting Folklore to Use*. Lexington: University Press of Kentucky.

Kapchan, Deborah A. 1995. Performance. *Journal of American Folklore* 108:479–508.

Kartchner, Kenner C. 1990. *Frontier Fiddler: The Life of a Northern Arizona Pioneer*. Edited by Larry V. Shumway. Tucson: University of Arizona Press.

Kennedy, Stetson. [1942] 1989. *Palmetto Country*. Tallahassee: Florida A&M University Press.

Kirshenblatt-Gimblett, Barbara. 1992. Mistaken Dichotomy. In *Public Folklore*, edited by Robert Baron and Nicholas Spitzer, 29–48. Washington, D.C.: Smithsonian Institution Press.

Klug, Slats, and Stephen Miller. 1997. *Liar's Bench: Musical Portraits of Brown County.* Nashville, Ind.: Ghosts of Brown Count Productions.

Krassen, Miles. 1973. *Appalachian Fiddle.* New York: Oak Publications.

———. 1983. *Masters of Old-Time Fiddling.* New York: Oak Publications.

Kundera, Milan. 1990. *Immortality.* Translated by Peter Kussi. New York: Harper Perennial.

———. 1991. *The Joke.* Translated by Michael Henry Heim. Reprint edition. New York: Harper Perennial.

Kurin, Richard. 1997. *Reflections of a Culture Broker: A View from the Smithsonian.* Washington, D.C.: Smithsonian Institution Press.

Lamme, Ary J. III. 1984. The Image of Florida. In *First Citizens and Other Florida Folks: Essays on Florida Folklife,* edited by Ronald Foreman, 17–22. Publications of the Florida Division of Archives, History and Records Management, No. 1. White Springs: Bureau of Florida Folklife Programs.

Lau, Kimberly J. 2000. Serial Logic: Folklore and Difference in the Age of Feel-Good Multiculturalism. *Journal of American Folklore* 113:70–82.

Lawrence, Elizabeth Atwood. 1982. *Rodeo: An Anthropologist Looks at the Wild and the Tame.* Chicago: University of Chicago Press.

Leary, James P. 1991. *Midwestern Folk Humor.* Little Rock, Ark.: August House Publishers, Inc.

Lévi-Strauss, Claude. 1995. *The Story of Lynx.* Translated by Catherine Tihanyi. Chicago: University of Chicago Press.

Linzee, Jill. 1990. *A Reference Guide to Florida Folklore from the Federal WPA Deposited in the Florida Folklife Archives.* Edited by Ormond H. Loomis and Deborah S. Fant. White Springs: Florida Department of State/Bureau of Florida Folklife Programs.

Lord, Albert B. 2000. *The Singer of Tales.* 2nd edition. Cambridge: Harvard University Press.

Lyons, Ernest F. 1969. *My Florida.* South Brunswick, N.J.: A. S. Barnes and Company.

Malone, Bill C. 1985. *Country Music USA.* Rev. ed. Austin: University of Texas Press.

———. 1993. *Singing Cowboys and Musical Mountaineers: Southern Culture and the Roots of Country Music.* Athens: University of Georgia Press.

Malone, Bill C., and David Stricklin. 2003. *Southern Music/American Music.* Revised and expanded edition. Lexington: University Press of Kentucky.

Manlove, Donald C., ed. 1982. *The Best of James Whitcomb Riley.* Bloomington: Indiana University Press.

Marshall, Howard, and John Williams. 1999. Fiddling Missouri. Seattle: Voyager Recordings. Compact disc VRCD 344.

Martin, Philip. 1994. *Farmhouse Fiddlers: Music and Dance Traditions in the Rural Midwest.* Mount Horeb, Wis.: Midwest Traditions, Inc.

Mazo, Jeffrey Alan. 1996. "A Good Saxon Compound." *Folklore* 107:107–8.

McGregory, Jerrilyn. 1997. *Wiregrass Country.* Folklife in the South Series, edited by William Lynwood Montell. Jackson: University Press of Mississippi.

McLaughlin, Thomas. 1996. *Street Smarts and Critical Theory: Listening to the Vernacular.* Madison: University of Wisconsin Press.

McLuhan, Marshall. 1964. *Understanding Media: The Extensions of Man.* New York: New American Library Publishers.

McWhorter, Frankie, and John R. Erickson. 1992. *Cowboy Fiddler.* Lubbock: Texas Tech University Press.

Melchert, Norman. 1994. *Who's to Say? A Dialogue on Relativism.* Indianapolis: Hackett Publishing.

Menuhin, Yehudi. 1996. *The Violin.* Translated by Ed Emery. New York: Flammarion.

Michael, Nancy. 1989. Preface to *A Teacher's Guide to the Duval County Folklife in Education Program* by Gregory Hansen. White Springs: Florida Department of State/Bureau of Florida Folklife Programs.

Milanich, Jerald T. 1996. *The Timucua.* The Peoples of America, ed. Alan Kolata and Dean R. Snow. Cambridge, Mass.: Blackwell Publishers, Inc.

Milnes, Gerald. 1999. *Play of a Fiddle: Traditional Music, Dance, and Folklore in West Virginia.* Lexington: University Press of Kentucky.

Momaday, N. Scott. 1969. *The Way to Rainy Mountain.* Illustrated by Al Momaday. Albuquerque: University of New Mexico Press.

Monroe, Bill. 1994. *The Music of Bill Monroe from 1936 to 1994.* The Country Music Foundation. Universal City, Calif.: MCA Records, Inc. No. MCAD4–1148.

Montell, William Lynwood. 1970. *The Saga of Coe Ridge: A Study in Oral History.* Knoxville: University of Tennessee Press.

Morris, Alton. 1950. *Folksongs of Florida.* Gainesville: University of Florida Press.

Nettl, Bruno. 1965. *Folk and Traditional Music of the Western Continents.* Prentice Hall History of Music Series, ed. H. Wiley Hitchcock. Englewoods Cliffs, N.J.: Prentice-Hall, Inc.

Neustadt, Kathy. 1992. *Clambake: A History and Celebration of an American Tradition.* American Folklore Society Publication Series. Amherst: University of Massachusetts Press.

Noles, Randy. 1998. She's the Fastest Train on the Line: The Untold Story of Ervin Rouse, Chubby Wise and the Legendary "Orange Blossom Special." *Jacksonville Today,* September.

——. 2002. *Orange Blossom Boys: The Untold Story of Ervin T. Rouse, Chubby Wise and the World's Most Famous Fiddle Tune.* Anaheim Hill, Calif.: Centerstream Publishing.

Nusz, Nancy, ed. 1991. Folklife in Education. *Southern Folklore* 48.

Orlean, Susan. 1998. *The Orchid Thief.* New York: Ballantine Books.

Paredes, Américo, and Richard Bauman, eds. 2001. *Toward New Perspectives in Folklore.* Bloomington: Trickster Press.

Pearson, Barry Lee. 1984. *"Sounds So Good to Me": The Bluesman's Story*. Philadelphia: University of Pennsylvania Press.

Phelts, Marsha Dean. 1997. *An American Beach for African Americans*. Gainesville: University Press of Florida.

Piccalo, Jack. 1997. Richard Seaman Is a Treasure. *Midnight Flier*. Monthly Newsletter of the North Florida Bluegrass Music Association, Inc. Jacksonville, August.

Pirsig, Robert M. 1974. *Zen and the Art of Motorcycle Maintenance: An Inquiry into Values*. New York: Bantam Books.

Porter, Peter, ed. 1990. *Great Irish Poetry: W. B. Yeats, the Last Romantic*. New York: Clarkson N. Potter, Inc.

Prabhavananda, Swami, and Christopher Isherwood. 1972. *The Song of God: Bhagavad-Gita*. New York: Mentor Books.

Propp, Vladímir. 1968. *Morphology of the Folktale*. Translated by Laurence Scott. Austin: University of Texas Press.

Quigley, Colin. 1995. *Music from the Heart: Compositions of a Folk Fiddler*. Athens: University of Georgia Press.

Rahula, Walpola. 1974. *What the Buddha Taught*. New York: Grove Press.

Randolph, Vance. 1951. *We Always Lie to Strangers: Tall Tales from the Ozarks*. Illustrated by Glen Rounds. New York: Columbia University Press.

Rawlings, Marjorie Kinnan. 1939. *The Yearling*. New York: Charles Scribner's Sons.

———. 1942. *Cross Creek*. New York: Charles Scribner's Sons.

Reaver, J. Russell, ed. 1987. *Florida Folktales*. Gainesville: University of Florida Press.

Renwick, Roger deV. 2001. *Recentering Anglo-American Folksong: Sea Crabs and Wicked Youths*. Jackson: University of Mississippi Press.

Riddle, Almeda. 1970. *A Singer and Her Songs*. Edited by Roger Abrahams. Baton Rouge: Louisiana State University Press.

Rosenberg, Neil V. 1985. *Bluegrass: A History*. Urbana: University of Illinois Press.

———, ed. 1993. *Transforming Tradition: Folk Music Revivals Examined*. Urbana and Chicago: University of Illinois Press.

Rothrock, Joseph T., and Jane Rothrock. 1984. *Chesapeake Odysseys: An 1883 Cruise Revisited*. Centreville, Md.: Cornell Maritime Press.

Rowe, Anne E. 1992. *The Idea of Florida in the American Literary Imagination*. Gainesville: University Press of Florida.

Rumble, John W., ed. 1994. The Music of Bill Monroe from 1936 to 1994. Produced by the Country Music Foundation. MCA Records, Inc. MCAD4–11048.

Rymer, Russ. 1998. *American Beach: A Saga of Race, Wealth, and Memory*. New York: HarperCollins.

Seaman, Richard. 1988. Tape-recorded interview with Gregory Hansen, Jacksonville, Florida, August 10. Deposited at the Florida Folklife Archives, Tallahassee.

———. 1991. Tape-recorded interview with Gregory Hansen, Jacksonville, Florida, September 28. Deposited at the Florida Folklife Archives, Tallahassee.

———. 1992. Videotaped interview with Glen Fisher, Jacksonville, Florida, October 16. Broadcast on WJKS First Coast News.

———. 1998. Tape-recorded interviews with Gregory Hansen, Jacksonville, Florida, May 18–19. Deposited at the Florida Folklife Archives, Tallahassee.

———. 1999. Tape-recorded interview with Gregory Hansen, Jacksonville, Florida, December 17. Deposited at the Florida Folklife Archives, Tallahassee.

Simons, Elizabeth Radin. 1990. *Student Worlds/Student Words: Teaching Writing Through Folklore.* Portsmouth, N.H.: Boynton/Cook and Heinemann.

Simons, Glen, and Laura Ogden. 1998. *Gladesmen: Gator Hunters, Moonshiners, and Skiffers.* Gainesville: University Press of Florida.

Siporin, Steve. 2000. On Scapegoating Public Folklore. *Journal of American Folklore* 113:86–89.

Skillman, Amy E. 1992. "She Oughta Been a Lady": Women Old-time Fiddlers in Missouri. *Missouri Folklore Society Journal* 13–14:123–32.

Smart, Barry. 1993. *Postmodernity.* New York: Routledge.

Sokal, Alan, and Jean Bricmont. 1999. *Fashionable Nonsense: Postmodern Intellectuals' Abuse of Science.* New York: Picador USA.

Stahl, Sandra Dolby. 1989. *Literary Folkloristics and the Personal Narrative.* Bloomington: Indiana University Press.

Stanfield, Peter. 2002. *Horse Opera: The Strange History of the 1930s Singing Cowboy.* Urbana: University of Illinois Press.

Staub, Shalom. 1994. Cultural Conservation and Economic Recovery Planning: The Pennsylvania Heritage Parks Program. In *Conserving Culture: A New Discourse on Heritage,* edited by Mary Hufford, 229–44. Publications of the American Folklife Center at the Library of Congress. Urbana: University of Illinois Press.

Ste. Clair, Dana. 1998. *Cracker: The Cracker Culture in Florida History.* Daytona Beach: Museum of Arts and Sciences.

Sting. 1987. History Will Teach Us Nothing. . . . *Nothing Like the Sun.* A & M Records, Inc. SP-6402.

Sunstein, Bonnie Stone, and Elizabeth Chiseri-Strater. 2002. *Fieldworking: Reading and Writing Research.* 2nd ed. Boston: Bedford/St. Martin's.

Swann, Brian, ed. 1994. *Coming to Light: Contemporary Translations of the Native Literatures of North America.* New York: Vintage Books.

Taylor, David A. 1985. Duval County Folklife. Public document produced for the Duval County Folk Arts in Education Program. White Springs: Florida Department of State/Bureau of Florida Folklife Programs.

Tebeau, Charles W. 1996. *The New History of Florida.* Gainesville: University Press of Florida.

Thede, Marion. 1967. *The Fiddle Book.* New York: Oak Publications.

Thomas, Jean. 1938. *The Singin' Fiddler of Lost Hope Hollow.* New York: E. P. Dutton and Company, Inc.

Thomas, Lowell. 1945. *Tall Stories: The Rise and Triumph of the Great American Whopper.* Illustrated by Herb Roth. New York: Harvest House.

Thompson, Stith. 1946. *The Folktale.* New York: Dryden.

———. 1955-58. *Motif-Index of Folk Literature.* 6 vols. Bloomington: Indiana University Press.

———. 1961. *The Types of the Folktale.* 2nd rev. ed. Helsinki: Folklore Fellows Communication no. 184.

Thomson, Robert. 1984. *Non Nimium Credendum Antiquitati*: But Don't Throw the Baby Out with the Bathwater. In *First Citizens and Other Florida Folks: Essays on Florida Folklife,* ed. Ronald Foreman, 35–43. Publications of the Florida Division of Archives, History and Records Management, No. 1. White Springs: Bureau of Florida Folklife Programs.

Titon, Jeff Todd. 2001. *Old-Time Kentucky Fiddle Tunes.* Lexington: University Press of Kentucky.

Tönnies, Ferdinand. [1887] 1993. *Community and Society.* Translated by Charles P. Loomis. New Brunswick, N.J.: Transaction Publishers.

Tribe, Ivan M. 1984. *Mountaineer Jamboree: Country Music in West Virginia.* Lexington: University Press of Kentucky.

Turner, Graeme. 1990. *British Cultural Studies: An Introduction.* New York: Routledge.

Turner, Patricia A. 1993. *I Heard It Through the Grapevine: Rumor in African-American Culture.* Berkeley: University of California Press.

Tyler, Paul L. 1992. "Sets on the Floor": Social Dance as an Emblem of Community in Rural Indiana. Ph.D. dissertation, Indiana University.

Watson, Bruce. 1993. This Here's All for Foot Tappin' and Grin Winnin'. *Smithsonian* 23:68–80.

West, Patsy. 1998. *The Enduring Seminoles: From Alligator Wrestling to Ecotourism.* Gainesville: University Press of Florida.

Whisnant, David E. 1983. *All That Is Native and Fine: The Politics of Culture in an American Region.* Chapel Hill: University of North Carolina Press.

———. 1988. Public Sector Folklore as Intervention: Lessons from the Past, Prospects for the Future. In *The Conservation of Culture: Folklorists and the Public Sector,* edited by Burt Feintuch, 229–43. Lexington: University Press of Kentucky.

———. 1990. Letting Loose of Liberalism: Some Thoughts on Cultural Work and the Limits of Polite Discourse. *Southern Changes* 12:1–11.

Wiggins, Gene. 1987. *Fiddlin' Georgia Crazy: Fiddlin' John Carson, His Real World, and the World of His Songs.* Urbana: University of Illinois Press.

Will, Lawrence E. 1978. *Okeechobee Boats and Skippers.* St. Petersburg, Fla.: Great Outdoors Publishing Co.

Williams, Michael Ann. 2004. *Homeplace: The Social Use and Meaning of the Folk Dwelling in Southwestern North Carolina.* Charlottesville: University Press of Virginia.

Williams, Raymond. 1977. *Marxism and Literature.* Oxford: Oxford University Press.

Wilson, Charles Reagan, and William Ferris, eds. 1989. *Encyclopedia of Southern Culture*. Chapel Hill: University of North Carolina Press.

Wilson, Joe, and Lee Udall. 1982. *Folk Festivals: A Handbook for Organization and Management*. Knoxville: University of Tennessee Press.

Wise, Chubby. 1994. *Chubby Wise in Nashville*. Orlando, Fla.: Pinecastle Records.

Wolfe, Charles K. 1977. *Tennessee Strings: The Story of Country Music in Tennessee*. Knoxville: Tennessee Three Star Books.

———. 1997. *The Devil's Box: Masters of Southern Fiddling*. Nashville, Tenn.: Vanderbilt University Press/Country Music Foundation Press.

Yoder, Don. 1963. The Folklife Studies Movement. *Pennsylvania Folklife* 13:42–57.

Youmans, Julie. 1992. Warming the Cold Notes: Style and Boundaries in Old-Time Fiddling. *Missouri Folklore Society Journal* 13–14:133–49.

Zach, Paul, ed. 1987. *Florida: Insight Guide*. New York: APA Productions.

Index

~

Abrahams, Roger, 4
Acosta, Tom, 90–94, 148
African-American folklore, 65, 80, 85, 179
"Alabama Jubilee," 137, 145
Alligators, 20, 77, 78
"Amazing Grace," 49, 143
American Folklife Center, 2
American Indians, 15–16, 73, 80, 85, 168
Ammidown, Margot, 165
Anderson, John, 147
Anderson, Miss, 130, 169
"Annie Seaman Waltz," 7, 13, 119–20, 120,
   141, 199, 201
"Arkansas Traveler," 138
Arlington neighborhood, 103
"At a Georgia Camp Meeting," 146
"Aunt Dina's Quilting Party," 143, 145
authenticity, 137, 138
Avondale neighborhood, 99, 198

Baldwin, Florida, 18
Ballymenone, Ireland, 29
Barber, Joe, 108, 109, 112

Barber, Ross, 109
Barbour, George M., 175, 176, 180
bass, 66–67
Basso, Keith, 73
Bauman, Richard, 4, 140
Bayard, Samuel Preston, 134, 135, 144
Beaver Falls, Pennsylvania, 19
bees, 12, 78–79
Bennett, Earnest, 194
Bennington, Floyd, 194
"Big John in the Barroom," 137
"Bile Them Cabbage Down," 138, 139
"Bill Cheatem," 138
"Billy in the Lowground," 136
Bivins, T. K., 197, 198
bluegrass music, 2–3, 41, 50–53, 110, 146
blues music, 52, 157, 178, 179
Blume, George, 194
Bridal Street, Jacksonville, 96, 200
Briggs, Charles, 140
Bronner, Simon, 193
Brookville, Florida, 175
"Bully of the Town," 137

Burch, Wandley, 194
Bureau of Florida Folklife Programs, x, 1, 2, 10, 33, 151, 199
Burke, Kenneth, 4
busking, 43, 89

Campbell, George, 190
"Carroll County Blues," 157, 179
cattle, x, 60, 61, 157, 158
Chesapeake Bay, 55
Chester, Pennsylvania, 55
"Chicken Reel," 137
Chomsky, Noam, 4
Christianity, 49, 56, 192, 193, 195
"Cindy," 136, 139, 140, 153, 154
Civil War, 87, 137, 167, 169, 177
Clements, Vassar, 147
Clewiston, Florida, 170
community aesthetic, 133, 136
community ethos, 28–32, 188, 191
core repertory, 132–49
corn, 11, 71, 158
"Cotton Bagging." See "Shear 'Em."
"Cotton-Eyed Joe," 136
"crackers," 7, 166, 167, 174–77
Cruse, Wade, 89
Custer, George, 4, 34–54, 133, 148, 200

Dale, Greg, 150
"Dance All Night with a Bottle in My Hand," 136, 202
dance halls, 94–95
dance parties, 13, 17, 19–21, 24, 25, 38, 45, 47, 89, 95, 100, 109, 110, 145, 146, 148, 156, 176, 179–80, 183
Daniels, Charlie, 147
Danielson, Linda, 136
Dann, Carl, 176
"Darling Nelly Gray," 145
Darsey, Barbara, 179
debt peonage. See peonage
Deetz, James, 6
devil, 27, 28,
Disney World, 166, 172
Disston, Hamilton, 55
"Dixie," 136
dogs, 67–70, 170

dogtrot house, 61
Dolby, Sandra, 138
"Don't Be Angry with Me Darling," 141, 142
"Don't Let Your Deal Go Down," 44,
Dorson, Richard, 62, 64, 79
"Down Yonder," 36, 136
Dundes, Alan, 134
Duval County Folk Arts (Folklife) in Education Program, 1–3, 8, 59, 162

Eatonville, Florida, 169
epistemology, 59, 73, 83–85, 190
ethnopoetics, 58, 59, 192
Evans, Thomas, 172
Everglades, 64

"Faded Love," 44, 45, 143
Farley, Frank, 182–85
Faulkner, William, 61
Feintuch, Burt, 30
fiddle beaters, 27, 47, 48, 112, 113, 130, 153, 154, 177
fiddlers' contests, 90–92, 144
fiddle tune lyrics, 117, 120, 139–40, 201–8
fiddling techniques: aesthetics, 27, 39, 106, 112, 120–22; bounce, 113–14; long-bow/short-bow, 114–15; melody lines, 116–18; noting, 107, 108; ornamentation, 118, 119, 121; playing by ear, 108–11, 115, 133, 134; shuffles, 114; tuning and keys 115, 116; variations, 46, 117, 118
fieldwork methodology, ix, x, 3–5, 18
fights, 31, 94, 95, 145
Fisher, Glen, 189
fish fry, 31
fishing, 31, 65–67, 70, 74
"Flop-Eared Mule," 13, 106, 135, 153, 184
Florida Fiddlers Association, 60
Florida Folk Festival, ix, 34, 59, 163, 164, 182–86, 200
Florida Folk Heritage Awards, 164, 200
Florida Folklife Council, 163, 200
Florida Folklife Program. See Bureau of Florida Folklife Programs
Florida frolics. See dance parties
Florida Keys, 66
Florida's Boom, 86

Florida's Gulf Coast, 66
folk belief, 27–28, 72
Folklife in Education programming,
    7, 150, 151, 189
Folklife festivals, 9–17, 41, 105, 167, 182–87
folk music revivals, 51, 191, 192
"Footprints in the Snow," 52, 53
Ford, Henry, 178
Forrester, Howdy, 35, 36, 44, 52, 179
Forrester, Joe, 44
Fountain of Youth, 166
"Fourteen Days in Georgia," 15, 137
Francis Grill, 94
Freeman, "Old Man," *126*
frogs, 73–74, 76–77, 160, 161

Gainesville, Florida 52
Gemeinschaft, 95
Gesellschaft, 95
Georgia Slim and the Texas Roundup, 44
Gimble, Johnny, 45
"Girl I Left Behind," 138
Glassie, Henry, 4
"Golden Slippers," 137
Goodman, Harold, 43
gopher tortoise, 68
Gorrie, John, 63
Grand Old Opry, 35, 42, 43, 52, 146
Grant, Ulysses, S., 175
Great Depression, 6, 88, 93, 95–97
Griffin, W. H., 91
Guntharp, Matthew, 132, 134

Hansen, Gregory, *129*
Harris, Taylor J., 90
hillbilly stereotype, 165
Hinduism, 194
hoedown genre, 2, 12, 57, 106, 116–19, 138,
    141, 147, 163
hog-callers' contest, 90, 91, 144
honey, 12, 79
horses, 15–16, 24–25, 29, 80, 81, 109, 156
house parties. *See* dance parties
Housewright, Wiley, 179, 180
"How Great Thou Art," 144, 148, 161
hunting, 67–70, 72–73, 75
hurricanes, 37, 106, 155

Hurston, Zora Neale, 65, 169, 171
Hustvedt, Sigurd Bernhard, 163

"Ida Red," 136
"I Don't Love Nobody," 12, 136, 146
"I'll Fly Away," 144
"I'm Going Where the Roses Never
    Fade," 145
"In the Garden," 144
"In the Good Old Summertime," 143, 145
International Association of Machinists,
    Number 257, 99
Irish folklore, 29, 72, 85
"Irish Washerwoman," 136, 141, 152, 153
Ives, Edward D., 4

Jacksonville, 1, 28, 39, 46, 60, 86, 140, 148,
    168, 183, 187, 199
Jacksonville Beach, 90
Jacksonville Landing, 9, 34, 158, 162
jig-couplet, 139
Jim Crow Era, 169
"John Brown's Body," 178
Johnson, Abner, 56
Johnson, Queenie Husky, 56
jokes, 12–14, 59, 81, 82
Jones, Willie, 208

KBOO Radio, 43
KRLD Radio, 44
"Katy Hill," 52, 136
Kennedy Space Center, 104, 187
Kennedy, Stetson, 57, 63, 177
"Kentucky Waltz," 141
Kershaw, Doug, 147
Key West, 187
Kirkland, Clyde, 89, 92, 147
Kissimmee, 11, 13, 14, 37, 46, 56, 97, 138,
    152, 171, 172, 183
Kissimmee Park, 1, 6, 14, 20, 25, 28, 56,
    60, 75, 76, 86, 89, 94, 100, 108, 109, *123*,
    125–28, 135, 137, 140, 148, 157, 166, 176,
    184, 195
Kissimmee Prairie, 15, 80, 166
Kissimmee River, 65, 74
Kopp, I. Sheldon, 9
Kundera, Milan, 82

labor strikes, 99
Lackawanna School, 102, 162
Lake City, Florida, 90
Lake Okeechobee, 171
Lake Tohopekaliga, 19, 55, 56, 64, 87, *125*, 170, 172
Lassiter, Ella, 179
Lee, Robert E. 178
"Liberty," 11, 12, 53, 137
lies. *See* tall tales
"Life is Like a Mountain Railway," 144
lightning, 72
Lincoln, Abraham, 178
"Listen to the Mockingbird," 143
Live Oak, Florida, 60
lizards, 65–66
Lofton, Florida, 171

Mann, Tappan, 57
Mann, T. C., 57
"Maple Sugar," 116, 137, 185
"Marching Through Georgia," 136
Marshall, Howard, 179
Mazo, Jeffrey, 150
McCool, Billy, *127*
McCool, Jean, *125*
McCool, William, 19, 55, *125*
McCool's Grove, 55, 87
McLaughlin, Thomas, 187
Melody Makers, 92, 93, 144
Memphis, 147
Menéndez, Pedro, 168
Miami, 15, 64
Michael, Nancy, 8
Miccosukees, 168
"Mississippi Sawyer," 12, 135, 153, 183
mockingbird, 77
"Mockingbird Hill," 143
"Molly Darling," 143
Momaday, N. Scott, 73
Monroe, Bill, 3, 6, 33, 42, 51–53, 114, 179
moonshine, 47, 96–97, 145
mosquitoes, 20, 79–80
Mossy Lee Bluegrass Band, 53
motifs, (D2156.2), 61; (F816), 63; (F968), 72; (F989.17), 80; (J426.2), 74; (T589.7.1),

80; (X1121), 73, 75; (X1122.2), 73; (X1124), 67, 72; (X11303.3), 76; (X1150), 65, 74; (X1153), 65, 71, 74; (X1215), 67; (X1215.8), 67; (X1241), 80; (X1242), 72; (X1250), 67, 77; (X1268), 78; (X1286), 79; (X1342), 74, 76; (X1411.1), 71; (X1455), 71; (X1455.1), 71; (X1522.1), 64; (X1606.1), 76; (X1623), 76; (X1633.1), 61
mules, 11, 13, 24, 71–72, 158, 185
Museum of Science and History, (Jacksonville) 34–50
music, sheet, *117*, *120*, *201–8*

Nashville, 52, 148
Nassau County, Florida, 97
National Endowment for the Arts, 1
Native Americans. *See* American Indians
nativism, 167, 168, 178, 179, 187
neighborliness, 29–32, 191
"New Five Cent," 138
"Nigger in the Woodpile," 173
"Nightingale's Song," 196
"No Name Waltz," 146

Ocala, Florida, 90
occupational folklife: citrus grove care-
takers, 55, 87; cowboys, 57, 87, 88, 174; farmers, 56, 61–65, 71, 87, 184; railroad-ers, 87, 88, 97, 98, 102; watermen, 56, 65, 66
"Old Hen Cackled," 136, 139
"Old Joe Clark," 136
"Old Spinning Wheel," 143, 148
old-time music, 2, 141
Old Town, Florida, 45
oral/aural tradition, 51, 105, 133, 134
oral history, 5
"Orange Blossom Special," 39–41, 156, 162
Orlando, 152, 170, 172
Orlean, Susan, 187
Osceola County, Florida, 18, 61, 86, 158
"Osceola's Rag," 138
"Over the Waves," 42

"Paddy on the Turnpike," 136
Paganini, Niccolò, 28, 106

Palatka, Florida, 90
parlor Tunes, 143
Parson, Joe, 100
Paschal and Shaw's Hardware, 104
Pensacola, Florida, 90, 91
peonage, 169, 172
performance theory, 4
Perlman, Itzhak, 106
personal aesthetic, 134
personal experience narratives, 86
Piccalo, Jack, 1, 10–16, 33, 59, *123*, 163, 182–85, 200
Piccalo, Troy, 2
Pirsig, Robert M., 182
Pitts, Jack, 92, 148
political economy of education, 151, 162
Polk County, Florida, 57, 180
popcorn, 62, 158
"Pop Goes the Weasel," 51, 119, 136
preachers, 14, 15, 81–82
prison labor, 169–71
Prohibition, 94, 97
public sector folklore, 5, 151, 164, 167, 178, 179, 185, 186, 189
pumpkins, 63–64, 159
Purcell, E. O. "Fiddlin'," 91

Quine, Jim, 35, 36, 41

"Rabbit in a Pea Patch," 136
Race Relations, 169–73, 180
radio broadcasts, 20, 92, 93, 144, 145, 164
"Ragtime Annie," 136, *204*
Rainbow Ranch Girls, 102
ranching, 87–88
Randolph, Vance, 62
Rawlings, Marjorie Kinnan, 78
recordings, 144, 145
recursion, 63, 70, 71, 82, 118
Reddy, David, 10
"Red River Valley," 143
"Red Wing," 143, 145
regional speech, 41, 43, 46, 67
regional stereotypes, 174–77
representation of folk culture, 164, 180
Ribault, Jean, 164

Riley, James Whitcomb, 105
Roberts, Henry W., 90
Robertson, Eck, 135
Rodgers, Jimmie, 147
Rogers, Gamble, 147
Roosevelt, Franklin D., 88
Rosenberg, Neil, 146
Rosewood, Florida, 169
Rouse, Ervin, 40, 41, 147
Rouse, Gordon, 40
"Rubber Dolly," 137, 147
"Run Nigger Run," 173 *See also* "Trouble Amongst the Yearlings"
Rutland, Georgia Slim, 35, 36, 43–44

Saddle Mountain Roundup, 43
"Sally Gooden," 106, 135, 140, *205*
Salt Run Bluegrass Band, 35, 53
Salt Springs, Florida, 35
"San Antonio Rose," 143
Seaboard Air Line, 40, 97, 196
Seaman, Anne, 56, *124*, *128*
Seaman, Annie Johns Bivins, 10, 25, 81, 97, *131*, 192, 193, 196–99
Seaman, Daisy, 92, 94–96, 99, 100, 143, 163, 196
Seaman, (Daisy) Jean, 99, 101, 104, 143
Seaman, Lewis, 19, 55, 87, 111–12, *125–28*
Seaman, Lulu, 19, 55, 183
Seaman, Richard, *123*, *124*, *127–31*
Seaman, Richard Keith, Jr., 99, 101, 104
Sebring, Florida, 179
Seminoles, 168
Sessions, Erik, 150
Sharpe, Elizabeth, 177
"Shear 'Em," 26, 45, 46, 57, 109–11, 116, *117*, 119, 135, 140, 145, *206*
sheet music. *See* music, sheet
Sherman, William Tecumseh, 178
"Silver Bell," 143, 145
"Skip to My Lou," 136
slavery, 168–69, 171, 179
snakes, 73–74, 82, 83, 107
Sneed, Taylor, 172
"Soldier's Joy," 12, 136, 153, 184
South Land Trail Riders, 101–3, 145–49

Spanish-American War, 87, 174
Spirit of the Suwannee Campground, 60
square dance, 13, 17, 19, 20, 21–24, 25, 26,
    27, 30–31, 38, 47, 89, 92, 95, 109, 139, 145,
    177, 183
square dance calling, 22, 30, 177
squirrels, 72–73
St. Augustine, Florida, 35, 90, 168
St. Clair, Dana, 166
Stephen Foster Folk Culture Center State
    Park, ix, 182
Stern, Isaac, 114
St. Johns River, 9, 34, 66, 151
Stone, Robert, 6, 33–54
"Stoney Point," 136, *203*
storytelling style, 69, 74–75, 83, 189–91
string bands, 25
Structuralism, 61, 70, 71
Suwannee River, ix, 45, 182
"Sweet Bunch of Daisies," 145
systematic cultural intervention, 8

"Take Me Back to Tulsa," 46
tale types, (1242), 82; (1414), 14; (1889M),
    82; (1890), 75; (1891), 67, 72; (1920),
    62, 65, 82; (1920A), 63; (1920F), 67,
    68; (1960D), 64, 65; (1960M), 78;
    (1960M2), 79
Tallahassee, 199
tall tales, 11–17, 58, 59, 157–61
taxonomy of animals, 69, 77, 80
Taylor, David, 1
television, 100, 154
"Tennessee Waltz," 141
Texas-style fiddling, 44
Thomas, Lowell, 74
Thomas's Swamp, 96
Thompson, Stith, 72
Tift County, Georgia, 38
Timucua, 168
Tingle, Philip, 86
Tönnies, Ferdinand, 95
"Too Young to Marry," 110
transcribed music. *See* music, sheet
trick fiddling, 50
"Trouble Amongst the Yearlings," 138, 173
trout, 66–67

Tubb, Ernest, 102, 146
turpentine camps, 171–72

Udall, Lee, 188
"Unnamed tune learned from Willie
    Jones," *208*
"Up Jumped Trouble/the Devil," 16, 138,
    145, 147, 185

Valdosta, Georgia, 35
violin compared to fiddle, 106, 114

waltz, 119–20, 141, 142
"Waltz You Saved for Me," 141, 154, 185
"Washington and Lee Swing," 143
watermelons, 11, 71, 159, 185
"Watermelon on the Vine," 136
"Wednesday Night Waltz," 141
Western swing, 43
"Westphalia Waltz," 14, 141, 142, 154, 184
"What a Friend We Have in Jesus," 51
"When It's Lamp Lighting Time in the
    High Country," 43
"When the Work's All Done this Fall," 143
"When You and I Were Young Maggie,"
    143, 145, 148
Whisnant, David, 8
"Whistling Rufus," 135, 138, *207*
White Springs, Florida, ix, 33, 58, 59,
    90, 182
Whitford, Windy, 132
William, Martin J., 90
Wills, Bob, 6, 45, 46, 146
Wilson, Joe, 188
Wise, Robert "Chubby," 6, 14, 35–54, 114,
    133, 138, 142–43, 148, 179, 200
Wise, Rossi, 35
WJAX Radio, 92
"Won't You Come Home Bill Bailey," 143
World War II, 43, 99, 144, 145
WRUF Radio, 52

Yankees, 173–75
Yeats, William Butler, 18
"Yellow Gals," 11, 48, 119, 136
Yulee's Hill-Billies, 52